ADVANCES IN ACCOUNTING BEHAVIORAL RESEARCH

ADVANCES IN ACCOUNTING BEHAVIORAL RESEARCH

Series Editor: Khondkar E. Karim

Recent Volumes:

Volumes 5–14:	Edited by Vicky Arnold
Volumes 15–20:	Edited by Donna Bobek Schmitt
Volumes 21–26:	Edited by Khondkar E. Karim

ADVANCES IN ACCOUNTING BEHAVIORAL RESEARCH
VOLUME 27

ADVANCES IN ACCOUNTING BEHAVIORAL RESEARCH

EDITED BY

KHONDKAR E. KARIM

University of Massachusetts Lowell, USA

United Kingdom – North America – Japan
India – Malaysia – China

Emerald Publishing Limited
Emerald Publishing, Floor 5, Northspring, 21-23 Wellington Street, Leeds LS1 4DL

First edition 2024

Editorial matter and selection © 2024 Khondkar E. Karim.
Published under exclusive licence by Emerald Publishing Limited.
Individual chapters © 2024 by Emerald Publishing Limited.

Reprints and permissions service
Contact: www.copyright.com

No part of this book may be reproduced, stored in a retrieval system, transmitted in any form or by any means electronic, mechanical, photocopying, recording or otherwise without either the prior written permission of the publisher or a licence permitting restricted copying issued in the UK by The Copyright Licensing Agency and in the USA by The Copyright Clearance Center. Any opinions expressed in the chapters are those of the authors. Whilst Emerald makes every effort to ensure the quality and accuracy of its content, Emerald makes no representation implied or otherwise, as to the chapters' suitability and application and disclaims any warranties, express or implied, to their use.

British Library Cataloguing in Publication Data
A catalogue record for this book is available from the British Library

ISBN: 978-1-83608-281-1 (Print)
ISBN: 978-1-83608-280-4 (Online)
ISBN: 978-1-83608-282-8 (Epub)

ISSN: 1475-1488 (Series)

Printed and bound by CPI Group (UK) Ltd, Croydon, CR0 4YY

INVESTOR IN PEOPLE

CONTENTS

List of Contributors   *vii*

Fairness in Cost Allocations: Proportionality vs. Equality   *1*
Sachin Banker, Rajiv D. Banker, Angelika Dimoka and Eunbin
Whang

**The Influence of a Family Firm Structure on Auditor Judgments:
Effects of Managerial Control and Ownership Concentration**   *29*
Jingyu Gao, Anna M. Rose, Ikseon Suh and Min Zhang

**Corporate Social Responsibility as Insurance: Its Limitations and
Risk of Backfiring**   *55*
L. Emily Hickman and Bernard Wong-On-Wing

**The Effect of Academic Performance, Internship Experience,
Gender, and Being a Transfer Student on Early Job Attainment of
Accounting Graduates**   *97*
Hossein Nouri and Carolyn M. Previti

**The Association Between Budgetary Participation With
Competitive Advantage: A Sequential Mediation Model**   *115*
Sophia Su, Kevin Baird and Nuraddeen Nuhu

**Good Jobs Finding Bad Guys: An Exploration of the Work of
Special Agents of the Internal Revenue Service Using the Job
Characteristics Model**   *137*
Robert A. Warren and Timothy J. Fogarty

Index   *159*

LIST OF CONTRIBUTORS

Sachin Banker	University of Utah, USA
Rajiv D. Banker	Temple University, USA
Angelika Dimoka	University of Houston, USA
Eunbin Whang	Widener University, USA
Jingyu Gao	Capital University of Economics and Business, China
Anna M. Rose	University of Northern Colorado, USA
Ikseon Suh	University of Nevada Las Vegas, USA
Min Zhang	Renmin University of China, China
L. Emily Hickman	California Polytechnic State University, USA
Bernard Wong-On-Wing	Washington State University, USA
Hossein Nouri	The College of New Jersey, USA
Carolyn M. Previti	Seton Hall University, USA
Sophia Su	Macquarie University, Australia
Kevin Baird	Macquarie University, Australia
Nuraddeen Nuhu	Macquarie University, Australia
Robert A. Warren	Radford University, USA
Timothy J. Fogarty	Case Western Reserve University, USA

FAIRNESS IN COST ALLOCATIONS: PROPORTIONALITY VS. EQUALITY

Sachin Banker[a], Rajiv D. Banker[b], Angelika Dimoka[c] and Eunbin Whang[d]

[a]University of Utah, USA
[b]Temple University, USA
[c]University of Houston, USA
[d]Widener University, USA

ABSTRACT

Allocation problems in accounting require joint costs to be allocated among participating agents. In this setting, however, unfair allocations can stifle cooperation and lead to inefficient group outcomes. Then, what qualifies as fair enough for individual agents to agree to cooperate and extract joint benefits? Building on prior analytical literature that has offered perspectives involving joint cost allocations, we experimentally evaluate two common notions of fairness that present competing predictions in the cost allocation context – proportionality and equality. We operationalize two notions of fairness using a behavioral approach and examine which fairness notion prevails in cost allocation problems. More specifically, we examine fairness considerations in the cost allocation context using a modified ultimatum game, where joint cost savings can only be acquired through cooperation between two agents and individual contributions are varied transparently. Our experimental evidence suggests that fairness considerations in cost allocations coincide more with the proportionality notion when individuals make different contributions to create joint benefits. These findings provide important insights on the key rationale underlying the prevalent cost allocation method in accounting practices and the design of fair cost allocations that promote cooperation among agents.

Keywords: Fairness; equality; proportionality; cost allocation; behavioral accounting; cooperation

---

Advances in Accounting Behavioral Research, Volume 27, 1–28
Copyright © 2024 by Emerald Publishing Limited
All rights of reproduction in any form reserved
ISSN: 1475-1488/doi:10.1108/S1475-148820240000027001

INTRODUCTION

Cost allocations are pervasive in accounting practice where participating agents incur joint costs with a shared goal of achieving cost savings. Tracing jointly incurred costs directly to each participating agent is often costly, demanding, and impractical. Firms, therefore, routinely allocate these joint costs to participating agents based on some convenient, reasonable cost drivers. Building on prior analytical work that yields game theoretical joint cost allocations schemes (Banker, 1981; Billera & Heath, 1982; Hamlen et al., 1980; Roth & Verrecchia, 1979; Shapley, 1953), our current study takes a behavioral approach to examine fairness considerations associated with cost allocation schemes.

Understanding the fairness considerations associated with cost allocation problems has become increasingly important. As the sharing economy rapidly transforms traditional notions of work (Etter et al., 2019), individuals are encountering new and consequential forms of cost sharing problems. For example, the growing popularity of co-working and co-living environments (e.g., WeWork, Impact Hub) raises issues around how to appropriately allocate costs across participating agents who use various services with different frequencies. In addition, issues regarding the increasing number of gig workers who benefit from coordination offered through digital platforms (e.g., Uber/Lyft, TaskRabbit, Instacart) but also contribute their own personal resources raise complex questions around the allocation of costs associated with delivering these services to consumers (Chai & Scully, 2019). Although reaching mutual agreements between participating agents often generates greater economic value for all agents (Forcadell, 2005; Garriga, 2009; Gemser & Leenders, 2011; Singh, 1997), cooperation is frequently stifled by concerns for fairness. People are in fact quite willing to give up materially significant financial benefits in order to reject practices or outcomes that they deem to be unfair (Bellemare et al., 2008; Fehr & Gächter, 2000; Güth et al., 1982). We adopt a behavioral accounting approach toward understanding how individuals perceive fair and unfair cost allocations.

Our objectives in this paper are threefold. First, we experimentally operationalize two common fairness notions – proportionality and equality – drawing on the game theoretical solutions prescribed for cost allocation problems. In particular, we focus on the analytical solutions driven from the Shapley value (Shapley, 1953) and Banker's modified Shapley value (Banker, 1981) that provide competing predictions in alignment with the proportionality and equality notions of fairness. Second, using the controlled experiment, we document experimental evidence suggesting proportionality as the prevailing fairness notion in the cost allocation context. Third, we provide insights into the role of fairness as a key rationale underlying the prevalence of the proportionality allocation method in accounting practices.

In our study, we are particularly interested in two common notions of fairness – proportionality and equality – within the context where individual contributions vary transparently.[1] We experimentally identify which of the two fairness notions prevails and promotes cooperation. Understanding fairness considerations in allocation problems is important because perceptions of fairness can drive cooperative behavior. Unfairness in allocation problems can be costly if inequity provokes resentments and conflicts (Dawes & Thaler, 1988; Fehr & Gächter, 2000; Fehr & Schmidt, 1999), as many of these conflicts end up in courts. Most court decisions for allocation problems often side with either the equality notion of fairness or the proportionality notion, aligning with the fairness notions of our interest. We introduce two examples of legal cases below to highlight the common application of both the equality notion and proportionality notion of fairness in allocation problems that involves costly economic consequences for the involved parties.

State Contracting & Engineering Corp v. Condotte America, Inc. is an example where the equality notion of fairness is applied. Two counsels worked on a patent infringement case together and had a disagreement on the attorney fee allocation, one demanding more than the other based on their contributions. Since no official evidence existed to prove clear distinction in individual contribution levels, the court concluded that the attorney fee be split equally between the two counsels. For the case *United States v. Atlas Minerals and Chemicals, Inc. et al.* where the United States sued corporations that contaminated a landfill by disposing the hazardous waste, the court applied the proportional allocation method to split the cost among the sued corporations. The court held those corporations responsible for the cleanup cost based on the relevant "equitable factors" such as the relative volume and toxicity of the waste disposed by each corporation. These two cases illustrate that when information on individual contribution levels is available, legal arguments can justify the proportionality notion of fairness in allocation problems.

In our study, unlike these legal cases, we evaluate fairness notions in the cost allocation context where individual contribution levels are known, and conflict or resentment induced by unfair allocations is designed to drive the involved agent's decision to either accept or reject cooperation. Yet, these court rulings are useful for our study because they provide us with social, institutional, and normative grounds to formulate our conjecture that the proportionality notion often prevails and promotes cooperation in cost allocation problems where individual contributions vary and are known. We conduct an experiment to examine which notion of fairness between proportionality and equality better aligns with individual fairness considerations in such cost allocation problems where individual contributions vary and are known. More specifically, we use a modified, anonymous, one-shot ultimatum game as an experimental tool to examine fairness considerations in economic decision-making. This controlled experiment setting allows us to focus on fairness considerations as a sole driver for cooperation, excluding alternative explanations for cooperation including reputation, reciprocity, or relationship building (Güth et al., 1982).

In a typical two-player, one-shot ultimatum game (Güth et al., 1982), the proposer allocates a sum of money between the proposer and the responder and offers allocations to the responder. The responder either *accepts* the offer (if deemed to be sufficiently fair) or *rejects* the offer (if deemed to be sufficiently unfair). If the responder accepts the offer, both players economically benefit from cooperation. If the responder rejects the offer, both players walk away with nothing. In our study, we modify the typical ultimatum game by casting a cost allocation problem within an ultimatum game framework. Utilizing special features of a cost allocation problem, we set up our experiment so that we can address our specific research question: Which notion of fairness prevails in cost allocation problems and drives cooperation when individual contributions vary? In our modified context, instead of asking our participants to allocate an endowment, we frame the joint benefit as a cost savings that requires the cooperation of both players to realize. Each player incurs inevitable costs at varying degrees and if both players cooperate, they can both benefit from cost savings. In our context, not achieving cooperation thus becomes more costly for both players. Therefore, unfair cost allocations that lead players to reject cooperation have direct negative economic consequences to the players. We operationalize two notions of fairness as experimental treatments and compare the rate of rejection between the two treatments. Using the modified ultimatum game, we find that fairness considerations coincide more with the proportionality notion when individuals make different contributions to achieve join benefits through cooperation.

We derive our experimental treatments from the game theoretical solutions prescribed by the Shapley value (Shapley, 1953) and Banker's (Banker, 1981) modified Shapley value in a two-person cooperative game. The Shapley value allocates joint benefits or cost savings equally to the players in a two-person cooperative game, taking into account all possible orders of entry of the players into the game to allocate the expected marginal contribution. In contrast, Banker's modified Shapley value, which incorporates additional information on individual contribution levels, allocates joint benefits or cost savings in proportions with individual contribution levels. In our study, we design two experimental conditions based on these analytical allocation solutions. In one condition, cost savings are split between two participating agents equally, regardless of the individual contribution levels, yet as prescribed by the Shapley value and supported by the equality notion of fairness. In the other condition, cost savings are allocated between two agents proportionally based on their individual contributions, as prescribed by Banker's solution and as supported by the proportionality notion of fairness. Our study is the first to evaluate these competing fairness notions that align with the corresponding allocation solutions and experimentally identify which notion prevails in the cost allocation context.

With our study, we contribute to the accounting literature by shifting the focus beyond what has been done in accounting research so far. In accounting practices, joint cost allocation has been pervasive for a long time and accounting researchers have recognized the importance of the design of joint cost allocation in pricing decisions, cost control and management, and fostering desired behavior at the managerial level (Banker, 1981; Banker et al., 1988; Hamlen et al., 1977, 1980; Roth & Verrecchia, 1979; Zimmerman, 1979).[2] However, the importance of fairness considerations underlying the design of allocations has not yet received the kind of attention it deserves in the accounting literature. By examining fairness considerations in allocation problems experimentally at an agent level, our findings provide important insights into fairness not only as a key rationale underlying the prevalence of the proportional allocation method in accounting practices but also as a central component in designing allocations that promote and sustain cooperation.

Our study also adds to the behavioral economics literature on other-regarding preferences, by exploring the cost allocation problem in a special context where cost contribution levels differ. More specifically, previous findings show that if the allocation share is considerably below the equal split (usually below 30% of the total endowment), most individuals perceive such allocation scheme as unfair and prefer to forego the material benefit that can only be achieved by cooperating with the other party. However, our study shows that in the cost allocation context where individual contribution levels vary and can be distinguished, the proportional split is rather more acceptable than the equal split. Thus, in the cost allocation context, more unequal (but proportional) allocation proposals can actually be perceived as fairer, leading to greater cooperation with the other party.

We proceed to the next section by introducing the discussion of fairness considerations in allocation problems in various fields of studies, including accounting, economics, behavioral economics, and the wider social sciences. Then, we describe our experiment and develop hypotheses to examine which allocation solution represents individual notion of fairness in the context where individual contribution levels vary. We conclude our paper with results and discussion.

LITERATURE ON FAIRNESS CONSIDERATIONS AND ALLOCATIONS

Accounting Literature

Joint cost allocation has a long history of practice in accounting (Ahmed & Scapens, 2000; Balachandran & Ramakrishnan, 1996; Dasgupta & Tao, 1998; Hamlen et al., 1977; Moriarity, 1975). In the cost accounting context, a joint cost allocation problem arises when at least two agents use shared resources. Total costs incurred jointly are then allocated to each party based on the resource usage level, ideally. In practice, since tracking and measuring shared resource usage levels can be costly or impossible, joint costs are often allocated to each party based on the most appropriate cost driver (Balachandran & Ramakrishnan, 1981; Gangolly, 1981; Tijs & Driessen, 1986; Zimmerman, 1979). Because the allocation process involves estimation to some extent, fairness becomes a particularly important concern in joint cost allocation problems, yet this factor has still been overlooked in accounting research (Horngren et al., 2002; Young, 1994).

Cost allocation is important in making managerial decisions such as budgeting decisions (e.g., Baldenius et al., 2007; Pfaff, 1994; Rajan, 1992; Zimmerman, 1979), pricing decisions (e.g., Cohen & Loeb, 1990; Lere, 1986), control and management systems (e.g. Gordon, 1951; Suh, 1987), financial reporting (e.g., Khumawala et al., 2005; Tinkelman, 1998), and performance evaluations (e.g. Reichelstein, 1997; Rogerson, 1997; Wei, 2004). Therefore, it is critical that the cost allocation method charges each responsible party a fair share of the total cost, reflecting true cost incurred by each party. Unfair allocations may create disutility and psychological tension in the workplace, which can result in undesired management behavior and decisions. Although the cost allocation method in accounting research, driven from the economic game theory, has been evaluated for its efficiency, optimality, and practicality, little has been studied as to whether the allocation is perceived as fair. Our study uses a behavioral approach to examine fairness considerations associated with the cost allocation methods.

Economics Literature: Game Theory

Using an axiomatic approach, scholars have proposed allocation solutions that align with both the equality and proportionality notions of fairness. The equal distribution of resources among players can be seen as a Nash equilibrium solution to the classic Nash bargaining game (Nash, 1950). Nash equilibrium is a set of each player's strategy that generates the best possible outcome for every player, taking into account other players' decisions. The equal distribution is also the outcome prescribed by the Shapley value mechanism in situations involving two players (Shapley, 1953).

The Shapley value is a unique solution to the cooperative n-player game that satisfies Shapley's axioms of symmetry, efficiency, and additivity (see Appendix A). The "symmetry" axiom implies that it is only the value added to the game by the player that matters in determining the allocation, not any other characters of the player – that is, if any two players add the same value to any coalition, they should get the same allocations. The "efficiency" axiom states that the total amount distributed to all players adds up to the total value yielded by the cooperative game. The "additivity" axiom states that adding the allocations of two independent games yields the solution of the sum of those games. The Shapley value is the unique solution satisfying these axioms. It allocates to a player i the amount given by $\sum_{S \subset N} \frac{(s-1)!(n-s)!}{n!} [v(S) - v(S-i)]$, where N is the set of all n players, S is a subset of N comprising s players, and $v(S)$ is the value generated by the subset S of players. In effect, this method allocates the expected marginal contribution to each player. In the n-player setting, the Shapley value is determined considering all possible orders of entry of the players into the game, giving each player the expected marginal contribution. In the two-player case subset, the mechanism reduces to the solution that each player receives an equal allocation of the costs or benefits – same as the Nash equilibrium.

Analogous to Shapley's axiomatic approach to the justification of the Shapley value method, Banker (1981) proposes the proportional allocation method in the form of a unique mechanism that satisfies a set of axioms similar to the Shapley axioms (see Appendix A). Banker states Shapley's "efficiency" axiom as the "full cost allocation" axiom, which requires that $\sum_{i=1}^{n} x_i = c$, where c is the total cost (or benefit) to be allocated. This full cost allocation axiom ensures that all of the costs (or benefits) are allocated to the players – total burden is shared by all participants. The "symmetry" axiom requires that individuals who consume (or contribute) the same level of resources should be responsible for the same share of the costs (or benefits) – or more formally, that $q_1 = q_2 \rightarrow x_1 = x_2$, where q_i is the size of player i and x_i is the amount allocated to player i. Finally, Banker modifies Shapley's "additivity" axiom as the "additivity of players (or cost centers)" axiom, which requires that if a specific player (or cost center) k is subdivided into two players (or cost centers), f and g, such that $q_k = q_f + q_g$, then the sum of costs allocated to each of the two component players (cost centers), f and g, should be the same as the cost allocated solely to k, unless their resource consumption levels change.

Banker proposes the "additivity of cost centers" axiom to replace Shapley's "additivity" axiom because the Shapley value method determines allocations that are determined by the way players are organized rather than their resource consumption levels. Banker argues that unless the resource consumption levels of different players (or "cost centers") change, consolidating players into one player should not influence the amount allocated to other players. For example, consider two players, A and B, and their sub-players, A1 and A2 under A, B1 and B2 under B, who agreed to share the cost of using a shared resource. The best way to split the cost is to allocate it based on the number of days each sub-player uses the shared resource, as each needs to use the resource for a certain number of days. According to Banker's assertion, unless the number of days used by each sub-player changes, whether player A1 and player A2 enter the agreement as a single party or as two separate sub-parties should not influence the cost amount allocated to player B. However, according to the Shapley value method, the allocated cost amount for player B differs from when sub-player A1 and A2 play as a single party against B to when they play as two separate sub-parties.

The axioms of the Shapley value – especially the "additivity" axiom – has been subject to criticism when applied to various situations and contexts in which the Shapley value does not necessarily seem to yield fair allocations (Banker, 1981). An alternative mechanism to allocate costs or benefits is the proportional allocation method. Proportional allocation method is widely applied in cost accounting systems. This method takes into account additional information on q_i, the relative magnitudes of resource consumption (or contribution) by each individual player i (Banker, 1981). If additional information on individual consumption (or contribution) levels is permitted to enter into the specification of the allocation mechanism, the common accounting method prescribes fair allocations to be in the proportions of the consumption (or contribution) by each player.

Based on these game theoretical solutions, we design our experiment to examine which notion between the equality notion and the proportionality notion better represents individual notion of fairness.

Behavioral Economics Literature

A classic demonstration of the fact that fairness matters is provided by the ultimatum game, first studied by Güth et al. (1982). In a two-player ultimatum game, a proposer is given an endowment, y (usually in the amount of $10 in laboratory experiments), and the proposer offers a proportion of the endowment, x, to the responder. The responder can either accept or reject the offer, x. If the responder accepts the offer, the responder takes x and the proposer is left with $y-x$. If the responder rejects the offer, both players are left with a payoff of zero. Theoretically, a unique subgame-perfect Nash equilibrium predicts that when the game is played as a one-shot anonymous interaction game, a rational economic responder is expected to accept any offer $x > 0$ from the proposer since rejection of the offer would forego the material benefit of x. Behavioral findings, however, deviate significantly from these theoretical predictions: if the offer, x, is below 30% of the endowment, y, responders reject the offer at rates of around 40%–60% (Camerer & Thaler, 1995).

These findings suggest that individuals often prefer the fair solution to the rational solution. When offered an unfair allocation, individuals prefer an inefficient outcome (getting zero) to an efficient but unfair outcome (getting $x > 0$). This indicates that motivations to achieve fairness can indeed outweigh self-interested materialistic desires. These findings are very robust and have been demonstrated in a number of industrialized societies and with stakes as much as several months' expenditures, giving further sustenance to the power and fundamental nature of the aspirations for fairness (Cameron, 1999; Hoffman et al., 1996; Roth et al., 1991).

Motivations to achieve fair outcomes promote socially efficient, cooperative outcomes. Research findings, both at the behavioral level and at the neural level, suggest that cooperation and fairness may be desirable in and of itself, not because of the subsequent material benefits. Behavioral studies document that when disciplinarian players – who are seriously concerned about achieving fair outcomes over unfair outcomes even at their own costs – are given the opportunity to sanction selfish players by imparting punishments for their selfish acts, those strongly motivated disciplinarians may be able to rationally induce some of the selfish players to realize fair outcomes that are socially efficient and eventually to cooperate toward achieving fair outcomes (Fehr & Gächter, 2000; Gürerk et al., 2006; Kahneman et al., 1986).[3]

Recent studies employing neuroimaging methods have even begun to uncover the proximal mechanisms involved in the implementation of the motivation to achieve fair outcomes. In particular, some evidence has revealed that mutual cooperation and the realization of fair outcomes can be intrinsically rewarding experiences, while unfairness can be distressing. For example, implementing a cooperative outcome in a prisoner's dilemma game yielded increased activations in brain regions implicated in reward processing, including nucleus accumbens, caudate nucleus, and ventromedial orbitofrontal cortex (Rilling et al., 2002). Similar patterns were documented using a modified ultimatum game – in response to fair rather than unfair offers, increased activations in brain regions related to reward processing were observed, including ventral striatum, ventromedial prefrontal cortex, and orbitofrontal cortex (Tabibnia et al., 2008). Furthermore, transfers of money that generate equitable outcomes yielded increased activations in ventral striatum and ventromedial prefrontal cortex (Tricomi et al., 2010). However, when individuals receive unfair offers in an ultimatum game, they can experience more negative emotion, yielding increased activations in the right anterior insula that is associated with an increased likelihood to reject unfair offers (Sanfey et al., 2003). Finally, individuals tend to find it rewarding to punish players who behave toward unfair outcomes in a trust game, thus motivated to actually scold defectors and maintain fair and efficient outcomes (Quervain et al., 2004).

A wide swathe of behavioral evidence supports the importance of fairness considerations in allocation problems. Our study takes a closer look at fairness by examining two typical notions of fairness – equality and proportionality – in a cost allocation setting important in accounting. In our modified ultimatum game, we vary individual contribution levels and the proposed offer, such that if individual notion of fairness is better represented by the equality notion, equal allocations will be preferred regardless of the individual contribution level. On the other hand, if individual notion of fairness is better represented by the proportionality notion, allocations that are proportional to the individual contribution level will be preferred to the equal split. We find that individual notion of fairness is subject to change depending on the context and that the proportionality notion prevails when individual contributions vary in achieving joint benefits.

Philosophy and Sociology Literature

Philosophers and sociologists have recognized both equality and proportionality as appropriate notions of fairness. Although equal allocations have been justified as the fairest on moral grounds (see the expositions of Carens, 1981; Nielsen, 1979; Rawls, 1971), unequal allocations can also be regarded as fair, as long as inequalities can be justified by suitable rights, duties, and conditions in basic social institutions (Adams, 1965; Boulding, 1958, 1962; Lamont, 1994; Nozick, 1974; Rawls, 1971). Boulding (1962) suggested two general principles underlying fairness perceptions in allocations, emphasizing the importance of one's need and contribution level when determining fair allocations. Rawls (1971) focused on one's need in fair allocation problems, asserting that the fairest allocation is the one that makes the most disadvantaged in society as comfortable as possible. On the other hand, Nozick (1974) focused on one's contribution level, postulating that a proportional allocation based on one's contribution or production is the fairest.

Adams (1965) postulates that individuals feel distress when the ratio of their rewards relative to their input is unequal to that of their colleagues.[4] Building on Adams' equity theory, the proportionality notion has been applied to a number of socio-economic settings as a fair allocation method, in settings such as scheduling (Moulin, 2008) and the rationing of indivisible goods (Moulin, 2002). Proportional allocations are also incorporated as fair allocations in behavioral economic preference models as well (Cappelen et al., 2007; Frohlich et al., 2004; Ho & Su, 2009; Konow, 2000). Frohlich et al. (2004) extend the inequity-aversion model of preference (Fehr & Schmidt, 1999) by including additional terms that generate disutility to a proposed allocation if the offered amount is below the proportional amount contributed, for either the proposer or the responder. Konow (2000) builds on the accountability principle from equity theory to prescribe the fair allocation of gains based on the proportion of input contributed by player i. Cappelen et al. (2007) provide a more general specification that allows each individual to hold one's own fairness ideal, whether it be strictly egalitarian (considering equal allocations as fair), libertarian (giving each person exactly what he or she produces), or liberal egalitarian (corresponding to the Konow (2000) proportional specification) and characterizes disutility for unfair allocations as a convex function of deviations relative to the fairness ideal. Ho and Su's (2009) peer-induced fairness model is also built on a fairness principle similar to original equity theory ideas, calling for those that put in equal effort to be rewarded equally.

Connecting Prior Literature to Our Study

Drawing on prior studies from various fields on allocations and fairness, our study evaluates two common notions of fairness – proportionality and equality – in cost allocation problems. While prior studies suggest analytical solutions to joint cost allocation problems, our study is the first to use a behavioral approach to examine fairness considerations in the allocation schemes prescribed for accounting practices. We use a two-person cooperative game to evaluate fairness considerations underlying the two competing allocation methods that are prescribed analytically for accounting practices. Although our experimental design simplifies the key features of complex real-world allocation problems, we choose to use a controlled experiment because it allows us to directly compete two notions of fairness by operationalizing the analytical prescriptions for allocations as experimental conditions that align with either proportionality or equality notion of fairness. If individual conceptions of fairness in cost allocation problems coincide more with equality notion, participating agents will prefer equal allocations driven from the Shapley value. On the other hand, if individual conception of fairness in cost allocation problems coincide more with the proportionality notion, individuals will exhibit greater preference for proportional allocations driven from Banker's modified Shapley value. This design allows us to compare the acceptance rate of an equal allocation and the acceptance rate of a proportional allocation to experimentally identify the prevailing fairness notion in the cost allocation context.

Fairness considerations in allocation problems arise from comparing one's own allocation to the other. When, *ceteris paribus*, one's allocation is not equal to the other's, aversion to inequity surfaces, and allocations are assessed as unfair based on the equality notion of fairness. Many formal accounts of fairness motivations invoke this simple notion that equality is fair. For example, many political philosophers have endorsed equality as fair in political domains including opportunity, fundamental human worth, and basic moral rights (e.g. Boulding, 1958, 1962; Carens, 1981; Nielsen, 1979; Nozick, 1974; Rawls, 1971). In game theory, equal allocations are prescribed by Nash (1950) equilibrium and the Shapley value (1953) based on the axiomatic properties that a fair, desirable allocation mechanism should satisfy.[5] The notion of equality in allocation problems has been studied in the economic decision-making setting where people use equality as a heuristic (Allison & Messick, 1990; Messick, 1993, 1995;

Messick & Schell, 1992). Equal sharing of monetary benefits or costs is commonly observed in the business practice context including profit sharing among joint venture partners (Dasgupta & Tao, 1998; Veugelers & Kesteloot, 1996). Although the perception of unfairness often converges with inequality, in a variety of circumstances, equality does not always lead to fair allocations. After recognizing inequalities in allocations with a discrepancy, differences in contributions are often evaluated to resolve the discrepancy. Enter the proportionality notion of fairness.

The proportionality notion often competes with the equality notion in assessing fairness in the context where one may deserve more than the other. For example, when Partner A of a joint venture contributes disproportionately more capital and greater contribution than Partner B, it is intuitively conceivable that Partner A may "deserve" a greater share of the total profit. The proportionality notion of fairness prescribes allocations to be matched with the usage levels or contribution levels and is at the core of accounting methods for cost allocations. In business practices, multiple parties often share resources or facilities to achieve economies of scale. Then, each party is charged a share of total costs that were incurred jointly, called joint costs or common costs. Since not all costs can be traced directly to a specific cost object, these joint costs are assigned to cost objects using an allocation method. In accounting practices, the proportional allocation method, among many others, has been used pervasively – costs are allocated in proportion to the cost objects' contribution levels based on the most reasonable, appropriate, and convenient cost drivers. The proportional allocation solution has also been rationalized within the political philosophy and sociology literature on the grounds that since individuals differ in their contribution, resources, and welfare, each involved party should meet the input requirements in order to share the outcome equally (e.g., Adams, 1965; Boulding, 1958, 1962; Lamont, 1994; Rawls, 1971). The axiomatic justifications have also been provided based on the axioms similar to the Shapley value (1950) except for a slightly modified additivity property (Banker, 1981). In our study, we directly compete these two notions of fairness using a controlled experiment to study which notion prevails in an allocation problem and leads to cooperation.

Both the equality and proportionality notions of fair allocations can be supported by several different arguments and are widely applied in maintaining social institutions. In this paper, we design and conduct an experiment to examine whether equal allocations or proportional allocations better represent individual notion of fairness in a cost allocation problem that is cast as the two-person one-shot anonymous ultimatum game. We describe the experimental design and develop research hypotheses in the following section.

EXPERIMENTAL DESIGN AND HYPOTHESES

We conduct an experiment to study individual intuition about fairness toward allocations determined by either the Shapley value method or the proportional allocation method based on Banker's modifications to the Shapley value axioms.

Our experimental setting employs the ultimatum game framework as it allows for a calibrated assessment of the perceptions of fair outcomes that influence individual decisions for cooperation. The ultimatum game represents the cooperative problem by focusing on allocating the potential benefits that can be achieved only through collaboration. In a two-player ultimatum game, the proposer offers some of the benefits to the responder, who can decide to either accept or reject the offer. Only when the responder accepts the offer, both players are able to realize the benefits according to the agreed terms. In case the responder rejects the offer, both players receive zero. Within this ultimatum game framework, we design our experiment using the cost allocation problem.

The cost allocation problem can be cast as an ultimatum game. Consider two players, Player 1 and Payer 2, sharing a common resource. Sharing this common resource will cost only c in total, whereas if they operated separately, it would cost c_1 for Player 1 and c_2 for Player 2, for total cost of $c < c_1 + c_2$. Therefore, by sharing a common resource, they can benefit from total cost savings of y, where $y = (c_1 + c_2 - c)$. When this cost allocation problem is cast as an ultimatum game, the proposer offers a portion of total cost savings, x, so that $0 \leq x \leq y$, to the responder. If the responder accepts the offer, cost allocations are in effect. Player 1 bears the cost $c_1 - (y - x)$ and Player 2 the cost $(c_2 - x)$, so that $c_1 - (y - x) + c_2 - x = c$. Similar representations can translate multiplayer cost sharing situations into ultimatum games by designating one player as the proposer and the other as a responder, with the understanding that a common pooled resource sharing proposal will be agreed upon if and only if no responder rejects the offer. In addition, an independent external party can be cast as the proposer with all players in the cost sharing acting as responders. While this is not the only way the cost allocation game may be played, representing the cost allocation problem in this manner enables us to draw on the vast amount of experimental evidence accumulated in the behavior of players in the ultimatum game and calibrate how individuals perceive fairness of proposed cost allocations.

Participants were asked to play the responder role and decide whether to accept or reject the predetermined allocation offer. Every participant was given two scenarios of modified ultimatum games – in a randomized order – where players consumed resources equally in one scenario and unequally in the other. Individual preferences for various allocations offered in both the equal consumption and unequal consumption scenarios were assessed in a two-player setting. To examine participants' perceptions of fair allocations in different settings, we implemented a fractional factorial design (2×2) in which participants were randomly assigned to one of the four experimental conditions (see Table 1). We varied the following across the participants:

- The contribution level: All participants completed two tasks. In one task, all participants contributed (or consumed) an equal amount as the other player – "Contributed 50%." In the other task, the relative contribution level was varied and participants were randomly assigned to either the "Contributed 80%" condition, in which participants contributed four times more than the other, or

Table 1. Experimental Conditions.

Offered %	Contributed %	Conditions	N
Offered 20%	Contributed 20%	[c20o20]	179
	Contributed 50%	[c50o20]	179
Offered 50%	Contributed 50%	[c50o50]	177
	Contributed 80%	[c80o50]	177
Total			356

the "Contributed 20%" condition, in which participants contributed four times less than the other player.

• The proposed offer: Participants were randomly assigned to either an equal split of the savings (50% of total) or lower offer (20% of total). The proposed offer remained the same in two tasks that each participant completed so that we can measure the within-subject difference for the same offer amount between two tasks – one task with equal contribution level ("Contributed 50%") and the other task with unequal contribution level (either "Contributed 80%" or "Contributed 20%").

We counterbalanced the order of the equal consumption and unequal consumption games. In addition, participants were randomly assigned either to a condition in which the offer was proposed by the other player or to a condition in which the offer was proposed by an external arbitrator; because the rejection rates in both games did not differ based on the order or the proposer type (χ^2s < 1), we report collapsed analyses in the results section for ease of exposition. Table 1 summarizes the four key experimental conditions by contribution levels and offers.

A total of 356 undergraduate students participated in our experiment for partial class credit. Every participant assumed the responder role in a modified two-person ultimatum game and was asked to either accept or reject the offer proposed. Each participant was asked to complete two tasks – one task in which both players contributed equally (Contributed 50%) and the other task in which one player contributed more (Contributed 80%) than the opponent (Contributed 20%). Each participant was randomly assigned to one of the two offers – either 20% or 50% of total benefit – and the offer remained the same for both tasks. For both tasks, either the opponent or an arbitrator proposed the offer. Since neither the task order effect nor the arbitrator effect was statistically significant, we collapse the conditions into four and each subject made decisions in two conditions (tasks) that correspond to the randomly assigned offer. For example, Participant A, who was randomly assigned to the offer amount of 20%, was asked to make a decision whether to reject or accept the 20% offer in two conditions: [c20o20], where A contributed 20% and was offered 20%, and [c50o20], where A contributed 50% and was offered 20%. Participant B, who was randomly assigned to the offer amount of 50%, decided whether to reject of accept the 50% offer in two conditions: [c50o50], where B contributed 50% and was offered 50%, and [c80o50], where B contributed 80% and was offered 50%.

In the two-player setting, when both players consume equal amounts of resources, the Shapley method yields the same allocations as those yielded by the proportional allocation method: equal sharing of the total cost savings between the two. Each participant was asked to decide whether to accept or reject an offer made by the other player, where the players' resource consumption levels were randomly determined to be either equal or unequal. The responder's decision and behavior are of particular interest in our study because the responder's acceptance indicates not only the desire to cooperate but also fairness perception – the responder accepts the offer because the offer is perceived to be fair enough to motivate the responder to work toward cooperation. In many cooperative games, such as public goods games, uncertain anticipation of unfair outcomes prevents participation. In our ultimatum game interpretation, since we specify the offer as given (predetermined and will not change) to the responder, we eliminate any risk of uncertainty for the responder. Therefore, our setting has the advantage that responder behavior reveals a desire to cooperate in conjunction with fairness perceptions toward allocations determined by either allocation method.

The predictions for our experimental conditions are summarized in Table 3 Panel A. If individual perception about fairness aligns better with the equality notion, cooperation will be achieved more frequently when offered an equal split. On the other hand, if individuals find their ideas about fairness more consistent with the proportionality notion, cooperation will be achieved more frequently when offered an allocation amount proportional to the contribution level. More specifically, if it is true that fairness is based on the equality notion (E), the rejection rate for a particular offer should be the same regardless of the contribution level:

Under the hypothesized assumption that fairness is based on the equality notion,

$H1E$ (null): The 20% offer is rejected with the same frequency when the individual contributed 50% (or R[c50o20]) as when the individual contributed 20% (or R [c50o20]).

$H2E$ (null): The 50% offer is rejected with the same frequency when the individual contributed 80% (or R[c80o50]) as when the individual contributed 50% (or R [c50o50]).

Under the hypothesized assumption that fairness is based on the proportionality notion,

$H1P$ (alternative): The 20% offer is rejected more frequently when the individual contributed 50% (or R[c50o20]) than when the individual contributed 20% (or R[c50o20]).

$H2P$ (alternative): The 50% offer is rejected more frequently when the individual contributed 80% (or R[c80o50]) than when the individual contributed 50% (or R[c50o50]).

METHOD

Participants

A total of 356 undergraduate students (45% female and 55% male) participated in the study for partial class credit. Table 2 shows the descriptive statistics of the participants who answered the demographic questionnaires. Participants (mean age = 21) categorized themselves in an above-middle economic condition (mean = 4.65 on a 7-point scale); 49% of the participants majored in Accounting, 40% in Marketing, and 9% in Finance. For our analysis, because we are interested in the within-subject difference between the two conditions in which the contribution levels are different, only those who completed both tasks could be included (N = 353).

Upon the completion of two tasks, participants answered five items in regards to their feelings of compassion on the Dispositional Positive Emotions Scale compassion subscale (DPES; Shiota et al., 2006; α = 0.53) and six items relating to their feelings of self-righteousness (Falbo & Belk, 1985; α = 0.41). All 11 items were rated on a 7-point Likert type scale ranging from 1 (strongly disagree) to 7 (strongly agree), with 4 indicating neutral. Subsequently, participants answered demographic questions. The economic condition was self-reported on a scale of 1–7, where 1 indicated that the participant felt "distressed" and 7 indicated that the participant felt "comfortable." Here, we show the descriptive statistics for only those who reported their information.

Procedure

Participants were randomly assigned to one of the four conditions (see Table 1) to play the responder role in two modified ultimatum games (or tasks) in the context of a cost allocation problem. For each task, participants read a hypothetical scenario in which they were considering a joint purchase decision with the other player, or a hypothetical roommate. The order of the two tasks given was randomized. In one task, participants were asked to consider the equal consumption scenario where both players consumed equal amounts of steak ("Contributed 50%") in our experiment. In the other task, participants were asked to consider the unequal consumption scenario where two players consumed unequal amounts of energy drinks – some were asked to assume the role of a roommate consuming only a quarter of the other roommate's consumption level ("Contributed 20%") and others were asked to assume the role of a roommate consuming four times more than the other roommate's consumption level ("Contributed 80%"). In both tasks, the amount of total possible cost savings was $10, in case participants accepted the offer as a responder. After deciding whether to accept or reject the offer, participants provided their minimum acceptable offer (between $0 and $10) and indicated the amount that they would have offered if they played the proposer role instead. These allocation values were selected to correspond to prior literature on the ultimatum game in the behavioral economics literature.

Participants subsequently answered five items relating to their feelings of compassion on the Dispositional Positive Emotions Scale compassion subscale (DPES; Shiota et al., 2006; α = 0.53) and six items relating to their feelings of

Table 2. Descriptive Statistics.

Demographic Variables	N	Mean	Std. Dev.	Min	Max
Age	345	21.02	2.70	18	45
Economic condition	341	4.65	1.52	1	7
Educational level	347	2.72	0.75	1	5
Compassion	352	0.057	0.867	−2.658	1.613
Self-righteousness ("I" or "me")	342	−0.002	0.853	−1.913	2.564
Self-righteousness ("people")	342	0.172	0.787	−2.116	2.164
Gender	344	Male = 55%; Female = 45%			

self-righteousness (Falbo & Belk, 1985; $\alpha = 0.41$). All 11 items were on a scale of 1–7, where 1 indicated that participants strongly disagreed, 4 indicated that they were neutral, and 7 indicated that they strongly agreed (see Appendix B for 11 items). Finally, participants answered demographic questions (See Table 2).

RESULTS

The main results are summarized in Table 3, panel B and Fig. 1.

We graph the rejection rate of the offer in four conditions, by offer amount. When individuals are offered a 20% share (dotted line) of total benefits, the offer is rejected as frequently as 72% when they contribute the same amount (50%) as the other player in the game. However, when they contribute 20% to generate the total benefits and are offered a 20% share, the rejection rate drops to 34%. When individuals are offered an equal split (solid line) of total benefits, the 50% offer is

Table 3. Hypotheses and Results.

Panel A. Hypotheses

Offer	Hypothesized assumption (E): Fairness is based on equality	Hypothesized assumption (P): Fairness is based on proportionality
Offered 20%	$H1E$ (null): R[c50o20] = R[c20o20]	$H1P$ (alternative): R[c50o20] > R[c20o20]
Offered 50%	$H2E$ (null): R[c50o50] = R[c80o50]	$H2P$ (alternative): R[c50o50] < R[c80o50]

Panel B. Paired t-Test Results

Offer	Hypothesized assumption (P): Fairness is based on proportionality
Offered 20% ($N = 177$)	$H1P$ (alternative): R[c50o20] > R[c20o20] 72% > 34% difference = 38% ($t = 7.49$)
Offered 50% ($N = 176$)	$H2P$ (alternative): R[c50o50] < R[c80o50] 12% < 32% difference = −20% ($t = -4.84$)

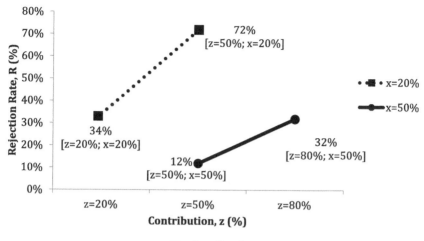

Fig. 1. Results.

rejected at a rate of 12% when the contribution level is also 50%. The rejection rate then goes up to 32% when they are offered 50% but contributed 80%. These results support the hypothesized assumption that fairness is based on proportionality:

H1P (alternative): R[c50o20] > R[c20o20]
72% > 34%   difference = 38% ($t = 7.49$)
H2P (alternative): R[c50o50] < R[c80o50]
12% < 32%   difference = -20% ($t = -4.84$)

We postulate two sets of hypothesized assumptions based on the two notions of fairness – equality and proportionality. Based on the equality notion, the rejection rate of an offer – whether it be 20% or 50% – is not influenced by the contribution level and we state our hypotheses under the equality notion as nulls. Based on the proportionality notion, on the other hand, the rejection rate of an offer is affected by the contribution level, such that for the same amount of an offer, when the contribution level is higher than the offer, the rejection rate will be higher. The 20% offer is rejected more frequently when individuals contributed 50% than when contributed 20% (*H1P*). The 50% offer is rejected more frequently when individuals contributed 80% than when contributed 50% (*H2P*).

Because we examine the within-subject difference between the two conditions with different contribution levels for each subject, we require that each subject completes both tasks to be included in our analysis. Two subjects were excluded from the 20% offer ($N = 177$) and one subject from the 50% offer ($N = 176$). We used the two-sided test although our hypotheses call for a one-sided test.

Participants, who were proposed the 20% offer (refer to the results reported in a dotted line), rejected the offer at a significantly higher rate when they contributed equal amount as the other player (R[c50o20] = 72%) than when they contributed only 20% toward the total cost savings (R[c20o20] = 34%). When participants were offered 50% of the total savings (refer to the results reported in a solid line), they rejected the 50% offer at a significantly higher rate when they contributed 80% (R[c80o50] = 32%) than when they contributed 50% (R[c50o50] = 12%). These main results support our hypothesized assumption for proportionality and show that when contribution levels are different, proportional allocations better represent the individual notion of fairness.

In addition, we observe some interesting between-subject differences. When the contribution level is the same, the 20% offer was rejected at a significantly higher rate than the 50% offer (R[c50o20] = 72% vs. R[c50o50] = 12%; difference = 60%, $t = 14.35$). When the contribution level differs, those who contributed more toward the total savings than the other player rejected the relatively lower offer as frequently as those who contributed 20% and were offered 20% (R[c80o50] = 32% vs. R[c20o20] = 34%).

As an additional analysis, we present a logit regression analysis (see Table 4) in which we control for additional participant characteristics, such as personality (in terms of compassion and self-righteousness), age, gender, economic condition,

Table 4. Logit Models With Control Variables.

DV = Reject	Model (1)*	Model (2)*	Model (3)*
[c50o20]	**2.939**		**3.035**
	(0.000)		**(0.000)**
[c20o20]	**1.323**		**1.278**
	(0.000)		**(0.000)**
[c80o50]	**1.228**		**1.263**
	(0.000)		**(0.000)**
Age		0.057	0.062
		(0.092)	(0.115)
Female		0.082	−0.083
		(0.621)	(0.659)
Economic Condition		−0.044	−0.053
		(0.425)	(0.399)
Education Level		−0.039	−0.078
		(0.756)	(0.578)
Compassion		−0.067	−0.034
		(0.482)	(0.754)
Self-righteousness_me		0.046	−0.028
		(0.635)	(0.799)
Self-righteousness_ppl		−0.072	−0.141
		(0.495)	(0.235)
Unequal consumption task first			−0.028
			(0.878)
Arbitrator			−0.017
			(0.926)
Intercept	**−1.999 (0.000)**	−1.426 (0.040)	**−2.774 (0.001)**
N	709	656	656
Pseudo R^2	0.159	0.006	0.171

education level, whether the proposer was the other roommate or a third party (*Arbitrator*), and the order effect (*Unfair consumption task first*). We first run a logit regression (column (1) of Table 4) on whether participants rejected the offer or not in four conditions, using [c50o50] as our baseline (indicated by intercept). We find that participants are significantly more likely to reject the offer when they are in conditions [c50o20], [c20o20] and [c80o50] and less likely to reject the offer when they are in condition [c50o50]. In Model (2), we run the logit regression on whether the rejection choice is affected by individual characteristics and find no significant association with any characteristics (column (2) of Table 4). In the last column, (3), when we include all the condition variables and individual characteristics, we find that after controlling for individual characteristics, the experimental condition effects are robust, confirming that our results are not driven by individual demographic characteristics.

Examining all conditions simultaneously, we show the condition effect on the likelihood of rejecting the offer, after controlling for individual characteristics. In all three models, the dependent variable is *Reject*, a binary variable (i.e. Reject = 1 if the offer was rejected and 0 if accepted). In Model (1), we first show the condition effect where the [c50o50] condition is the base line (refer to the intercept). [c50o20], [c20o20], and [c80o50] are binary variables. In Model (2), we examine whether individual demographic characteristics affect the rejection choice. Finally, in Model (3), we include the condition variables and demographic variables.

$$\text{Model}(1) : \text{Reject} = \alpha_0 + \alpha_1 \, [c50o20] + \alpha_2 \, [c20o20] + \alpha_3 \, [c80o50] + \epsilon$$

$$\begin{aligned}
\text{Model}(2) : \text{Reject} = {} & \beta_0 + \beta_1 \, \text{Age} + \beta_2 \, \text{Female} + \beta_3 \, \text{Economic Condition} \\
& + \beta_4 \, \text{Education Level} + \beta_5 \, \text{Compassion} \\
& + \beta_6 \, \text{Self} - \text{righteousness}_{\text{me}} \\
& + \beta_7 \, \text{Self} - \text{righteousness\_ppl} + \epsilon
\end{aligned}$$

$$\begin{aligned}
\text{Model}(3) : \text{Reject} = {} & \gamma_0 + \gamma_1 \, [c50o20] + \gamma_2 \, [c20o20] + \gamma_3 \, [c80o50] \\
& + \gamma_4 \, \text{Age} + \gamma_5 \, \text{Female} + \gamma_6 \, \text{Economic Condition} \\
& + \gamma_7 \, \text{Education Level} + \gamma_8 \, \text{Compassion} \\
& + \gamma_9 \, \text{Self} - \text{righteousness}_{\text{me}} \\
& + \gamma_{10} \, \text{Self} - \text{righteousness\_ppl} \\
& + \gamma_{11} \, \text{Unequal consumption task first} \\
& + \gamma_{12} \, \text{Arbitrator} + \epsilon
\end{aligned}$$

CONCLUSION

Various allocation methods have been proposed on analytical, social, institutional, and moral grounds to settle cost allocation problems. Our study focuses on fairness considerations associated with two competing allocation methods that are commonly applied in economic decision-making contexts – the equal allocation method and the proportional allocation method. Based on our experimental evidence, we conclude that individual conception of fairness seems to coincide more with the notion of proportionality in the context where the contribution levels of the involved agents are different and can be distinguished. We find that when both players contribute equally, equal allocations are perceived to be fair, which coincide with both notions of fairness. However, when the players contribute unequally, allocating the outcome proportional to the contribution level is perceived to be fair, which coincides more with the proportionality notion of fairness.

Allocation problems are prevalent in business practices where cooperation is imperative. Cooperation is critical for an organization's success as it enables the involved parties to achieve greater economic benefits despite the costs involved (Forcadell, 2005; Garriga, 2009; Gemser & Leenders, 2011; Rustagi et al., 2010; Singh, 1997). In the process of cooperation, multiple parties – for example, corporations, joint venture partners, member-owners of cooperative entities, business unit managers, or project managers – bring individual contributions in the form of effort, time, and resources to accomplish a shared goal of acquiring benefits that are greater when achieved jointly than when achieved individually. Nevertheless, cooperative problems are often accompanied by a tension between self-interest and collective interests. This tension arises because costs are incurred at the individual level, while benefits are acquired jointly and shared among the cooperators. Thus, if joint benefits are allocated unfairly, individuals often exhibit aversion to one's own disadvantage by rejecting cooperation, which leads to a suboptimal outcome (Bellemare et al., 2008; Fehr & Schmidt, 1999; Güth et al., 1982).

Cooperation is a fundamental social behavior that holds human societies together (Fehr & Fischbacher, 2004; Henrich et al., 2001; Tomasello & Vaish, 2013). Many philosophical speculations and evolutionary theories have been developed around the puzzle of human tendency for maintaining cooperation. One theory points out that cooperation has proven to be the winning evolutionary strategy for human civilizations to thrive on many accounts – including foraging, hunting, carrying on wars, and building bridges and railroads – and has become an ethical social norm that has preserved social institutions (Boyd et al., 2010; Henrich, 2006; Hill, 2002; Hirshleifer, 1985; Holländer, 1990; Tomasello et al., 2012; Tomasello & Vaish, 2013). Regardless of whether it is in human nature to cooperate or it is to embody an ethical social norm, humans tend to maintain cooperation (Bear & Rand, 2016; Bowles & Gintis, 2002; Fehr & Fischbacher, 2004; Henrich et al., 2001; Rand et al., 2012; Rand & Nowak, 2013; Tomasello & Vaish, 2013).

Despite the positive outcomes of cooperation that human societies have benefitted from throughout many centuries of our history, in many cases, cooperation is not strictly preferred (De Cremer & Van Knippenberg, 2002; Fehr & Rockenbach, 2003; Fehr & Schmidt, 1999; Henrich, 2006; Hill, 2002). This is mainly due to the clash between self-interests and collective interests, especially when economic incentives are involved. Cooperators are expected to bring contributions and restrict self-interests at the individual level to achieve a collective goal. This tension between self-interests and collective interests tends to peak when individuals perceive unfairness in allocations of joint benefits (Fehr & Schmidt, 1999; Güth et al., 1982). If potential cooperators perceive allocations to be unfair, they often exhibit aversion to inequity by rejecting cooperation, leaving everyone worse off, even at their own expenses (Balliet et al., 2011; Boyd et al., 2010; Fehr & Gächter, 2000). As such, fairness considerations that facilitate cooperation and promote achieving greater benefits are particularly important in business practices. Our study provides experimental evidence that individual fairness considerations in the cost allocation context coincide with the proportionality notion of fairness when individual contributions vary transparently.

Our findings suggest that the equity principle manifested in the proportional allocation method is preferred to the equality principle in accounting practice because it is perceived as fair, thus promotes cooperation that enables an organization to thrive. Cost allocation problems are ubiquitous in accounting practice as multiple agents or divisions share firm resources mainly to achieve cost savings from the economies of scale. When agents share facilities or resources and individual usage level can be distinguished or estimated, firms allocate joint costs to each agent based on the usage level of cost drivers. This practice not only reduces cost distortions but also is perceived to be fair as allocated costs influence managerial decisions for performance evaluations, budgeting, and resource allocations. Thus, fairness considerations in cost allocations are crucial in facilitating cooperation among agents, which is imperative in achieving organizational success in the long term.

Our results also provide support for the common legal practice of applying both equality and proportionality notions of fairness depending on the context. In the case of allocating the attorney fee between the attorney and co-counsel, who is discharged before the settlement of case, because there is no supporting evidence that distinguishes the contribution level of each agent toward legal representation, the court rules that the fee be split equally between the two agents. In the case of allocating the cleaning costs of contaminated landfill, because the contribution level of each party is distinguishable based on the "equitable factors," total cost is allocated proportionally to each corporation's contribution level toward contamination.

Future research could examine cost allocation problems in greater complexity. While the current study controlled a number of complicating factors, further research could explore in more depth how aspects such as imperfectly observed costs, cooperation among a greater number of agents, or opportunities for repeated interactions and/or sanctioning may moderate behavior in the cost allocation context. Each of these dimensions could help to describe different classes of cost allocation problems that individuals encounter in the modern marketplace.

When designing allocations, fairness is an important consideration. The meaning of fairness has been given due consideration for a long time, going as far back as Plato's *The Republic*, in which the concept of fairness is explored through Socrates' lengthy dialogs. While the definition of fairness may seem to be straightforward, various contexts in which fairness perceptions are formed make the concept dynamic. Therefore, it is important to understand notions of fairness and which notion of fairness best represents individual intuition about fairness in a particular context so that the appropriate notion of fairness is considered when designing cost allocations.

ACKNOWLEDGMENTS

We are grateful for valuable comments from the anonymous reviewers, Dan Weiss (discussant), Matthew Sooy (discussant), and participants at the 2019 Management Accounting Section Midyear Meeting, the 2019 Conference on the Convergence of Financial and Managerial Accounting, and the 2019 American Accounting Association Annual Meeting.

NOTES

1. In this paper, we use "contribution" and "consumption" interchangeably as we refer to a cost driver based on which joint benefits or cost savings are allocated using the proportional allocation method.

2. For example, in the United Kingdom, the surviving evidence of cost allocations goes back to the business records of Welsh companies that engaged in metal work and iron manufacturing between 1700 and 1830 (Jones, 1985).

3. However, the same motivations that enable these disciplinarians may also prevent them from participating at all, sometimes leading to rapid degeneration in cooperation. An individual, who desires to achieve fair outcomes but anticipates others to behave in a selfish way, may choose not to participate at all, resulting in lower total contribution levels and inefficient outcomes. This behavior is observed in repeated public goods games and is especially apparent when punishment opportunities are available: while contribution levels in the first interaction toward the group investment are around 40%–60%, these levels drop dramatically after observing others deviate from cooperation, to around 20% in subsequent interactions (Fehr & Gächter, 2000). This finding is alarming since it shows that the presence of a small number of selfish, uncooperative individuals may quickly lead to the deterioration of group collaboration.

4. More formally, distress is thought to be experienced when $\exists i, j$ s.t. $\frac{x_i}{q_i} \neq \frac{x_j}{q_j}$, where x denotes the reward for each individual i and j, and q denotes their inputs.

5. The Nash (1950) solution in a bargaining game yields equal allocation to two symmetric players. The widely applied Shapley value (Shapley, 1953) solution to n-player cooperative games prescribes distributions of payoffs corresponding to the weighted average of the marginal benefits that a player provides upon joining different sub-coalitions. When only two players are involved, the Shapley value solution reduces to Nash equilibrium, assigning an equal share of benefits to each player, conditional on both players choosing to cooperate.

REFERENCES

Adams, J. S. (1965). Inequity in social exchange. In L. Berkowitz (Ed.), *Advances in experimental social psychology* (Vol. 2, pp. 267–299). Academic Press. https://doi.org/10.1016/S0065-2601(08)60108-2

Ahmed, M. N., & Scapens, R. W. (2000). Cost allocation in Britain: Towards an institutional analysis. *European Accounting Review, 9*(2), 159–204. https://doi.org/10.1080/09638180050129864

Allison, S. T., & Messick, D. M. (1990). Social decision heuristics in the use of shared resources. *Journal of Behavioral Decision Making, 3*(3), 195–204. https://doi.org/10.1002/bdm.3960030304

Balachandran, B. V., & Ramakrishnan, R. T. (1981). Joint cost allocation: A unified approach. *The Accounting Review*, 85–96.

Balachandran, B. V., & Ramakrishnan, R. T. (1996). Joint cost allocation for multiple lots. *Management Science, 42*(2), 247–258.

Baldenius, T., Dutta, S., & Reichelstein, S. (2007). Cost allocation for capital budgeting decisions. *The Accounting Review, 82*(4), 837–867. https://doi.org/10.2308/accr.2007.82.4.837

Balliet, D., Mulder, L. B., & Van Lange, P. A. M. (2011). Reward, punishment, and cooperation: A meta-analysis. *Psychological Bulletin, 137*(4), 594–615. https://doi.org/10.1037/a0023489

Banker, R. (1981). Equity considerations in traditional full cost allocation practices: An axiomatic perspective. In S. Moriarity (Ed.), *Joint cost allocations* (pp. 110–130). University of Oklahoma.

Banker, R. D., Datar, S. M., & Kekre, S. (1988). Relevant costs, congestion and stochasticity in production environments. *Journal of Accounting and Economics, 10*(3), 171–197. https://doi.org/10.1016/0165-4101(88)90002-X

Bear, A., & Rand, D. G. (2016). Intuition, deliberation, and the evolution of cooperation. *Proceedings of the National Academy of Sciences, 113*(4), 936–941. https://doi.org/10.1073/pnas.1517780113

Bellemare, C., Krger, S., & van Soest, A. (2008). Measuring inequity aversion in a heterogeneous population using experimental decisions and subjective probabilities. *Econometrica, 76*(4), 815–839. https://doi.org/10.1111/j.1468-0262.2008.00860.x

Billera, L. J., & Heath, D. C. (1982). Allocation of shared costs: A set of axioms yielding a unique procedure. *Mathematics of Operations Research, 7*(1), 32–39.

Boulding, K. E. (1958). *Principles of economic policy*. Prentice Hall.

Boulding, K. E. (1962). *Conflict and defense: A general theory*. Harper.

Bowles, S., & Gintis, H. (2002). The inheritance of inequality. *The Journal of Economic Perspectives, 16*(3), 3–30.

Boyd, R., Gintis, H., & Bowles, S. (2010). Coordinated punishment of defectors sustains cooperation and can proliferate when rare. *Science, 328*(5978), 617–620. https://doi.org/10.1126/science.1183665

Camerer, C., & Thaler, R. H. (1995). Anomalies: Ultimatums, dictators and manners. *The Journal of Economic Perspectives, 9*(2), 209–219. https://doi.org/10.1257/jep.9.2.209

Cameron, L. A. (1999). Raising the stakes in the ultimatum game: Experimental evidence from Indonesia. *Economic Inquiry, 37*(1), 47–59. https://doi.org/10.1111/j.1465-7295.1999.tb01415.x

Cappelen, A. W., Hole, A. D., Sørensen, E. Ø., & Tungodden, B. (2007). The pluralism of fairness ideals: An experimental approach. *The American Economic Review, 97*(3), 818–827. https://doi.org/10.1257/aer.97.3.818

Carens, J. H. (1981). *Equality, moral incentives, and the market: An essay in utopian politico-economic theory*. University of Chicago Press.

Chai, S., & Scully, M. A. (2019). It's about distributing rather than sharing: Using labor process theory to probe the "sharing" economy. *Journal of Business Ethics, 159*(4), 943–960.

Cohen, S. I., & Loeb, M. (1990). Implicit cost allocation and bidding for contracts. *Management Science, 36*(9), 1133–1138.

Dasgupta, S., & Tao, Z. (1998). Contractual incompleteness and the optimality of equity joint ventures. *Journal of Economic Behavior & Organization, 37*(4), 391–413. https://doi.org/10.1016/S0167-2681(98)00117-6

Dawes, R. M., & Thaler, R. H. (1988). Anomalies: Cooperation. *The Journal of Economic Perspectives, 2*(3), 187–197. https://doi.org/10.1257/jep.2.3.187

De Cremer, D., & Van Knippenberg, D. (2002). How do leaders promote cooperation? The effects of charisma and procedural fairness. *Journal of Applied Psychology, 87*(5), 858–866. https://doi.org/10.1037/0021-9010.87.5.858

Etter, M., Fieseler, C., & Whelan, G. (2019). Sharing economy, sharing responsibility? Corporate social responsibility in the digital age. *Journal of Business Ethics, 159*(4), 935. https://doi.org/10.1007/s10551-019-04212-w

Falbo, T., & Belk, S. S. (1985). A short scale to measure self-righteousness. *Journal of Personality Assessment, 49*(2), 172–177. https://doi.org/10.1207/s15327752jpa4902_13

Fehr, E., & Fischbacher, U. (2004). Social norms and human cooperation. *Trends in Cognitive Sciences, 8*(4), 185–190. https://doi.org/10.1016/j.tics.2004.02.007

Fehr, E., & Gächter, S. (2000). Cooperation and punishment in public goods experiments. *The American Economic Review, 90*(4), 980–994. https://doi.org/10.1257/aer.90.4.980

Fehr, E., & Rockenbach, B. (2003). Detrimental effects of sanctions on human altruism. *Nature, 422*(6928), 137–140. https://doi.org/10.1038/nature01474

Fehr, E., & Schmidt, K. M. (1999). A theory of fairness, competition, and cooperation. *Quarterly Journal of Economics, 114*(3), 817–868.

Forcadell, F. J. (2005). Democracy, cooperation and business success: The case of Mondragón Corporación Cooperativa. *Journal of Business Ethics, 56*, 255–274.

Frohlich, N., Oppenheimer, J., & Kurki, A. (2004). Modeling other-regarding preferences and an experimental test. *Public Choice, 119*(1), 91–117. https://doi.org/10.1023/B:PUCH.0000024169.08329.eb

Gangolly, J. S. (1981). On joint cost allocation: Independent cost proportional scheme (ICPS) and its properties. *Journal of Accounting Research, 19*(2), 299–312. https://doi.org/10.2307/2490866

Garriga, E. (2009). Cooperation in stakeholder networks: Firms' 'tertius iungens' role. *Journal of Business Ethics, 90*(S4), 623–637. https://doi.org/10.1007/s10551-010-0596-9

Gemser, G., & Leenders, M. A. A. M. (2011). Managing cross-functional cooperation for new product development success. *Long Range Planning, 44*(1), 26–41. https://doi.org/10.1016/j.lrp.2010.11.001

Gordon, M. J. (1951). Cost allocations and the design of accounting systems for control. *The Accounting Review, 26*(2), 209–220.

Gürerk, O., Irlenbusch, B., & Rockenbach, B. (2006). The competitive advantage of sanctioning institutions. *Science, 312*(5770), 108–111. https://doi.org/10.1126/science.1123633

Güth, W., Schmittberger, R., & Schwarze, B. (1982). An experimental analysis of ultimatum bargaining. *Journal of Economic Behavior & Organization, 3*(4), 367–388. https://doi.org/10.1016/0167-2681(82)90011-7

Hamlen, S. S., Hamlen, W. A., & Tschirhart, J. (1980). The use of the generalized Shapley allocation in joint cost allocation. *The Accounting Review, 55*(2), 269–287.

Hamlen, S. S., Hamlen, W. A., & Tschirhart, J. T. (1977). The use of core theory in evaluating joint cost allocation schemes. *The Accounting Review, 52*(3), 616–627.

Henrich, J. (2006). Costly punishment across human societies. *Science, 312*(5781), 1767–1770. https://doi.org/10.1126/science.1127333

Henrich, J., Boyd, R., Bowles, S., Camerer, C., Fehr, E., Gintis, H., & McElreath, R. (2001). In search of homo economicus: Behavioral experiments in 15 small-scale societies. *The American Economic Review, 91*(2), 73–78. https://doi.org/10.1257/aer.91.2.73

Hill, K. (2002). Altruistic cooperation during foraging by the ache, and the evolved human predisposition to cooperate. *Human Nature, 13*(1), 105–128. https://doi.org/10.1007/s12110-002-1016-3

Hirshleifer, J. (1985). The expanding domain of economics. *The American Economic Review, 75*(6), 53–68.

Ho, T.-H., & Su, X. (2009). Peer-induced fairness in games. *The American Economic Review, 99*(5), 2022–2049. https://doi.org/10.1257/aer.99.5.2022

Hoffman, E., McCabe, K., & Smith, V. L. (1996). Social distance and other-regarding behavior in dictator games. *The American Economic Review, 86*(3), 653–660.

Holländer, H. (1990). A social exchange approach to voluntary cooperation. *The American Economic Review, 80*(5), 1157–1167.

Horngren, C. T., Bhimani, A., Datar, S. M., & Foster, G. (2002). *Management and cost accounting.* Financial Times/Prentice Hall Harlow.

Jones, H. (1985). *Accounting, costing, and cost estimation in Welsh industry.* University of Wales Press.

Kahneman, D., Knetsch, J. L., & Thaler, R. (1986). Fairness as a constraint on profit seeking: Entitlements in the market. *The American Economic Review, 76*(4), 728–741.

Khumawala, S. B., Parsons, L. M., & Gordon, T. P. (2005). TRACKS assessing the quality of not-for-profit efficiency ratios: Do donors use joint cost allocation disclosures? *Journal of Accounting, Auditing and Finance, 20*(3), 287–309. https://doi.org/10.1177/0148558X0502000305

Konow, J. (2000). Fair shares: Accountability and cognitive dissonance in allocation decisions. *The American Economic Review, 90*(4), 1072–1091. https://doi.org/10.1257/aer.90.4.1072

Lamont, J. (1994). The concept of desert in distributive justice. *The Philosophical Quarterly, 44*(174), 45–64. https://doi.org/10.2307/2220146

Lere, J. C. (1986). Product pricing based on accounting costs. *The Accounting Review, 61*(2), 318–324.

Messick, D. M. (1993). Equality as a decision heuristic. In B. A. Mellers & J. Baron (Eds.), *Psychological perspectives on justice: Theory and applications* (pp. 11–31). Cambridge University Press.

Messick, D. M. (1995). Equality, fairness, and social conflict. *Social Justice Research, 8*(2), 153–173. https://doi.org/10.1007/BF02334689

Messick, D. M., & Schell, T. (1992). Evidence for an equality heuristic in social decision making. *Acta Psychologica, 80*(1), 311–323. https://doi.org/10.1016/0001-6918(92)90053-G

Moriarity, S. (1975). Another approach to allocating joint costs. *The Accounting Review, 50*(4), 791–795.

Moulin, H. (2002). The proportional random allocation of indivisible units. *Social Choice and Welfare, 19*(2), 381–413. https://doi.org/10.1007/s003550100118

Moulin, H. (2008). Proportional scheduling, split-proofness, and merge-proofness. *Games and Economic Behavior, 63*(2), 567–587. https://doi.org/10.1016/j.geb.2006.09.002

Nash, J. F. (1950). The bargaining problem. *Econometrica, 18*(2), 155–162.

Nielsen, K. (1979). Radical egalitarian justice: Justice as equality. *Social Theory and Practice, 5*(2), 209–226. https://doi.org/10.5840/soctheorpract1979523

Nozick, R. (1974). *Anarchy, state and utopia*. Blackwell Publishers.

Pfaff, D. (1994). On the allocation of overhead costs. *European Accounting Review, 3*(1), 49–70. https://doi.org/10.1080/09638189400000003

Quervain, D. J.-F. D., Fischbacher, U., Treyer, V., Schellhammer, M., Schnyder, U., Buck, A., & Fehr, E. (2004). The neural basis of altruistic punishment. *Science, 305*(5688), 1254–1258. https://doi.org/10.1126/science.1100735

Rajan, M. V. (1992). Cost allocation in multiagent settings. *The Accounting Review, 67*(3), 527–545.

Rand, D. G., Greene, J. D., & Nowak, M. A. (2012). Spontaneous giving and calculated greed. *Nature, 489*(7416), 427–430. https://doi.org/10.1038/nature11467

Rand, D. G., & Nowak, M. A. (2013). Human cooperation. *Trends in Cognitive Sciences, 17*(8), 413–425. https://doi.org/10.1016/j.tics.2013.06.003

Rawls, J. (1971). *A theory of justice*. Harvard University Press.

Reichelstein, S. (1997). Investment decisions and managerial performance evaluation. *Review of Accounting Studies, 2*(2), 157–180. https://doi.org/10.1023/A:1018376808228

Rilling, J. K., Gutman, D. A., Zeh, T. R., Pagnoni, G., Berns, G. S., & Kilts, C. D. (2002). A neural basis for social cooperation. *Neuron, 35*(2), 395–405. https://doi.org/10.1016/S0896-6273(02)00755-9

Rogerson, W. P. (1997). Intertemporal cost allocation and managerial investment incentives: A theory explaining the use of economic value added as a performance measure. *Journal of Political Economy, 105*(4), 770–795. https://doi.org/10.1086/262093

Roth, A. E., Prasnikar, V., Okuno-Fujiwara, M., & Zamir, S. (1991). Bargaining and market behavior in Jerusalem, Ljubljana, Pittsburgh, and Tokyo: An experimental study. *The American Economic Review, 81*(5), 1068–1095.

Roth, A. E., & Verrecchia, R. E. (1979). The Shapley value as applied to cost allocation: A reinterpretation. *Journal of Accounting Research, 17*(1), 295. https://doi.org/10.2307/2490320

Rustagi, D., Engel, S., & Kosfeld, M. (2010). Conditional cooperation and costly monitoring explain success in forest commons management. *Science, 330*(6006), 961–965. https://doi.org/10.1126/science.1193649

Sanfey, A. G., Rilling, J. K., Aronson, J. A., Nystrom, L. E., & Cohen, J. D. (2003). The neural basis of economic decision-making in the ultimatum game. *Science, 300*(5626), 1755–1758. https://doi.org/10.1126/science.1082976

Shapley, L. S. (1953). The value of an N-person game. In H. W. Kuhn & A. W. Tucker (Eds.), *Contributions to the theory of games*. Princeton University Press.

Shiota, M. N., Keltner, D., & John, O. P. (2006). Positive emotion dispositions differentially associated with big five personality and attachment style. *The Journal of Positive Psychology, 1*(2), 61–71. https://doi.org/10.1080/17439760500510833

Singh, K. (1997). The impact of technological complexity and interfirm cooperation on business survival. *Academy of Management Journal, 40*(2), 339–367.

Suh, Y. S. (1987). Collusion and noncontrollable cost allocation. *Journal of Accounting Research, 25*, 22–46. https://doi.org/10.2307/2491077

Tabibnia, G., Satpute, A. B., & Lieberman, M. D. (2008). The sunny side of fairness: Preference for fairness activates reward circuitry (and disregarding unfairness activates self-control circuitry). *Psychological Science, 19*(4), 339–347. https://doi.org/10.1111/j.1467-9280.2008.02091.x

Tijs, S. H., & Driessen, T. S. (1986). Game theory and cost allocation problems. *Management Science, 32*(8), 1015–1028.

Tinkelman, D. (1998). Differences in sensitivity of financial statement users to joint cost allocations: The case of nonprofit organizations. *Journal of Accounting, Auditing and Finance, 13*(4), 377–393. https://doi.org/10.1177/0148558X9801300401

Tomasello, M., Melis, A. P., Tennie, C., Wyman, E., & Herrmann, E. (2012). Two key steps in the evolution of human cooperation: The interdependence hypothesis. *Current Anthropology, 53*(6), 673–692. https://doi.org/10.1086/668207

Tomasello, M., & Vaish, A. (2013). Origins of human cooperation and morality. *Annual Review of Psychology, 64*(1), 231–255. https://doi.org/10.1146/annurev-psych-113011-143812

Tricomi, E., Rangel, A., Camerer, C. F., & O'Doherty, J. P. (2010). Neural evidence for inequality-averse social preferences. *Nature, 463*(7284), 1089–1091. https://doi.org/10.1038/nature08785

Veugelers, R., & Kesteloot, K. (1996). Bargained shares in joint ventures among asymmetric partners: Is the Matthew effect catalyzing? *Journal of Economics, 64*(1), 23–51. https://doi.org/10.1007/BF01237524

Wei, D. (2004). Inter-departmental cost allocation and investment incentives. *Review of Accounting Studies, 9*(1), 97–116. https://doi.org/10.1023/B:RAST.0000013630.18838.04

Young, H. P. (1994). Cost allocation. *Handbook of Game Theory with Economic Applications, 2*, 1193–1235.

Zimmerman, J. L. (1979). The costs and benefits of cost allocations. *The Accounting Review, 54*(3), 504–521.

APPENDIX A

AXIOMS FOR SHAPLEY VALUE (1953) AND BANKER'S (1981) MODIFIED AXIOMS FOR PROPORTIONAL ALLOCATION METHOD

(1) Axioms for Shapley Value (1953)

Axiom 1 ("Symmetry"). The value is essentially a property of the abstract game. For each x in $\pi(U)$,

$$\emptyset_{xi}[xv] = \emptyset_i[v] \text{ (all } i \in U).$$

Axiom 2 ("Efficiency"). For each carrier N of v,

$$\sum_N \emptyset_i[v] = v(N).$$

Axiom 3 ("Law of Aggregation"). For any two games v and w,

$$\varnothing[v + w] = \varnothing[v] + \varnothing[w].$$

(2) Banker's (1981) Modified Axioms for Proportional Allocation Method

Axiom A1 ("Full Cost Allocation"). The costs allocated to the user departments add up to the total cost of providing the service,

$$\text{i.e. } \sum_{j=1}^{n} x_j = c$$

Axiom A2 ("Symmetry"). If the amount of service provided to two user departments is the same, then the costs allocated to them must be the same,

$$\text{i.e. } q_f = q_g \rightarrow x_f = x_g$$

Axiom A3 ("Additivity of Cost Centers"). If a cost center k is subdivided into two cost centers f and g, such that $q_k = q_f + q_g$; then the costs allocated to each of the remaining cost centers remains the same as before when k was considered as a single entity. In other words, we do not want the allocation to change unless or until the amount of service usage changes with the reorganization.

APPENDIX B

EXPERIMENTAL MATERIAL – PERSONALITY SCALES

After completing the two tasks, participants answered 11 items below relating to their feelings of compassion and self-righteousness. The first five items (Items 1 thru 5) were adopted from the Dispositional Positive Emotions Scale compassion subscale (DPES; Shiota et al., 2006; $\alpha = 0.53$). The next six items (Items 6 thru 11) had to do with participants' feelings of self-righteousness (Falbo & Belk, 1985; $\alpha = 0.41$). All 11 items were on a scale of 1–7, where 1 indicated that participants strongly disagreed, 4 indicated that they were neutral, and 7 indicated that they strongly agreed with the statement. In our analysis, two separate variables were used for the self-righteousness items – *self-righteousness_me* for items focusing on oneself (Items #6, 7, and 11) and *self-righteousness_ppl* for items focusing on others (Items #8, 9, and 10).

Please indicate your level of agreement with the following statements. Answer with 7 if you strongly agree, with 0 if you strongly disagree, and with 4 if you are neutral.

Strongly Disagree	1	2	3	4 Neutral	5	6	7	Strongly Agree

(1) It's important to take care of people who are vulnerable.
(2) When I see someone in need, I feel a powerful urge to take care of them.
(3) Taking care of others gives me a warm feeling inside.

(4) I never notice people who need help.
(5) I am a very compassionate person.
(6) People who disagree with me are usually wrong.
(7) I can benefit other people by telling them the right way to do things.
(8) One person's opinions are just as valid as the next person's.
(9) Most people naturally do the right thing.
(10) People generally make few mistakes because they do know what is right or wrong.
(11) When people disagree with me, I figure they're just not up to my level of thinking.

THE INFLUENCE OF A FAMILY FIRM STRUCTURE ON AUDITOR JUDGMENTS: EFFECTS OF MANAGERIAL CONTROL AND OWNERSHIP CONCENTRATION

Jingyu Gao[a], Anna M. Rose[b], Ikseon Suh[c] and Min Zhang[d]

[a]*Capital University of Economics and Business, China*
[b]*University of Northern Colorado, USA*
[c]*University of Nevada Las Vegas, USA*
[d]*Renmin University of China, China*

ABSTRACT

We employ an experiment with experienced Chinese auditors to examine how family firm structures influence auditors' reliance on management's explanations for evidence and their assessments of fraud risk. Our findings indicate that for firms with family ownership, high levels of family managerial control cause auditors to rely less on management's explanations and assess higher levels of fraud risk when a firm's control environment is strong. However, when the control environment is weak, auditors' judgments are not influenced by family firm structure.

Keywords: Control environment risk; family firms; fraud risk; managerial control; ownership concentration

INTRODUCTION

Family firms are a dominant form of business entity in the global economy (Bennedsen et al., 2015; Hope et al., 2012; Prencipe et al., 2014), and little is known about the effects of family firm structure on auditors' judgments. We leverage the advantages of the experimental research methodology to investigate

---

Advances in Accounting Behavioral Research, Volume 27, 29–53
Copyright © 2024 by Emerald Publishing Limited
All rights of reproduction in any form reserved
ISSN: 1475-1488/doi:10.1108/S1475-148820240000027002

the influence of family firm structure and control environment risk on practicing auditors' judgments. Our sample consists of 116 highly experienced Chinese auditors who are primarily audit managers and partners. China offers a perfect setting for the research because family firms account for 55.8% of listed firms, making Chinese auditors highly familiar with family firm clients (Chen et al., 2008; Cheng, 2014; Yuan, 2010).

Our findings indicate that the effects of family firm structure on auditor judgments depend upon the level of control environment risk. When control environment risk is high, practicing auditors' judgments are not influenced by family firm structure. Once auditors perceive significant problems with a firm's control environment, there is little effect of family firm structure on evaluations of management explanations or assessments of fraud risk. Results are very different, however, when the control environment risk is low. Auditors are less likely to accept management explanations for audit evidence and assess higher levels of fraud risk when a firm has high levels of family ownership and high family managerial control, relative to when a firm has high levels of family ownership and low levels of family managerial control.[1] These results indicate that increased family managerial control causes auditors to be concerned about management's potential agency behavior, such as incentives to conceal the firm's true financial performance and protect private control benefits at the expense of minority (nonfamily) shareholders' interests.

In contrast, we find no significant differences in auditor judgments between nonfamily firms and firms with a high level of family ownership but a low level of family control. These results are important and further indicate that auditors perceive that less family control of management is indicative of family owners' stewardship motivations and decreased risks of fraud. Collectively, our findings provide support for social embeddedness theory (Le Breton-Miller & Miller, 2009) and reveal that when a firm is owned by family members, increased family control of management causes auditors to be concerned about agency conflicts and increased audit risks. Thus, while prior auditing research finds evidence that auditors perceive higher risks for family firms relative to nonfamily firms (e.g., Krishnan & Peytcheva, 2019), we find that family control of management is a primary source of these perceived risks.

Prior to our study, the limited auditing literature related to family firm structure has provided mixed evidence in support of either a stewardship theory or agency theory perspective. Stewardship theory portrays family business owners and managers as prioritizing stakeholders' interests over private economic interests (Arrègle et al., 2007; Le Breton-Miller & Miller, 2009), thereby increasing the likelihood that external auditors may perceive family firms to be less concerned with earnings manipulation and more focused on long-term social and organizational performance (Ghosh & Yang, 2015; Martin et al., 2016; Niemi, 2005; Suh et al., 2021). Alternatively, agency theory supports an entrenchment perspective of family firm governance, framing family business owners and managers as pursuing self-serving family interests at the expense of nonfamily shareholders (Miller & Le Breton-Miller, 2006; Prencipe et al., 2014). This perspective suggests that external auditors may view family firms skeptically, with the potential to affect earnings quality and increase audit risk (Hope et al., 2012; Krishnan & Peytcheva, 2019; Srinidhi et al., 2014).

One reason for conflicting views about the effects of family firms on auditors' judgments results from the design of prior research. Research has not investigated how specific elements of family firm structures affect auditors, and we extend the existing findings by examining how family control of management affects auditors' judgments for firms with family ownership. By examining the effects of family control of management, we provide insights into why auditors view risks differently in family firms versus nonfamily firms. According to PCAOB Auditing Standards No. 2110 (Para. 7), external auditors are required to "obtain an understanding of the company and its environment to understand the events, conditions, and company activities that might reasonably be expected to have a significant effect on the risks of material misstatement [whether due to errors or fraud]." In addition, based on International Standards on Auditing (ISA) 315 (Para. 19), the auditor "shall perform risk assessment procedures to obtain an understanding ... of the entity and its environment [including] the entity's organizational structure, ownership and governance, and its business model." Important factors to consider in the assessment of material misstatement risks are ownership attributes of the company such as family or nonfamily business environments (SAS 99, sec 37; ISA 315, Para. 19a). We also contribute by investigating how auditors evaluate the effects of family firms structures when other sources of audit risk vary (i.e., when there is a strong or weak control environment).

The results of this study add to the emerging but limited line of literature examining the effects of family firms on auditors' judgments (Ghosh & Yang, 2015; Hope et al., 2012; Kang, 2014; Khalil et al., 2011; Krishnan & Peytcheva, 2019; Niemi, 2005; Srinidhi et al., 2014; Suh et al., 2021). The use of an experiment enables us to address calls for research directed toward gaining insights into family businesses (Vazquez, 2018) and the effects of family firm structure on auditors' judgments (Prencipe et al., 2014). Finally, our findings highlight the importance of understanding what auditors perceive to be sources of risk and suggest that research that classifies family firms based only on ownership concentration or based on differentiating family firms versus nonfamily firms is likely to produce contradictory results if family managerial control is not measured and considered.

BACKGROUND AND DEVELOPMENT OF HYPOTHESES

External auditors represent one of the four cornerstones of corporate governance (Gramling et al., 2004). To promote effective corporate governance, auditors take an active role in monitoring risks and providing assurance regarding controls and the integrity of financial reporting (Hermanson & Rittenberg, 2003). During the planning stage, auditors must "obtain an understanding of the company and its environment to understand the events, conditions, and company activities that might reasonably be expected to have a significant effect on the risks of material misstatement" (PCAOB, 2010, AS No. 2110, Para. 7). The strategies and business processes established by family firms are likely to differ from those of nonfamily firms because family beliefs and culture influence the firm's decision processes (Sharma, 2004; Trotman & Trotman, 2010). These differences, in turn, are expected to have differential effects on auditing (Niemi, 2005; Trotman & Trotman, 2010). Nevertheless, auditing research on the influence of family firms on external auditors' judgment and decision-making is relatively under-represented as a field of inquiry (Bennedsen et al., 2015; Prencipe et al., 2014), despite family firms playing crucial roles in international economies and the global workforce (Bennedsen et al., 2015; Hope et al., 2012; Le Breton-Miller & Miller, 2009; Neckebrouck et al., 2018; Vazquez, 2018).

Family Firm Structure and Auditors' Judgments

There is no commonly accepted definition of "family business" (KMU Forschung Austia, 2008). Different definitions of family firms are applied in socioeconomic research to distinguish family firms from nonfamily firms, primarily focusing on ownership concentration or managerial control of the firm (KMU Forschung Austia, 2008). This dichotomous approach has also been employed by accounting and auditing researchers, who have operationalized a "family firm" using managerial control (Kang, 2014; Martin et al., 2016), ownership concentration (Firth et al., 2007; Jaggi et al., 2009), or both (Krishnan & Peytcheva, 2019; Srinidhi et al., 2014; Suh et al., 2021).

The use of various underlying dimensions of family firm structure in the existing literature is a potential cause of inconsistent results. To date, auditing research related to family firms, which is primarily archival, has provided contrasting results that support either a stewardship or agency theory perspective. Stewardship theory assumes that agents ("stewards") of the family are driven by goals other than sole private economic interests, such as social and emotional goals (Gomez-Mejia et al., 2007; Kets de Vries, 1993). This means that family owners and managers may have strong motivations to act for the long-term goals of the company and its stakeholders and the long-run benefit of the company (Le Breton-Miller & Miller, 2009; Martin et al., 2016). These incentives can influence the organization's behavior and performance, mitigating owner-manager conflicts or Type I agency problems (Le Breton-Miller & Miller, 2009; Prencipe et al., 2014) and resulting in higher earnings quality (Salvato & Moores, 2010).

Consistent with this view, findings of Niemi (2005) reveal that ownership controlled by the family is negatively associated with audit hours and audit fees. Ghosh and Yang (2015) also find that family firms, those either managed or controlled by the founding family, pay significantly less for the external audit services relative to nonfamily firms. These studies suggest that external auditors view management's ties to the family or concentrated family ownership positively and perceive family firms to have lower audit risk or more incentives to promote earnings quality (Martin et al., 2016; Salvato & Moores, 2010). Further corroborating the stewardship theory view, findings of Suh et al. (2021) indicate that external auditors' reliance on the internal audit function (IAF) and perceptions of internal auditor objectivity are not affected by the use of the IAF as a management training ground when key executives are members of the family and the founding family controls 60% of the voting shares.[2]

Alternatively, agency theory posits that family owners and managers have incentives to pursue the interest of the family at the expense of the organization and minority (nonfamily) shareholders (Bertrand & Schoar, 2006; Miller & Le Breton-Miller, 2006; Morck et al., 2005), thereby increasing owner-owner conflicts or Type II agency problems (Prencipe et al., 2014). From this perspective, family owners and/or managers are able to use their power to pursue self-serving transactions that are detrimental to the firm's strategy, core competency and long-term performance while avoiding the interference of minority shareholders (Bennedsen et al., 2007; Fan & Wong, 2002; Le Breton-Miller & Miller, 2009; Leuz et al., 2003; Pérez-González, 2006). Entrenched family owners and managers, in turn, have incentives to oversee the financial reporting process and manage earnings opportunistically by depriving minority shareholders of cash flow rights and lowering the firm's earnings quality (Leuz et al., 2003; Morck et al., 2005; Salvato & Moores, 2010).

In accordance with the agency theory view, Hope et al. (2012) find that private firms pay higher audit fees when their CEOs have close ties to the founding family. The results of Srinidhi et al. (2014), who identify a family firm as one in which family members have more than 20% of the voting rights and at least one member serving on the board, find similar results and identify strong board governance as a factor that mitigates the detrimental effects of family ownership on earnings quality. Krishnan and Peytcheva (2019) find that audit partners and managers with family firm clients, compared to auditors with nonfamily firm clients, assess fraud risk as higher and are less likely to make client acceptance decisions when the CEO of a potential audit client is closely related to the founder by blood and the founding family owns 60% of the voting shares.

The studies described above, either in support of stewardship theory or agency theory, do not separate the effects of family ownership and family managerial control, which makes it difficult to determine the causes of their findings. It is important to understand how the different dimensions of family firm structure affect auditor judgments such that the most appropriate measures are employed in future research. Social embeddedness theory (Le Breton-Miller & Miller, 2009; Le Breton-Miller et al., 2011) can be employed to reconcile the two opposing theoretical views of family firms and to better understand the dimensions of family firm structure that should influence the financial statement audit, in particular during the planning stage.

An alternative perspective on family firms (social embeddedness theory) is proposed by Le Breton-Miller and Miller (2009), who put forth the notion that "the strength of the influence of a family on a business will be a function of the extent to which the economic exchanges of the business are embedded within the social system of the family [structurally and politically]" (p. 1179).[3] Specifically, when more key actors of the firm, such as top executives and directors, are related to the founder or the founding family, their roles become more central to the firm's activities, and they are more likely to interact with and influence employees and shift their attention to the interest of the controlling family. Continual interactions with the family members, in turn, will likely influence attitudes and behavior of economic actors, potentially aligning their decisions with the family's priorities and needs (i.e., self-interest or agency behavior). In contrast, relatively few family members holding executive positions will likely drive economic actors to focus on social and organizational goals that are more consistent with the long-term interests of stakeholders (i.e., stewardship behavior). Further supporting this view, recent archival research suggests that family managerial control is one driver of agency conflicts that is recognized by the stock market (Purkayastha et al., 2019).

Purkayastha et al. (2019) measure principal-agency (PA) and principal-principal (PP) conflicts and investigate the effects of these conflicts on shareholder value (i.e., total market capitalization/total assets) for family-owned firms. Their findings indicate that adverse stock market responses can occur when there are more PA and PP conflicts (as measured by variables such as percentage of independent directors and percentage of voting shares owned by the largest shareholder, respectively). However, they also find that separating management control from family members reduces some of the negative impacts of PA and PP conflicts on market value, suggesting that investors have concerns about family-owned firms that are managed by family members.

Auditors make different types of judgments than investors (e.g., detailed assessments of risks of misstatement versus estimations of potential future market value), and auditors are highly trained to assess financial reporting risks, while investors are not. Further, auditors' judgments are not determined by market responses. The results of Purkayastha et al. (2019) do, however, lend support to the Social Embeddedness views of family firms. As a result of the predictions of social embeddedness theory and recent evidence indicating that investors view the separation of management control away from family members in family-owned firms as a positive signal, we expect that auditors will perceive more fraud risk and will be more skeptical of management when firms that have high levels of family ownership also have high levels of family managerial control, relative to low levels of family managerial control.

Hypothesis: Auditors will assess higher levels of fraud risk and place less reliance on client explanations when clients with high levels of family ownership also have high levels of family managerial control, relative to when clients have low levels of family managerial control.

Control Environment

We also expect that the effects of family firm structure on auditors' judgments will interplay with other audit risks such as control environment risk, and examination of this interaction is another contribution of the current study beyond archival findings with investors (Purkayastha et al., 2019). Auditing Standard No. 2110 (PCAOB, 2010) and ISA 315 Para. 21 (IAASB, 2019) require that auditors gain an understanding of the client's control environment, in particular management's commitment toward a culture of honesty, ethical behavior and accountability while overseeing effective controls over financial reporting. The control environment consists of top management's aggressive or conservative attitude toward business practices and the importance of internal controls in the entity (Arens et al., 2017).

There are potentially competing effects of control environment risks on auditors' perceptions of family firm structures. A strong control environment (or a low-risk control environment) could mitigate auditors' concerns about family firm structures because an effective system of controls will prevent families from being able to pursue family interests at the expense of other stakeholders. For example, Krishnan and Peytcheva (2019) find that auditors perceive more audit risk for family firms when the audit committee is weak, relative to when the audit committee is strong. From this perspective, family firm structure will have less effect on auditors' judgments when the control environment is strong, relative to when the control environment is weak. Alternatively, a strong control environment could increase auditors' attention to family firm structure because of the capacity for family control of management to override the system of internal control. From this perspective, a strong control environment would increase the effects family firm structures on auditor's perceptions of risk.

There are also potentially competing effects when the client's control environment is weak (or control environment risk is high). A weak control environment could increase audit risk to such an extent that perceptions of control risk dominate auditors' judgments. That is, a high-risk control environment could alarm auditors and, in turn, increase their suspicions about client explanations and assessment of fraud risk. Auditors' judgments would therefore not likely change for one family firm structure or another because of high levels of concerns about the firm's control environment. Alternatively, high control environment risks could cause auditors to become more concerned about family ownership and control, thereby increasing the effects of family firm structure on auditors' assessments of fraud risk.

Based upon these competing perspectives of the effects of control environment risk on auditors' considerations of family firm structure, we pose the following research question:

Research Question: Will control environment risk affect the influence of family firm structure on auditors' reliance on client explanations and assessments of fraud risk?

RESEARCH METHOD

Design

This study employs a 3×2 between-participant randomized experiment. The independent variables are *Family Firm Structure* and *Control Environment Risk*.[4] The dependent variables consist of (1) auditors' assessments of the likelihood that the explanation provided by the CFO properly explains unexpected account balance fluctuations (a proxy measure of auditors' decision to rely on client explanations), and (2) auditors' assessments of financial fraud risk. This study primarily focuses on two different indicators of auditor risk perceptions (reliance on client explanations and fraud risk assessment) because they have the capacity to be directly influenced by perceptions of family firm structure and control environment risk. The two measures also capture key determinants of audit quality because each judgment can significantly influence the outcome of the audit and the nature of audit procedures.

Participants

We conducted this study in China because family firms account for 55.8% of listed firms and 85.4% of private companies (Cambieri, 2011; Cheng, 2014), and US family and nonfamily firms have operated in China through joint ventures since 1979 (Luo, 1998). As such, it is very common for Chinese auditors to work with family firms, whether these firms are Chinese or foreign-invested companies (Yuan, 2010). Chinese laws and regulations do not require listed or private companies to hire auditors from Big 4 international public accounting firms.[5] As a result, auditors from non-Big 4 public accounting firms provide more assurance services to family firms, either public or private, than do auditors from the Big 4 international public accounting firms (Wei et al., 2009). We employed these non-Big 4 Chinese auditors as our participants. The initial pool of external auditor participants consisted of 121 seniors, managers and partners who had individually confirmed that they work at a non-Big 4 public accounting firm and were willing to participate. Five of these participants (4.1%) were excluded from the study because four failed to respond correctly to an attention check question related to a family firm treatment condition and one did not complete the task. Therefore, the final sample consisted of 116 external auditors, including 14 (12.1%) audit seniors, 71 (61.2%) audit managers, and 31 (26.7%) audit partners.

Experimental Task

The task was administered to participants at training sessions initiated by the Chinese Institute of Certified Public Accountants (CICPA) and held by the Chinese National Accounting Institute.[6] We randomly assigned participants to one of the treatment conditions, informed them of the anonymity of their responses, and instructed them to work independently. One of the authors was present at the training sessions and verified that all participants completed the task (and returned the instrument) within the designated time (average time: 20–25 minutes). All data collection sessions were conducted in Chinese, and all experimental materials were written in Chinese. To verify the instrument, a back-translation, an independent review, and a pretest were conducted.[7] The English translation of the instrument is described in the paper.

Participants read the case materials, which were based on the experiment used by Quadackers et al. (2014). The case consists of an assessment of the preliminary results of analytical review, evaluation of management's explanation for unexpected increase in the gross margin, and consideration of alternative reasons that could have caused the unusual fluctuation. We use an analytical review task because this task context is familiar to our experienced participants, and the task allows for assessment of multiple auditor judgments such as reliance on management's explanation, association of the unusual fluctuation in the gross margin with plausible financial fraud explanations, and assessment of fraud risk. Interacting with firms and seeking management explanations are also very common in the audit environment (Hirst & Koonce, 1996; Trompeter & Wright, 2010). Inquiries of management, for example, are often performed at the client's offices, and serve as the main source of explanations for unexpected fluctuation of account balances identified during audit planning (Hirst & Koonce, 1996; Rose et al., 2020). The analytical review task allows us to directly examine how auditors respond to management explanations in addition to examining auditors' related judgments.

Family firm structure and control environment risk were manipulated to create three levels of family firm structure and two levels of control environment risk. Following the case materials, participants were instructed to consider a client explanation for a variance discovered during the analytical review. Next, participants assessed fraud risk and then responded to debriefing items, a trust measure, and demographic questions.

Independent Variables

The first independent variable is *Family Firm Structure*. The case described a hypothetical listed company, the founding family's ownership levels, and the founding family's involvement in management. The *Family Firm Structure* variable was manipulated at three levels: (1) a nonfamily firm, (2) a firm with high family ownership concentration and outside professional managers (high ownership/low control), and (3) a firm with high family ownership concentration and high levels of family managerial control (high ownership/high control).[8]

The nonfamily firm condition informed participants that the founding family maintained less than 1% concentrated ownership and members of the founding family did not have active involvement in the firm's management. The high ownership/low control condition stated that the founding family maintained a 60% concentrated ownership of the firm and members of the founding family did not have active involvement in the firm's management but instead relied on outside professional managers. The high ownership/high control condition informed participants that the founding family maintained 60% concentrated ownership and family members held key executive positions. That is, the founder was the Chief Executive Officer (CEO) and Chairman of the Board, and three younger brothers were also owners and held the titles of Chief Financial Officer (CFO), Chief Operating Officer (COO), and marketing Vice President (VP), respectively.

The manipulation of *Family Firm Structure* is consistent with the current characteristics of Chinese family firms. Among the firms issuing their A-shares at the Shanghai and Shenzhen exchanges from 2003 to 2012, family firms had a much higher level of ownership concentration than nonfamily firms, and family members usually held top executive and director positions, inclusive of the CEO and CFO positions (Cheng, 2014). The Chinese Family Business Report (China Citic Press, 2011, 2015) defines a firm as a family firm when a family (or families) has control rights (or owns common stocks with voting rights) above 50%. The 2016 Global Family Business Index shows that large public Chinese family firms own, on average, 58.05% of shares.[9] Given these statistics, we used 60% ownership of shares to represent family ownership, and members of the founding family holding key executive positions within the firm (i.e., CEO and the Chairman of the board, CFO, COO, and marketing VP) to represent family managerial control.

The second independent variable is *Control Environment Risk*. We employed the approach used by Quadackers et al. (2014) and Rose et al. (2020) to manipulate the level of control environment risk (lower versus higher). Similar to Quadackers et al. (2014) and Rose et al. (2020), we expect that participants will assess fraud risk to be higher when control environment risk is high, relative to when risk is low.

Dependent Variables

We utilize participants' assessments of the likelihood (*0% to 100%*) that the explanation provided by the CFO properly explains the unexpected account balance fluctuation (*CFO-Provided Explanation*) and their assessments of financial fraud risk (*Fraud Risk*) for examining our hypothesis.[10]

Other Variables

Participants also responded to questions related to their level of disposition to distrust (i.e., *Suspicion of Humanity*). This variable is a composite scale reflecting the participating auditors' distrust of others when others are perceived to lie, act for self-interest, cheat on their income taxes, care more about themselves, and be dishonest (6 = a low level of suspicion and 42 = a high level of suspicion). We used *Suspicion of Humanity* as a control variable due to the findings of Quadackers et al. (2014). The authors demonstrated that presumptive doubt (or inverse scale of Rotter's Interpersonal Trust Scale) was a significant factor driving auditors' fraud risk assessments using a similar decision case. Prior research has also shown that distrust (i.e., skepticism) exists as a separate construct from trust (i.e., confidence) (McKnight et al., 2004). For more information on dispositional trust and distrust, see McKnight et al. (2004) and Goto (1996).[11]

We also coded other explanations that the participating auditors considered as reasons behind the unusual fluctuation in the gross margin (i.e., *Plausible Financial Fraud Explanations*). A research assistant (who was not aware of the treatment conditions) and one of the authors independently coded *Plausible Financial Fraud Explanations*.[12] We assessed the level of agreement between the tabulators by obtaining a single measure of inter-rater reliability (Kappa) of

0.827 ($p < 0.001$) for *Plausible Financial Fraud Explanations* (Fleiss, 1981; Howell, 2002; Shrout & Fleiss, 1979). Differences in the number of *Plausible Financial Fraud Explanations* between the two coders were examined and reconciled. After this reconciliation, we summed the percentage allocated to each *Plausible Financial Fraud Explanation* by the participating auditors to compute the total likelihood that plausible financial fraud explanations caused the unusual fluctuation in the gross margin (i.e., *Likelihood of Plausible Financial Fraud Explanation*). This variable, along with the *CFO-Provided Explanation* variable, was used in the mediation analysis (see the supplementary analysis section).

RESULTS

Descriptive Information

The external auditors in the final sample ($n = 116$) had, on average, 11.1 years of audit experience and 7.5 years of experience performing analytical reviews. Audit experience and analytical review experience for audit seniors are 7.8 years and 4.1 years, for audit managers, the experience levels are 9.7 years and 6.4 years, and for audit partners, they are 15.8 years and 11.7 years, respectively.[13] We performed Chi-Square analyses and a one-way ANOVA for the demographic data (*Gender, Years of Audit Experience*, and *Years of Analytical Review Experience*). Our results (un-tabulated) indicated that the participating auditors' demographic information did not differ significantly across the six treatment conditions (all $p > 0.48$).[14] A correlation analysis (un-tabulated) showed that demographic factors did not significantly correlate with auditors' decisions to rely on CFO-provided explanation or assessments of financial fraud risk.[15] Considering these results, our participants' demographic profile was balanced across the six treatment conditions.[16] Thus, we did not include demographic factors in further tests.

Preliminary Testing

Participants also responded to questions related to their perceptions of overall control risk and control environment effectiveness. The first question instructed participants to indicate their assessment of the level of *Overall Control Risk* (control risk at the level of the organization) based on the information provided in the case ($1 =$ very low control risk; $9 =$ very high control risk). On average, participants in the high control risk condition (mean $= 6.82$) evaluated higher risk compared to participants in the low control risk condition (mean $= 4.87$) (*t*-value $= -5.462, p < 0.001$). The second question pertains to participants' perceptions of the *Control Environment Effectiveness* ($1 =$ very ineffective; $9 =$ very effective). Participants in the high control risk condition (mean $= 3.58$) perceived the control environment less effective relative to participants in the low control risk condition (mean $= 4.76$) (*t*-value $= 3.685$, $p < 0.001$). These results indicate that the manipulation of control environment risk was effective. We also perform a correlation analysis and find that the *Control Environment Risk, Overall Control Risk,* and *Effectiveness of the Control Environment* variables are not significantly correlated with the *Family Firm Structure* variable (all $p > 0.30$). These results suggest that the *Control Environment Risk* variable, including its related dimensions, and the *Family Firm Structure* variable are capturing distinct constructs.

Hypothesis Testing and Analysis of Research Question

The hypothesis involves the potential effects of family firm structure on auditor judgments. We first performed two ANOVAs with *CFO-Provided Explanation* and *Fraud Risk* as the dependent variables and *Family Firm Structure* and *Control Environment Risk* as the independent variables. We also conducted Tukey tests to determine differences across the *Family Firm Structure* conditions. Treatment means and ANOVA results for the dependent variables are presented in Table 1, Panel A and Panel B. In addition, Figs. 1 and 2 graphically display the results.

Results of the ANOVAs reveal significant main effects of *Family Firm Structure* ($F = 8.06$, $p < 0.001$) and *Control Environment Risk* ($F = 15.56$, $p < 0.001$) and an insignificant interaction effect of *Family Firm Structure* and *Control Environment Risk* ($F = 1.67$, $p = 0.192$) for the *CFO-Provided Explanation* dependent variable. We also find significant main effects of *Family Firm Structure* ($F = 3.32$, $p = 0.040$) and *Control Environment Risk* ($F = 34.19$, $p < 0.001$) and an insignificant interaction effect of *Family Firm Structure* and *Control Environment Risk* ($F = 1.71$, $p = 0.186$) for the *Fraud Risk* dependent variable.[17] These results show significant differences in the dependent variables across the three treatment conditions of *Family Firm Structure*. Figs. 1 and 2 also indicate that auditors' reliance on client explanations and fraud risk assessments appear to vary for different combinations of family firm structure and control environment risk. While the significant main effects indicate that auditors' judgments are affected by *Family Firm Structure*, understanding the effects requires an examination of individual treatment differences.

Results of Tukey HSD tests, presented in Panels A and B of Table 2 show that the means for *CFO-Provided Explanation* and *Fraud Risk* do not differ significantly between the *nonfamily* condition and the *high ownership/low control* condition (both $p \geq 0.90$). In contrast, the participating auditors rely significantly less on *CFO-Provided Explanation* ($p = 0.002$) and assess higher *Fraud Risk* ($p = 0.048$) in the *high ownership/high control* condition compared to the *nonfamily* condition. Auditors' reliance decision on *CFO-Provided Explanation* is significantly higher ($p = 0.002$) and assessment of *Fraud Risk* is significantly lower ($p = 0.058$) in the *high ownership/low control* condition compared to *CFO-Provided Explanation* and *Fraud Risk* assessment under the *high ownership/high control* condition. These results collectively indicate that more family managerial control leads the participating auditors to be more skeptical about the client's explanation and to become more concerned about financial fraud risk. Further, the lack of evidence for a similar effect when family managerial control is low suggests that auditors do not perceive a firm's high level of ownership to be a significant source of agency problem threats. Overall, our results provide support for the study hypothesis.

To examine the research question, we analyze the interaction of *Family Firm Structure* and *Control Environment Risk*. While the interaction effects were not

JINGYU GAO ET AL.

Table 1. ANOVA Results.

Panel A: Dependent Variable = CFO-Provided Explanation

		Control Environment Risk		Row Mean
		Low	High	
Family Firm	Nonfamily	0.455	0.297	0.370
	High ownership/Low control	0.438	0.316	0.379
	High ownership/High control	0.282	0.240	0.258
Column Mean		0.395	0.281	0.334

Source	Sum of Square	df	Mean Square	F-Ratio	p-Value
Family Firm Structure	0.341	2	0.170	8.06	< 0.001
Control Environment Risk	0.329	1	0.329	15.56	< 0.001
Interaction (Family Firm Structure × Control Environment Risk)	0.071	2	0.035	1.67	0.192
Error	2.326	110	0.021		

Panel B: Dependent Variable = Fraud Risk

		Control Environment Risk		Row Mean
		Low	High	
Family Firm	Nonfamily	0.390	0.660	0.534
	High ownership/Low control	0.432	0.635	0.531
	High ownership/High control	0.559	0.680	0.629
Column Mean		0.466	0.661	0.566

Source	Sum of Square	df	Mean Square	F-Ratio	p-Value
Family Firm	0.216	2	0.108	3.32	0.040
Control Environment Risk	1.110	1	1.110	34.19	< 0.001
Interaction (Family Firm × Control Environment Risk)	0.111	2	0.056	1.71	0.185
Error	3.573	110	0.032		

(All p values are two-tailed.)

CFO-Provided Explanation =	The assessed likelihood that explanation provided by the CFO explains substantially all of the gross profit margin increase (0% to 100%)
Fraud Risk =	The assessed likelihood of financial fraud (0%–100%)
Family Firm Structure =	Nonfamily, High ownership/Low control, or High ownership/High control
Control Environment Risk =	Overall control environment risk

statistically significant in the ANOVA models, when manipulated factors in an experiment have more than two levels, ANOVAs are less sensitive to interactions, in particular ordinal interactions (Buckless & Ravenscroft, 1990; Guggenmos et al., 2018). Figs. 1 and 2 suggest ordinal interactions despite the insignificant interaction effects presented in Table 2. To better understand the pattern of auditor judgments across the three treatment conditions, we perform Tukey HSD tests on _CFO-Provided Explanation_ and _Fraud Risk_ for each _Control Environment Risk_ condition (high and low). Un-tabulated results of the Tukey HSD tests indicate that, when the _Control Environment Risk_ is high, the means for

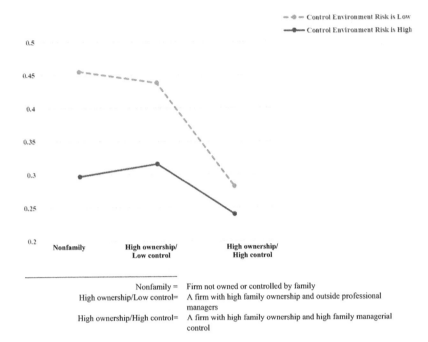

Fig. 1. Effects of Family Firm Structure and Control Environment Risk on Auditors' Reliance on CFO's Explanation.

CFO-Provided Explanation are not significantly different between the *nonfamily* (mean = 0.297, s.d. = 0.104) and *high ownership/low control* conditions (mean = 0.316, s.d. = 0.148) ($p = 0.899$), between the *nonfamily* and the *high ownership/high control* conditions (mean = 0.240, s.d. = 0.149) ($p = 0.330$), or between the *high ownership/low control* and the *high ownership/high control* conditions ($p = 0.199$). Likewise, the means for *Fraud Risk* do not differ significantly between the *nonfamily* (mean = 0.659, s.d. = 0.141) and the *high ownership/low control* conditions (mean = 0.635, s.d. = 0.191) ($p = 0.901$), between the *nonfamily* and *high ownership/high control* conditions (mean = 0.680, s.d. = 0.183) ($p = 0.906$), or between the *high ownership/low control* and *high ownership/high control* conditions ($p = 0.694$).

In contrast, when the control environment risk is low, the means of auditors' reliance on *CFO-Provided Explanation* do not differ significantly ($p = 0.948$) between the *nonfamily* (mean = 0.455, s.d. = 0.207) and *high ownership/low control* (mean = 0.438, s.d. = 0.141) conditions, but the means of the participating auditors' reliance on *CFO-Provided Explanation* decrease significantly from the *nonfamily* condition to the *high ownership/high control* condition (mean = 0.282, s.d. = 0.095) ($p = 0.005$) and from the *high ownership/low control* condition to the *high ownership/high control* condition ($p = 0.016$). Similarly, the means of auditors' assessment of *Fraud Risk* do not differ significantly ($p =$

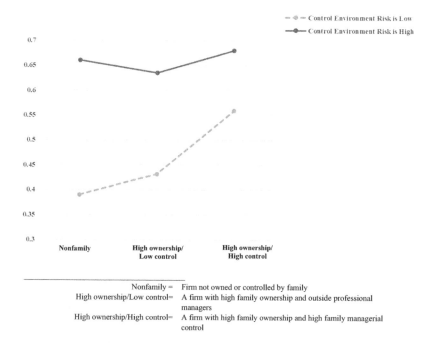

Fig. 2. Effects of Family Firm and Control Environment Risk on Auditors' Assessment of Financial Fraud Risk.

0.780) between the *nonfamily* (mean = 0.390, s.d. = 0.225) and *high ownership/ low control* (mean = 0.432, s.d. = 0.199) conditions and from the *high ownership/ low control* condition to the *high ownership/high control* conditions (mean = 0.559, s.d. = 0.128) ($p = 0.140$), but the means of *Fraud Risk* assessment increase significantly from the *nonfamily* condition to the *high ownership/high control* condition ($p = 0.026$). These results indicate that higher levels of family managerial control cause auditors to be concerned about managerial agency behavior, rely less on management's explanation for unusual fluctuation, and assess higher risk of financial fraud, but only in the low control environment risk condition.

Additional Analysis

We perform a mediation analysis to examine the potential for an indirect effect of *Family Firm Structure* on *Fraud Risk* through the variables of *CFO Provided-Explanation* and *Likelihood of Plausible Financial Fraud Explanation*. This analysis was conducted with the purpose of examining whether increased fraud risk assessments are the result (at least partially) of lack of trust in the CFO of family-controlled firms and/or alternative explanations of plausible financial fraud. Our subsamples in the high and low *Control Environment Risk* conditions were 62 and 54, respectively. When a subsample size is this small, the sampling distribution of the indirect effect may not be normal. In our case, it could cause us

Table 2. Tukey HSD Post-Hoc Tests.

Panel A: DV = CFO-Provided Explanation

(I) Family Firm Type	(J) Family Firm Type	Mean Difference (I–J)	Std. Error	p-Value	95% Confidence Interval	
					Lower Bound	Upper Bound
Nonfamily	High ownership/ Low control	−0.0088	0.03365	0.963	−0.0887	0.0712
	High ownership/ High control	0.1120*	0.03194	0.002	0.0361	0.1879
High ownership/ Low control	Nonfamily	0.0088	0.03365	0.963	−0.0712	0.0887
	High ownership/ High control	0.1208*	0.03419	0.002	0.0395	0.2020
High ownership/ High control	Nonfamily	−0.1120*	0.03194	0.002	−0.1879	−0.0361
	High ownership/ Low control	−0.1208*	0.03419	0.002	−0.2020	−0.0395

The error term is Mean Square (Error) = .022.
* The mean difference is significant at the .05 level.

Panel B: DV = Fraud Risk

(I) Family Firm Type	(J) Family Firm Type	Mean Difference (I–J)	Std. Error	p-Value	95% Confidence Interval	
					Lower Bound	Upper Bound
Nonfamily	High ownership/ Low control	0.0033	0.04171	0.996	−0.0957	0.1024
	High ownership/ High control	−0.0948*	0.03959	0.048	−0.1889	−0.0007
High ownership/ Low control	Nonfamily	−0.0033	0.04171	0.996	−0.1024	0.0957
	High ownership/ High control	−0.0981	0.04238	0.058	−0.1988	0.0025
High ownership/ High control	Nonfamily	0.0948*	0.03959	0.048	0.0007	0.1889
	High ownership/ Low control	0.0981	0.04238	0.058	−0.0025	0.1988

The error term is Mean Square (Error) = 0.032.
* The mean difference is significant at the 0.05 level.

(All p values are two-tailed)

to confirm the existence of a significant mediating effect of *CFO-Provided Explanation* and/or *Likelihood of Plausible Financial Fraud Explanation* when it is not present (Type I error).[18] To avoid this situation, we used the nonparametric resampling or bootstrapping procedure proposed by Preacher and Hayes (2008) that does not require the normality assumption of underlying data. Using 5,000 bootstrap samples, we were able to construct a 95% bias-corrected confidence interval for the indirect effect while controlling for the Type I error rate (Preacher & Hayes, 2008).

The results presented in Panel A of Table 3 show that when the control environment risk is high, the variables of *CFO-Provided Explanation* and *Likelihood of Plausible Financial Fraud Explanation* are not significant mediators for the relationship between *Family Firm Structure* and *Fraud Risk*, as the bias-corrected confidence interval contains zero, and the Z-test for the indirect effect is not significant ($p \geq 0.204$).[19] When the control environment risk is low, on the other hand, the results in Panel B of Table 3 indicate that the indirect effect of *Family Firm Structure* on *Fraud Risk* is through *Likelihood of Plausible Financial Fraud Explanation*. Its bias-corrected confidence interval does not contain zero and the Z-test for the indirect effect is statistically significant ($p = 0.0433$). These results reveal that,

Table 3. Total, Direct and Indirect Effects: Nonparametric Bootstrapping.

Panel A: High Control Environment Risk

	Effect	SE or Boot SE	t or Z Value	p-Value*	LLCI** (LL CI)	LLCI** (UL CI)
Total Effect of *Family Firm Structure* on *Fraud Risk*	0.011	0.026	$t = 0.457$	0.649	–0.0397	0.0633
Direct Effect of *Family Firm Structure* on *Fraud Risk*	–0.009	0.023	$t = -0.376$	0.708	–0.0545	0.0373
Indirect Effect through *CFO-Provided Explanation*	0.0029	Boot SE = 0.0078	$Z = 0.408$	0.683	–0.0068	0.0258
Indirect Effect through *Likelihood of Plausible Financial Fraud Explanations*	0.0175	Boot SE = 0.0127	$Z = 1.270$	0.204	–0.0006	0.0516

Panel B: Low Control Environment Risk

	Effect	SE or Boot SE	t or Z Value	p-Value*	LLCI** (LL CI)	LLCI** (UL CI)
Total Effect of *Family Firm Structure* on *Fraud Risk*	0.083	0.031	$t = 2.684$	0.0097	0.0210	0.1455
Direct Effect of *Family Firm Structure* on *Fraud Risk*	0.041	0.029	$t = 1.399$	0.1676	–0.0177	0.0991
Indirect Effect through *CFO-Provided Explanation*	0.003	Boot SE = 0.0123	$Z = 0.191$	0.8484	–0.0183	0.0331
Indirect Effect through *Likelihood of Plausible Financial Fraud Explanations*	0.039	0.024	$Z = 2.021$	0.0433	0.0042	0.0991

* All p values are two-tailed
** Boot (bootrapping) LL CI = Lower limit confidence interval, UL CI = Upper limit confidence interval

CFO-Provided Explanation =	The assessed likelihood that explanation provided by the CFO explains substantially all of the gross profit margin increase (0% to 100%)
Likelihood of Plausible Financial Fraud Explanation =	The assessed likelihood that plausible financial fraud explanation explains substantially all of the gross profit margin increase (0% to 100%)
Fraud Risk =	The assessed likelihood of financial fraud (0%–100%)
Family Firm Structure =	Nonfamily, High ownership/Low control, or High ownership/High control

rather than the *CFO-Provided Explanation* variable, it is the *Likelihood of Plausible Financial Fraud Explanation* variable that accounts for the relationship between *Family Firm Structure* and *Fraud Risk* when the control environment risk is low.

We also use partial least square structural equation modeling (PLS-SEM) to investigate the relationships between *Family Firm Structure, CFO-Provided Explanation, Likelihood of Plausible Financial Fraud Explanation,* and *Fraud Risk* while controlling for participants' demographic variables (*Gender, Level, Years of Audit Experience,* and *Years of AR Experience*) and level of dispositional trust (*Suspicion of Humanity*).[20] Goodness of fit measures presented in Fig. 3 indicate that the model presented in Fig. 3 is a good fit to the sample data.[21]

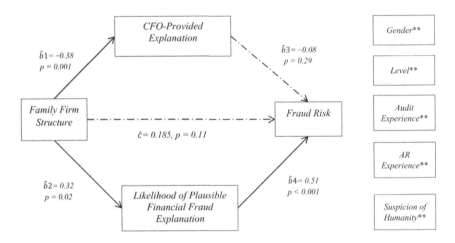

*	Path coefficients ($\hat{a}$ or $\hat{b}$) have standardized values between −1 and +1
**	None of the paths from the control variables to the dependent variables is significant ($p \geq 0.288$), except for the path from *Gender* to *CFO-Provided Explanation* ($\hat{b} = 0.253, p = 0.042$) and from *AR Experience* to *CFO-Provided Explanation* ($\hat{b} = -0.464, p = 0.082$). For the sake of parsimony, the paths from control variables to the dependent variables are not illustrated here.

Goodness of fit measures ***	Estimated Model	Acceptable fit criteria
Standardized root mean square residual (SRMR)	0.058	< 0.08
Geodesic discrepancy (d_G)	0.046	< 0.05
Chi-Square (χ^2)	$\hat{\chi}^2 = 12.037$	
Normed fit index (NFI)	0.923	> 0.90

	Specific Indirect Effect	*p*-Value
Family Firm Structure → *CFO Provided Explanation* → *Fraud Risk*	0.028	$p = 0.31$
Family Firm Structure → *Likelihood of Plausible Financial Fraud Explanation* → *Fraud Risk*	0.164	$p = 0.06$

*** See Henseler et al. (2016) for more information on the acceptable fit criteria.

Fig. 3. Path Model Mediation Analysis*: Low Control Environment Risk.

Un-tabulated results of PLS-SEM in the high *Control Environment Risk* condition indicate that the variables *CFO-Provided Explanation* and *Likelihood of Plausible Financial Fraud Explanation* are not significant mediators of the relationship between *Family Firm Structure* and *Fraud Risk* ($p \geq 0.324$). The paths from *Family Firm Structure* → *CFO-Provided Explanation* ($p = 0.157$), from *Family Firm Structure* → *Likelihood of Plausible Financial Fraud Explanation* ($p = 0.630$), from *CFO-Provided Explanation* → *Fraud Risk* ($p = 0.109$), and from *Likelihood of Plausible Financial Fraud Explanation* → *Fraud Risk* ($p = 0.289$) are not significant. The paths from the control variables to each dependent variable are also not significant ($p \geq 0.114$).

In contrast, when *the Control Environment Risk* is low, the PLS-SEM analyses and Fig. 3 indicate that participants rely less on *CFO-Provided Explanation* ($\hat{b}1 = -0.38, p = 0.001$), but perceive *Financial Fraud Explanations* to be more credible ($\hat{b}2 = 0.32, p = 0.02$) when family structure changes from *nonfamily* to *high ownership/low control* to *high ownership/high control*. The participating auditors, in turn, assess higher fraud risk when they find financial fraud explanations to be more plausible ($\hat{b}4 = 0.51, p < 0.001$), and their fraud risk judgments are not affected by the CFOs' explanation about unexpected fluctuation of gross margin ($\hat{b}3 = -0.08, p = 0.29$). The direct path from *Family Firm Structure* to *Fraud Risk* is not significant ($\hat{c} = 0.185, p = 0.11$), but the total indirect effect of *Family Firm Structure* on *Fraud Risk* is significant ($\hat{b}2 \times \hat{b}4 = 0.164, p = 0.06$). In sum, results of the nonparametric, bootstrapping approach (Preacher & Hayes, 2008) and PLS-SEM suggest that, when the control environment risk is low, increases in family control of management cause the participating auditors to be more skeptical about unusual fluctuations in gross income rather than their lack of trust in the CFO of family-controlled firms.

CONCLUSION AND DISCUSSION

Our findings reveal that the participating auditors rely less on CFO provided explanations and assess higher risk of fraud when firms have high family ownership concentration and high family managerial control, relative to nonfamily firms or when firms have outside professional managers but high family ownership concentration. These results suggest that increased levels of family managerial control cause participating auditors to be concerned about management's potential agency behavior. The agency behaviors that concern auditors involve the firm's pursuit of family interests at the expense of minority shareholders and misrepresentation of firm performance through earnings management. These concerns lead auditors to be more skeptical about management provided explanations and to assess higher levels of fraud risk.

Prior research suggests that a conflict of interest between insiders (e.g., family owners and managers) and outsiders (e.g., nonfamily, minority shareholders) can cause top management to misreport earnings (Gao et al., 2021;

Leuz et al., 2003; Wang, 2006). Gao et al. (2021), for example, find that Chinese public firm CFOs engage in aggressive reporting (i.e., unethical) behavior when their firms are owned and managed by family members. While prior research finds that family ownership concentration and family managerial control create agency conflicts for family firm managers, our findings indicate that the potential conflicts of interest between insiders and outside minority shareholders are most salient to auditors when an increased number of family members hold key executive positions (i.e., high management control).

We also find that the influence of family firm structure on auditor judgment is moderated by the presence of control environment risk. When control environment risk is high, auditor judgments are driven by concerns about internal controls, irrespective of the family firm structure. That is, when control environment risk is high, auditors' judgments are not influenced by family firm structure. However, when control environment risk is low, high levels of family managerial control cause auditors to be suspicious of the client and consider alternative plausible financial fraud explanations, causing them to rely less on the client's explanations for unusual fluctuations in the gross margin and to increase their assessments of fraud risk. Understanding how auditors react to the control environment of family firms and the firms' structures is vital to future research. For example, our findings reveal that classification of family firms based on ownership percentage controlled by the family could yield different and potentially misleading results compared to classifications that consider managerial control, and that the risk environment in which family firms are embedded could wane or wax the potential effects of family firm structures on auditor judgments.

There are limitations to our study. This study does not consider the effect of a large nonfamily ownership (e.g., institutional investors) on auditor judgments when family members hold key executive positions or own significant voting controls. Compared to individual investors, institutional investors (e.g., pension funds, investment banks and endowment funds) have more resources (i.e., reliance on professional analysts) and time to process and understand complex financial information (as well as corporate governance climate) and make investment decisions (Hirshleifer & Teoh, 2003; Utama & Cready, 1997). Institutional investors are likely to be more aware of PP conflicts or Type II agency problems that arise from the controlling family extracting private benefits at the expense of nonfamily shareholders (e.g., Gopalan & Jayaraman, 2012; Leuz et al., 2003). Institutional investors are also likely to be less inclined to invest in family firms than nonfamily firms (Fernando et al., 2014). Future research can extend our study and examine how auditors react to family ownership concentration and family managerial control when institutional investors closely monitor family firms' financial performance, inclusive of financial reporting quality. Our findings are also limited by the finite context of the experiment. Like any experimental study, the laboratory environment intentionally lacks a rich context such that experimental designs can isolate causal effects. In a more complex decision environment, other variables could influence how family firm environments affect audit judgments.

Despite these limitations, our findings expand our understanding of the family firm variables that drive auditors' judgments, and results indicate that different methods used to classify family firms in accounting research are likely to produce conflicting results. We find that family managerial control is perceived by auditors to be an important source of agency conflicts and audit risk, while family ownership concentration is not viewed as problematic when the family does not control key management positions. Future research could expand on these findings to examine issues such as how managerial control changes financial reporting behavior, how control system strength and managerial control are related, and how auditors change the nature of audit plans to respond to different levels of family managerial control.

NOTES

1. Family managerial control and family ownership are defined as "more family members work as key executives and directors" and "a significant portion of equity is held/controlled by the family," respectively (Gao et al., 2021, p. 100).

2. Other studies reveal that firms whose founders or family members hold key executive positions, work as directors, or own a significant block of stock are more likely to choose industry specialist auditors to signal their financial reporting quality (Kang, 2014), and they also experience a lower likelihood of auditor resignation (Khalil et al., 2011).

3. Cognitive embeddedness and cultural-normative embeddedness are the third and fourth ties to the controlling family proposed by social embeddedness theory (Le Breton-Miller & Miller, 2009). These social contexts of family firm's embeddedness are not discussed in this study because accounting and auditing research has operationalized a "family firm" primarily by focusing on structural embeddedness (family managerial power), political embeddedness (family ownership concentration) or both.

4. This study was approved by the Human Subjects Committee of the appropriate university Institutional Review Board (IRB).

5. The Company Law of the People's Republic of China (2006) requires that auditors be selected by the board of directors and a general meeting of shareholders (www.npc.gov.cn).

6. The main experiment was administered in one of the NAI training centers. Data were collected by one of the authors from the continuing professional education (CPE) session which was titled "Auditing and Consulting Practice," a general training for audit practice. This training was unrelated to auditing family firms. Participants came from all over the country (i.e., 14 provinces or states) and worked for different CPA firms located in different cities. The CPE was held in two training sessions that were 2 months apart. One of the authors cross-checked that there were no CPA firm offices that overlapped between the two training sessions and verified that trainees of the first and second sessions did not work for the same CPA firm office. Trainees who chose to participate in the study voluntarily completed the task in a controlled setting. The instrument was administered before the start of the training session to minimize any potential biases resulting from training.

7. We pilot tested the instrument with a small sample of auditors ($n = 23$) from the short-term training session held by the NAI. Feedback from the pilot test was used to modify the final case material to minimize ambiguity and improve clarity. These participants did not attend the general training offered by the NAI, and we did not include their responses in the final sample of this study.

8. We do not examine a condition with low family ownership and high family managerial control for two key reasons. First, the number of experienced participants available precluded a 3×3 design. Second, a design without this condition is more realistic because families without ownership lack the power to appoint family members in top management

roles, and it is rare for a family firm without family ownership control to have family managerial control (Mullins & Shoar, 2016).

9. Information on Chinese family firms is presented by the Global Family Business Center and can be accessed at http://familybusinessindex.com/

10. Consistent with the definitions of family managerial control and the actual characteristics of Chinese firms with high family managerial control, the firm with high family managerial control in the experiment has family members in the top executive positions (CEO, CFO, etc.). Therefore, the CFO explanation for a variance that the auditor participants evaluate comes from a family member in the condition where family managerial control is high. It is possible that the effects of family managerial control on auditors' reliance on statements from management could be weaker if the family did not control the key management positions of CEO and CFO. However, these roles are typically held by family members for firms with high managerial control.

11. The disposition to distrust variable (i.e., *Suspicion of Humanity*) is not statistically significant in any model ($p \geq 0.478$) and is not tabulated.

12. Plausible financial fraud explanation would be any reasonable explanation that could associate the ratio fluctuation with fraud.

13. Auditors in China spend more years at each level within the firm relative to U.S. auditors.

14. Chi-Square test results indicate that *Gender* ($\chi^2 = 2.352$, $p = 0.799$) does not differ significantly across the six treatment conditions. Results of a one-way ANOVA reveal that average *Years of Audit Experience* ($F = 0.510$, $p = 0.769$) and average *Years of Analytical Review Experience* ($F = 0.689$, $p = 0.633$) do not vary significantly across the six treatment conditions.

15. *Client-Provided Explanation* and *Fraud Risk Assessment* are both uncorrelated with (1) Gender, (2) Level, (3) Years of Audit Experience, and (4) Years of Analytical Review Experience (all p-values > 0.10).

16. In addition, preliminary MANCOVA analyses indicated that the effects of family firms on auditor judgments did not differ across levels of experience.

17. We also performed ANCOVAs with *CFO-Provided Explanation* or *Fraud Risk* as the dependent variable and *Family Firm, Control Environment Risk* as the independent variables and control variables for *Gender, Level, Years of Audit Experience, Years of AR Experience* and *Suspicion*. Results of ANCOVA are the same as those of ANOVA. We find significant main effects of *Family Firm* ($p \leq 0.043$) and *Control Environment Risk* ($p < 0.001$) and an insignificant interaction effect of *Family Firm* and *Control Environment Risk* ($p \geq 0.170$) for the *CFO-Provided Explanation* and *Fraud Risk* dependent variables. We find no significant effects of control variables on the dependent variables with the exception of *Years of AR Experience* ($p = 0.051$).

18. The Sobel test assumes that the sampling distribution of the indirect effect or the product-of-coefficients is normal. This assumption is not held when the sample size is not large enough (Preacher & Hayes, 2008).

19. A bias-corrected (BC) confidence interval (CI) is preferred to an ordinary confidence interval as the latter can be asymmetrical or skewed relative to a normal distribution, causing the distance between the upper confidence limit and the point estimate to be different from the distance between the lower confidence limit and the point estimate. The BC confidence interval corrects this problem. For more information, see Efron and Tibshirani (1998) and Hogg and Tanis (2001).

20. PLS-SEM is a multivariate analysis technique that has been increasingly used by management and business research in a wide range of research situations (Cepeda Carrión et al., 2016; Richter et al., 2015). PLS-SEM is a preferred over covariance-based structural equation modeling (CB-SEM) when sample sizes are small and complex models are used to estimate path relationships. Compared to CB-SEM, PLS-SEM (1) does not require assumptions about the distribution of the sample data, (2) uses ordinary least squares regression and (3) utilizes bootstrapping procedures while minimizing the error terms of the

endogenous constructs. For a more detailed description of PLS-SEM, see Sarstedt et al. (2014) and Henseler et al. (2016).

21. We also conduct an F test to determine whether the change in R^2 is significant from a base line model without the control variables to a super-set model with control variables. Un-tabulated results of F test indicate that impacts of control variables on *CFO-Provided Explanation*, *Likelihood of Plausible Financial Fraud Explanation* and *Fraud Risk* are not significant ($p \geq 0.62$). These results corroborate the overall insignificant effects of control variables on each dependent variable.

REFERENCES

Arens, A. A., Elder, R. J., Beasley, M. S., & Hogan, C. E. (2017). *Auditing and assurance services* (16th Global Edition). Pearson.

Arrègle, J.-L., Hitt, M., Sirmon, D., & Very, P. (2007). The development of organizational social capital: Attributes of family firms. *Journal of Management Studies*, *44*(1), 73–95.

Bennedsen, M., Fan, J. P. H., Jian, M., & Yeh, Y.-H. (2015). The family business map: Framework, selective survey, and evidence from Chinese family firm succession. *Journal of Corporate Finance*, *33*(C), 212–226.

Bennedsen, M., Nielsen, K. M., Pérez-González, F., & Wolfenzon, D. (2007). Inside the family firm: The role of families in succession decisions and performance. *Quarterly Journal of Economics*, *122*(2), 647–691.

Bertrand, M., & Schoar, A. (2006). The role of family in family firms. *The Journal of Economic Perspectives*, *20*(2), 73–96.

Buckless, F. A., & Ravenscroft, S. P. (1990). Contrast coding: A refinement of ANOVA in behavioral analysis. *The Accounting Review*, *65*(4), 933–945.

Cambieri, G. (2011). Family businesses are China's economic engine but face succession challenges, report. *Campden FB*. http://www.campdenfb.com/article/family-businesses-are-china-s-economic-engine-face-succession-challenges-report. Accessed on July 25, 2018.

Cepeda Carrión, G., Henseler, J., Ringle, C. M., & Roldán, J. L. (2016). Prediction-oriented modeling in business research by means of PLS path modeling: Introduction to a JBR special section. *Journal of Business Research*, *69*(10), 4545–4551.

Chen, S., Chen, X., & Cheng, Q. (2008). Do family firms provide more or less voluntary disclosure? *Journal of Accounting Research*, *46*(3), 499–536.

Cheng, Q. (2014). Family firm research – A review. *China Journal of Accounting Research*, *7*(3), 149–163.

China Citic Press. (2011). *Chinese family business report* (pp. 1–599). China Citic Press. ISBN: 9787508631585.

China Citic Press. (2015). *Chinses family business succession report* (pp. 1–392). China Citic Press. ISBN: 9787508655635.

Efron, B., & Tibshirani, R. J. (1998). *An introduction to the bootstrap*. Chapman and Hall/CRC.

Fan, J., & Wong, T. (2002). Corporate ownership structure and the informativeness of accounting earnings in East Asia. *Journal of Accounting and Economics*, *33*(3), 401–425.

Fernando, G. D., Schneible, R. A., & Suh, S. H. (2014). Family firms and institutional investors. *Family Business Review*, *27*(4), 328–345.

Firth, M., Fung, P. Y., & Rui, O. M. (2007). Ownership, two-tier board structure, and the informativeness of earnings—Evidence from China. *Journal of Accounting and Public Policy*, *26*(4), 463–496.

Fleiss, J. L. (1981). *Statistical methods for rates and proportions* (2nd ed.). John Wiley.

Gao, J., Masli, A., Suh, I., & Xu, J. (2021). The influence of a family business climate and CEO-CFO relationship quality on misreporting conduct. *Journal of Business Ethics*, *171*(1), 99–122.

Ghosh, A., & Yang, C. Y. (2015). Assessing financial reporting quality of family firms: The auditors' perspective. *Journal of Accounting and Economics*, *60*(1), 95–116.

Gomez-Mejia, L. R., Haynes, K., Nunez-Nickel, M., Jacobson, K., & Moyano-Fuentes, J. (2007). Socioemotional wealth and business risks in family-controlled firms: Evidence from Spanish olive oil mills. *Administrative Science Quarterly*, *52*(1), 106–138.

Gopalan, R., & Jayaraman, S. (2012). Private control benefits and earnings management: Evidence from insider controlled firms. *Journal of Accounting Research*, *50*(1), 117–157.

Goto, S. G. (1996). To trust or not to trust: Situational and dispositional determinants. *Social Behavior and Personality*, *24*(2), 119–132.

Gramling, A. A., Maletta, M. J., Schneider, A., & Church, B. K. (2004). The role of the internal audit function in corporate governance. *Journal of Accounting Literature*, *23*, 194–244.

Guggenmos, R. G., Piercey, M. D., & Agoglia, C. P. (2018). Custom contrast testing: Current trends and a new approach. *The Accounting Review*, *93*(5), 223–244.

Henseler, J., Hubona, G., & Ray, P. A. (2016). Using PLS path modeling in new technology research: Updated guidelines. *Industrial Management & Data Systems*, *116*(1), 2–20.

Hermanson, D. R., & Rittenberg, L. E. (2003). Internal audit and organizational governance. In *Research opportunities in internal auditing*. The Institute of Internal Auditors Research Foundation.

Hirshleifer, D., & Teoh, S. H. (2003). Herd behaviour and cascading in capital markets: A review and synthesis. *European Financial Management*, *9*(1), 25–66.

Hirst, D. E., & Koonce, L. (1996). Audit analytical procedures: A field investigation. *Contemporary Accounting Research*, *13*(2), 457–486.

Hogg, R. V., & Tanis, E. A. (2001). *Probability and statistical inference* (6th ed.). Prentice Hall.

Hope, O.-K., Langli, J. C., & Thomas, W. B. (2012). Agency conflicts and auditing in private firms. *Accounting, Organizations and Society*, *37*(7), 500–517.

Howell, D. C. (2002). *Statistical methods for psychology* (5th ed.). Duxbury.

International Auditing and Assurance Standards Board (IAASB). (2019). *ISA 315 (Revised), identifying and assessing the risks of material misstatement through understanding the entity and its environment*. IAASB.

Jaggi, B., Siney, L., & Ferdinand, G. (2009). Family control, board independence and earnings management: Evidence based on Hong Kong firms. *Journal of Accounting and Public Policy*, *28*(4), 281–300.

Kang, F. (2014). Founding family ownership and the selection of industry specialist auditors. *Accounting Horizons*, *28*(2), 261–276.

Kets de Vries, M. F. R. (1993). The dynamics of family controlled firms: The good and the bad news. *Organizational Dynamics*, *21*(3), 59–71.

Khalil, S. K., Cohen, J. R., & Trompeter, G. M. (2011). Auditor resignation and firm ownership structure. *Accounting Horizons*, *25*(4), 703–727.

KMU Forschung Austia. (2008). *Overview of family business relevant issues*. https://api.semanticscholar.org/CorpusID:152838970

Krishnan, G., & Peytcheva, M. (2019). The risk of fraud in family firms: Assessments of external auditors. *Journal of Business Ethics*, *157*(1), 261–278.

Le Breton-Miller, I., & Miller, D. (2009). Agency vs. stewardship in public family firms: A social embeddedness reconciliation. *Entrepreneurship Theory and Practice*, *33*(6), 1169–1191.

Le Breton-Miller, I., Miller, D., & Lester, R. H. (2011). Social embeddedness reconciliation of conduct and performance. *Organization Science*, *22*(3), 704–721.

Leuz, C., Nanda, D., & Wysocki, P. D. (2003). Earning management and investor protection: An international comparison. *Journal of Financial Economics*, *69*(3), 505–527.

Luo, Y. (1998). Joint venture successes in China: How should we select a good partner? *Journal of World Business*, *33*(2), 145–166.

Martin, G., Campbell, J. T., & Gomez-Mejia, L. (2016). Family control, socioemotional wealth, and earnings management in publicly traded firms. *Journal of Business Ethics*, *133*(3), 453–469.

McKnight, D. H., Kacmar, C. J., & Choudhury, V. (2004). Dispositional trust and distrust distinctions in predicting high-and low-risk internet expert advice site perceptions. *E-Service Journal*, *3*(2), 35–58.

Miller, D., & Le Breton-Miller, I. (2006). Family governance and firm performance: Agency, stewardship, and capabilities. *Family Business Review*, *XIX*, 73–87.

Morck, R. K., Wolfenzon, D., & Yeung, B. (2005). Corporate governance, economic entrenchment, and growth. *Journal of Economic Literature, 43*(3), 655–720.

Mullins, W., & Shoar, A. (2016). How do CEOs see their roles? Management philosophies and styles in family and non-family firms. *Journal of Financial Economics, 119*(1), 24–43.

Neckebrouck, J., Schulze, W., & Zellweger, T. (2018). Are family firms good employers? *Academy of Management Journal, 61*(2), 553–585.

Niemi, L. (2005). Audit effort and fees under concentrated client ownership: Evidence from four international audit firms. *The International Journal of Accounting, 40*(4), 303–323.

Pérez-González, F. (2006). Inherited control and firm performance. *The American Economic Review, 96*(5), 1559–1588.

Preacher, K. J., & Hayes, A. F. (2008). Asymptotic and resampling strategies for assessing and comparing indirect effects in multiple mediator models. *Behavior Research Methods, 40*(3), 879–891.

Prencipe, A., Bar-Yosef, S., & Dekker, H. C. (2014). Accounting research in family firms: Theoretical and empirical challenges. *European Accounting Review, 23*(3), 361–385.

Public Company Accounting Oversight Board (PCAOB). (2010). *AS 2110: Identifying and assessing risks of material misstatement.* PCAOB.

Purkayastha, S., Veliyath, R., & George, R. (2019). The roles of family ownership and family management in the governance of agency conflicts. *Journal of Business Research, 98*(3), 50–64.

Quadackers, L., Groot, T., & Wright, A. (2014). Auditors' professional skepticism: Neutrality versus presumptive doubt. *Contemporary Accounting Research, 31*(3), 639–657.

Richter, N. F., Cepeda, G., Roldán, J. L., & Ringle, C. M. (2015). European management research using Partial Least Squares Structural Equation Modeling (PLS-SEM). *European Management Journal, 33*(1), 1–3.

Rose, A., Rose, J., Suh, I., & Thibodeau, J. (2020). Analytical procedures in the era of data analytics: Are more good ideas always better for the audit? *Behavioral Research in Accounting, 31*(1), 37–49.

Salvato, C., & Moores, K. (2010). Research on accounting in family firms: Past accomplishments and future challenges. *Family Business Review, 23*(3), 193–215.

Sarstedt, M., Ringle, C. M., & Hair, J. F. (2014). PLS-SEM: Looking back and moving forward. *Long Range Planning, 47*(3), 132–137.

Sharma, P. (2004). An overview of the field of family business studies: Current status and directions for the future. *Family Business Review, 17*(1), 1–36.

Shrout, P. E., & Fleiss, J. L. (1979). Intraclass correlations, uses in assessing rater reliability. *Psychological Bulletin, 86*(2), 420–428.

Srinidhi, B., He, S., & Firth, M. (2014). The effect of governance on specialist auditor choice and audit fees in U.S. family firms. *The Accounting Review, 89*(6), 2297–2329.

Suh, I., Masli, A., & Sweeney, J. T. (2021). Will external auditors rely more on internal auditors from family firms? *Journal of Business Ethics, 173*(1), 205–227.

Trompeter, G., & Wright, A. (2010). The world has changed—Have analytical procedure practices? *Contemporary Accounting Research, 27*(2), 669–700.

Trotman, A. J., & Trotman, K. T. (2010). The intersection of family business and audit research: Potential opportunities. *Family Business Review, 23*(3), 216–229.

Utama, S., & Cready, W. M. (1997). Institutional ownership, differential predisclosure precision and trading volume at announcement dates. *Journal of Accounting & Economics, 24*(2), 129–150.

Vazquez, P. (2018). Family business ethics: At the crossroads of business ethics and family business. *Journal of Business Ethics, 150*(3), 691–709.

Wang, D. (2006). Founding Family Ownership and Earnings Quality. *Journal of Accounting Research (Wiley-Blackwell), 44*(3), 619–656.

Wei, Z., Li, C., & Zeng, A. (2009). Family control, audit supervision and corporate governance-evidence from supplement and correction announcements. *Auditing Research, 6*, 69–78.

Yuan, S. (2010). How to strengthen the audit in foreign invested companies. *Foreign Investment in China, 10*, 55–56.

CORPORATE SOCIAL RESPONSIBILITY AS INSURANCE: ITS LIMITATIONS AND RISK OF BACKFIRING

L. Emily Hickman[a] and Bernard Wong-On-Wing[b]

[a]*California Polytechnic State University, USA*
[b]*Washington State University, USA*

ABSTRACT

Prior research finds that firms disclosing a focus on corporate social responsibility (CSR) experience less negative reactions following a corporate misstep. We predict that this "insurance effect" is limited to cases of ordinary failures (i.e., failures not directly related to the social or environmental impacts of the firm) and may provide no protection when a failure is directly related to CSR. Further, we hypothesize a potential "backfire effect," where investors react more negatively to a CSR-focused firm in the case of a CSR-related failure than to a traditional firm experiencing the same failure. In-keeping with attribution theory and expectancy violations theory, our results support the predicted limitation of the insurance effect. In addition, we find that the limited insurance effect is mediated by reputational assessments. Although directionally consistent, the proposed backfire effect is not statistically significant. Overall, our results suggest that CSR is not a panacea for dampening the penalties associated with business missteps, and managers seeking to benefit from CSR engagement should be diligent in monitoring their firms' future CSR performance.

Keywords: Corporate social responsibility; environmental and social corporate activities; investor judgments; insurance effect; backfire effect

---

Advances in Accounting Behavioral Research, Volume 27, 55–96
Copyright © 2024 by Emerald Publishing Limited
All rights of reproduction in any form reserved
ISSN: 1475-1488/doi:10.1108/S1475-148820240000027003

INTRODUCTION

One intriguing rationale for pursuing corporate social responsibility (CSR) activities and for the publication of CSR reports is the "insurance hypothesis." The insurance hypothesis predicts that CSR engagement can act as a form of insurance for a firm, lessening the negative reactions of shareholders to a subsequent adverse event by establishing a "reservoir" of goodwill among the firm's stakeholders (Godfrey et al., 2008). Such an insurance effect is supported in both the theoretical and empirical literature (e.g., Brammer & Pavelin, 2005; Christensen, 2016; Godfrey et al., 2008; Kitzmueller & Shimshack, 2012; Minor & Morgan, 2012; Peloza, 2006; Sen & Bhattacharya, 2001; Werther & Chandler, 2005; Zahller et al., 2015). Missing from the literature, however, are tests of whether this quasi-insurance extends to all types of corporate failures.

In this study, we test whether the documented insurance effect generalizes to firm-specific CSR-related failures. Specifically, we examine whether following a CSR-related failure, a CSR-focused firm benefits from the insurance effect to the same extent as it does following an ordinary failure.[1] Moreover, we investigate whether a CSR-focused firm will suffer more negative investor reactions in the case of a CSR-related failure compared to a traditional firm experiencing the same failure. We refer to this as the "backfire effect" of CSR engagement.

From a practical standpoint, our study is particularly important to CSR-focused firms that expect to benefit from the insurance effect. Whether the insurance effect generalizes to all types of corporate failures or whether a CSR focus might actually backfire in the case of CSR-related failures is an empirical question. Answering this question is important since absent the benefit of the insurance effect, CSR-related failures can have significant negative repercussions for the reputation of CSR-focused firms.

Both attribution theory (Jones & Davis, 1965; Kelley, 1973) and expectancy violations theory (EVT) (Burgoon & Burgoon, 2001; Burgoon & Hale, 1988) provide the theoretical foundation for our predictions. The theories suggest that in the present context, after a company has publicly disclosed that it has a CSR focus, investors form an expectation of superior CSR performance from the firm.[2] If this expectation is violated by news of a CSR failure, negative reactions can be anticipated for the CSR-focused company. We posit that the negative investor reactions occur because of the damage to the reputation of the CSR-focused firm and its management. These negative investor reactions could offset the insurance effect of CSR engagement, or could potentially be so severe that the CSR strategy actually backfires on the firm when it violates the expectations that it originally sought to establish. These theoretical predictions are consistent with CSR-related incidents involving Volkswagen and Chipotle.[3]

Volkswagen, one of the world's largest automakers, had publicly emphasized sustainability as a core company value before admitting to manipulating the emissions testing in its "Clean Diesel" line of automobiles (Helper, 2015). The controversy cost the firm over $25 billion in market value in a matter of days and, amazingly, occurred only weeks after the firm was awarded best in class by the Dow Jones Sustainability Index. Similarly, Chipotle suffered a series of e-Coli outbreaks at its restaurants during 2015, an ironic turn of events for a firm that had sought to differentiate itself as the alternative to eating outlets that often source GMO-modified food from relatively less environmentally friendly factory farms (Wall Street Journal, 2015). Chipotle's stock fell over 25% in response to the food poisoning scandal.[4]

Our conjecture is that the dramatic investor responses to the Volkswagen and Chipotle incidents were prompted by the combination of the CSR nature of their failures and these firms' CSR positioning. Specifically, we reason that a CSR failure experienced by a CSR-focused firm represents a deviation from investors' expectations (i.e., an out-of-role behavior), which could lead them to conclude that earlier CSR activities were disingenuous, and that the firm's true disposition is not CSR-focused.

Based on the foregoing discussion, we predict that the documented "insurance effect" will not extend to protecting CSR-focused companies from missteps that are specifically related to the environmental or social aspects of corporate responsibility. Further, we hypothesize that the disclosed CSR commitment may actually backfire in cases of CSR-related failures.

We take advantage of the experimental method (Libby et al., 2002) to test the limits of the insurance effect and the potential backfire effect. Compared to archival studies, our experiment allows corporate failure type (CSR vs. Ordinary) and firm type (CSR vs. Traditional) to be manipulated independently. These manipulations are presented while holding the stated financial consequences constant across both types of failures. Fig. 1 illustrates our research design and how it tests the hypothesized limited insurance and backfire effects.

We sample MBA students as proxy nonprofessional investors (e.g., see Elliott et al., 2007) and find that investment judgments indicate that CSR commitment provides an insurance effect in cases of ordinary failures, but not when the failure is related to CSR. Unlike traditional firms which experience nearly identical average reactions across failure types, CSR firms suffer more from a CSR failure than an ordinary failure. In particular, while CSR firms enjoy significantly more favorable investor judgments relative to traditional firms in the case of an ordinary failure, they are not judged more favorably when the failure is related to CSR.[5] Thus, the insurance effect enjoyed by CSR-focused firms does not apply when the failure is CSR related. Indeed, investor judgments are actually less favorable (harsher) for CSR firms than traditional firms in the case of a CSR failure. This result is directionally consistent with the proposed backfire effect. Finally, the data also reveal that investors' perceptions of the reputation of a firm and of its management are significant mediators of the observed effects on investment judgments.

Our experimental results have implications for both research and practice. With respect to practice, our results suggest that the benefit of the insurance effect to CSR-focused firms is not generalizable to CSR-related failures. Further, we find directional evidence consistent with a backfire effect for CSR-focused firms experiencing a CSR-related failure. Moreover, our mediation results indicate that the negative investor reactions occur via the adverse effect on the reputation of CSR-focused firms and their management. The same effect is not observed among traditional firms. Together, our research indicates that managers seeking

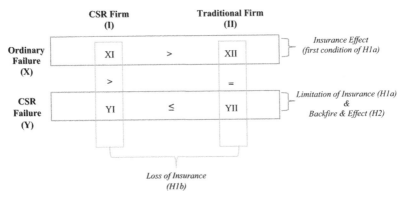

Fig. 1. Research Design Matrix. *Note:* Fig. 1 presents the 2 × 2 research design in relation to the hypotheses. The insurance effect is represented in row *X*, predicting that following an ordinary failure, investors will react less negatively in the case of a CSR firm than for a traditional firm (XI > XII). *H1a* and *H1b* predict the limitation of this insurance effect. Specifically, *H1a* predicts that the insurance effect (shown in row *X*) will not be observed following a CSR-related product failure (row *Y*), meaning that investors will no longer favor the CSR firm (YI will not be greater than YII). *H1b* also predicts the limitation of the insurance effect, predicting that traditional firms (column II) will experience equivalent investor reactions across failure types (XII = YII), while a CSR firm (column I) will experience a more negative reaction to a CSR failure than following an ordinary failure (XI > YI). *H2* predicts a potential backfire effect in the case of a CSR failure (row *Y*), wherein investors' reactions will be significantly more negative for a CSR firm than for a traditional firm following a CSR failure (YI < YII).

to take advantage of the insurance effect and other benefits of CSR engagement should be diligent in monitoring the future CSR performance of the firm.

The importance of monitoring social and environmental impacts is highlighted by the Canadian government in the CSR-related guidance posted on its Responsible Business Conduct Abroad webpage (Global Affairs Canada, 2021). The need to mitigate CSR-related risks has also been emphasized in the CSR literature (Chung & Cho, 2018). This study, therefore, not only underscores the importance of such monitoring but also indicates that the focus of the firm (traditional or CSR) can significantly affect the consequences of failing to monitor such CSR-related risks.

Our study also contributes to CSR research. First, we extend the work of Zahller et al. (2015) by providing evidence of the generalizability of the insurance effect by extending their findings to the context of firm-specific failures and also documenting a key boundary condition (i.e., cases of CSR-related failures). Second, we extend research on the investment-related effects of CSR events previously explored in archival studies (e.g., Krüger, 2015) by showing that investors' reactions can be conditioned upon the firm's overall CSR focus. Third, we provide evidence of the mechanism by which investors react to CSR failures. In particular, we find that following a CSR failure, the resulting reputational effects play a more important role for CSR-focused firms than for traditional firms. Thus, we document one of the "dynamic components that alter" the relationship between environmental disclosure and investor judgments; this contributes to filling a void in the literature noted by Brooks and Oikonomou (2018, p. 12).

In addition, our experimental evidence suggests that further work may prove fruitful in exploring whether the hypothesized backfire effect could be contingent on the relative magnitude or frequency of the CSR-related corporate transgressions. Perhaps whether there is a significant backfire effect depends on a company's CSR missteps being severe or frequent. In cases of more severe or repeated CSR-related failures, it is possible that the CSR failure would not only deteriorate the goodwill that has been built up by the firm's history of CSR commitment but could also result in the firm being significantly worse off than if it had never disclosed a CSR focus.

The remainder of this paper is organized as follows. The next section reviews the relevant literature and develops our hypotheses. In the third section of the paper, the experimental design and sample are described. The results of the study are then presented in the fourth section. In the conclusion, we discuss our findings, their limitations, and their implications.

LITERATURE REVIEW AND HYPOTHESES

Prior literature has documented a variety of ways in which a company's CSR engagement can influence investors. For instance, Elliott et al. (2014) find evidence that investors' assessments of a firm are positively affected by CSR reports that are, on balance, reporting positive performance and are negatively affected by negative-leaning CSR performance reports. Consistent with "affect as information" theory, these effects are most dramatic when the subjects of their experiment were not asked to explicitly consider the focal firm's CSR performance, indicating that an unintended behavioral component to valuation is elicited by CSR activity. While the valuation effect documented in Elliott et al. (2014) is unintentional, Cheng et al. (2015) investigate the impact of CSR performance in the context of its alignment with corporate strategy, testing whether CSR activity is more relevant to investors when it is seen as an integral part of the firm's strategic approach to business. Their experimental findings indicate that investors value CSR performance most when it is perceived to be aligned with, and supporting, a company's strategic focus. According to a study by Brown-Liburd and Zamora (2015), investors also consider the incentives of management and the authenticity of reported CSR performance. When management's pay is linked to CSR performance and the firm has invested significantly in CSR, investors appear to require a credibility signal – assurance of the CSR report – in order for the CSR information to increase investors' stock price assessments (Brown-Liburd & Zamora, 2015).

In another study, Krüger (2015) utilizes event study methodology and KLD ratings to examine the shareholder wealth effects of CSR-related incidents.[6] The study finds that negative CSR events are met with strongly negative stock market responses, and positive CSR events also elicit negative valuation effects, but these effects are much less dramatic.[7]

In contrast to the weak *negative* reactions to even *positive* CSR-related incidents documented in Krüger (2015), a growing body of evidence indicates that CSR activities and reports can contribute to firm performance and firm value (Brooks & Oikonomou, 2018; Dhaliwal et al., 2011; Li et al., 2018; Wang et al., 2016). For example, Dhaliwal et al. (2011) find that corporations which initiate CSR reporting subsequently benefit from lower costs of equity capital. In addition, CSR can act as a positive signal to potential employees, enabling the firm to attract a high-quality applicant pool, benefit from a greater likelihood of offer acceptance by the applicants, and assist in establishing a dedicated workforce, all contributing to a competitive advantage (Greening & Turban, 2000; Kitzmueller & Shimshack, 2012). Moreover, customers have been found to consider CSR when assessing a firm's products (Brown & Dacin, 1997), and companies reputed for CSR can enjoy increased sales (Lev et al., 2010).

Research also suggests that CSR activities can attract socially responsible investors (Glassman, 2012; Miralles-Quirós & Miralles-Quirós, 2017), which are a growing part of the investment community. Investment funds incorporating ESG (environmental, social, and governance) factors have grown from approximately \$12 billion in total net assets in 1999, to around \$569 billion by 2010, to about \$17.1 *trillion* by the end of 2019 (U.S. SIF, 2016, 2020). More generally, Qiu et al. (2016) find that social disclosures contribute to higher market values by increasing expectations of cash flow growth.

Given the benefits of CSR activities and reporting, firms have strong incentives to communicate a CSR focus.[8] Whether such communications reflect a genuine commitment to CSR has been questioned. In their review of the literature regarding voluntary disclosures, Merkl-Davies and Brennan (2007) highlight that some managers may make discretionary disclosures as part of an impression management effort. Researchers have long used the term "managerial capture" to refer to managers' use of CSR-related reporting for their own purposes (e.g., Adams & Larrinaga-González, 2007; Gray et al., 1997; Hickman & Cote, 2019). Cho et al. (2010) provide evidence of management using self-serving attributions in environmental disclosures. Indeed, prior research has documented cases of firms insincerely disclosing a commitment to CSR. For example, Larrinaga-González et al. (2001) provide evidence of firms engaging in environmental accounting without significantly improving their environmental practices.[9]

Importantly, Merkl-Davies and Brennan (2007) conclude from their review of the literature that it is investors' initial *perceptions* of voluntary disclosure strategies that make these communications value-relevant, and that investors subsequently revise their assessments upon receipt of additional information. Thus, investors' perceptions, but not the genuineness, of a firm's commitment to CSR are ostensibly the determinants of their investment judgments and decisions. Because the sincerity of a firm's CSR engagement cannot be directly observed, consistent with attribution theory, we posit that investors will initially infer the firm's disposition based on information about the firm's CSR activities and CSR reporting. Of interest in our study is how investors will react following CSR and non-CSR failures, conditional upon whether they perceived the firm as being CSR-focused or traditionally focused prior to learning of the failure. Therefore, our predictions and results would apply to a firm that has disclosed a focus on CSR in order to be *perceived* as being socially responsible, prior to experiencing a firm-specific failure. Hence, the hypothesized limited insurance and backfire effects could apply to either a sincerely CSR-committed firm, or to a firm that has disingenuously portrayed itself as being committed to CSR. We by no means condone disingenuous corporate behavior, nor do we intend to suggest that sincerely CSR-committed firms are equivalent to those that "greenwash." Rather, we refrain from distinguishing whether the company presented in our CSR firm treatment is sincere or insincere in its CSR-related actions and communications merely to enhance the realism and generalizability of the study.

In the next section, we review research that has documented the insurance effect. We then develop hypotheses related to the limitation of the insurance effect and the potential backfire effect.

The Insurance Effect

A well-documented benefit that CSR-focused firms enjoy is that of an "insurance effect," which mitigates the negative reaction to an adverse corporate event for firms that had previously disclosed a CSR focus (see Christensen, 2016; Godfrey et al., 2008; Minor & Morgan, 2012; Peloza, 2006). This effect is consistent with prior literature documenting that firms with favorable precrisis reputations suffer less negative reactions following a crisis than companies that had unfavorable pre-crisis reputations (e.g., Claeys & Cauberghe, 2015; Jones et al., 2000).

Kitzmueller and Shimshack (2012) state that CSR activities could be "...a hedge against the risk of future regulation or activism" (p. 59). Furthermore, literature suggests that many consumers are "robust to negative information" (e.g., Kitzmueller & Shimshack, 2012, p. 64; Sen & Bhattacharya, 2001) and have less negative reactions to service failures (Joireman et al., 2015) when the firm has portrayed itself as committed to CSR. In the same vein, Godfrey et al. (2008) assert that stakeholders will punish the firm when negative events occur, but that CSR activity can have an insurance-like effect "by encouraging stakeholders to give the firm the 'benefit of the doubt'" (p. 428). Werther and Chandler (2005) extend the insurance argument to multinational firms, reasoning that CSR expectations differ across cultures and that as globalization progresses and levels of affluence change, companies which rely on global brands ought to pursue CSR as insurance against managerial lapses.

Godfrey et al. (2008) test their hypothesis that, "In the context of a negative event, the decline in shareholder value is smaller for firms that engage in CSR activities than for firms that do not" (p. 429). Using event-study methodology and a sample of 178 negative corporate events, the authors find statistically significant support for the hypothesis. Additional empirical support for the insurance benefits of CSR activity is provided by Peloza (2006), who examined stock reactions to the World Trade Organization Riots in Seattle in 1999 and found that those firms targeted by the protests that had weak CSR reputations suffered twice the stock declines as firms with stronger CSR performance.

Minor and Morgan (2012) also conclude that CSR activities can provide valuable insurance against negative events when they test the stock price reactions to product recalls among S&P 500 firms. They find that firms with better CSR ratings have less negative wealth effects while firms with exceptional CSR performance suffer no reputational damage from the recalls. However, Minor and Morgan (2012) do not test for the potential that such insurance could be limited, and that there could be a backfire effect in the case of a CSR failure.[10]

Christensen (2016) focuses on the effect of a firm's CSR reporting on subsequent firm difficulties. Using archival data over an extended period (1999–2009) with over 15,000 firm-year observations, Christensen finds that (ii) accountability reporting (i.e., CSR-reporting) is associated with fewer instances of "high-profile misconduct," and that (ii) when high-profile misconduct does occur, the existence of accountability reporting reduces the magnitude of the negative stock response to the event.

Zahller et al. (2015) also find evidence of the insurance effect, which they term "social resilience." Their research tests whether greater accuracy and completeness of CSR disclosures is associated with greater organizational legitimacy, which in turn leads to social resilience in the event of an exogenous industry shock. A path analysis supports the hypothesized relationships. Specifically, Zahller et al. find support for the notion that high-quality CSR reports dampen the financial shock of an event outside the control of the firm's management. In sum, numerous prior studies have documented that CSR-focused companies benefit from an "insurance effect."

Limitation of the Insurance Effect and Potential Backfire Effect

Bebbington et al. (2008) assert that part of the benefit of CSR engagement is grounded in enhanced legitimacy, and Russo (2010) argues that the benefits of being a "mission-driven" company depend on the firm's authenticity. Thus, if circumstances cast doubt upon the legitimacy or authenticity of a firm's CSR focus, then perhaps the documented CSR "insurance" would be lost. Instead, according to Kitzmueller and Shimshack (2012) as well as Yoon et al. (2006), a firm's CSR focus could theoretically backfire in such circumstances.

Several studies of consumer and employee behavior provide evidence suggesting that observers' perceptions of the firm's underlying motivations for CSR engagement influence their reactions to the company, and that their reactions are consistent with attribution theory. For example, Yoon et al. (2006) show that when a company's motives for CSR engagement appear to be sincere, the firm is viewed more positively by consumers; when the motives are ambiguous, the CSR engagement does not benefit the firm; and when the motives are deemed to be insincere by consumers, the firm's image is harmed. Similarly, Newman et al. (2014) and Chernev and Blair (2015) demonstrate that customers' product evaluations are influenced by the firm's prosocial actions, and that the effect differs depending on consumer's beliefs regarding the company's motivations.

Other research has shown that employees' attributions regarding a company's motives for engaging in CSR can influence their work effort and their relationship with the firm (De Roeck & Delobbe, 2012; Story & Neves, 2015).

In the current study, we investigate whether a CSR failure experienced by a CSR-focused firm will lead investors to reevaluate the underlying disposition of the firm (i.e., whether the company is genuinely committed to CSR as its prior disclosure of a CSR-focus suggested, or whether that disclosure was perhaps insincere), resulting in the predicted loss of the insurance effect and a possible backfire effect. Thus, we compare firms that are seemingly committed to CSR (CSR-focused firms) to those that are not (traditional firms), basing our predictions on attribution theory and the cited studies of consumer and employee reactions to the CSR activities of firms.

As noted earlier, the true intentions of firms and their management cannot be directly observed. In such cases, attribution theory (Jones & Davis, 1965; Kelley, 1973) predicts that investors will initially infer whether a firm's CSR engagement is motivated by a sincere CSR-focus or not based on observable signals such as CSR activities and reporting. These inferences will then lead investors to expect the seemingly CSR-focused firms to be less likely to experience CSR failures relative to traditional firms. Consequently, when applied to our study, attribution theory would predict that a CSR failure within a CSR firm will be perceived as a deviation from expectations and seen as an out-of-role behavior. This will lead observers to conclude that earlier CSR activities were disingenuous and that the firm's true disposition is not CSR-focused. Thus, a CSR-related product failure could cause a re-interpretation of CSR activities as being a false signal of the company's underlying commitment, resulting in the loss of the CSR-related insurance and the potential for the previously disclosed CSR commitment to actually backfire on the firm.

Similarly, EVT predicts that individuals react more strongly when an expectation – established based on prior communications – is violated (Burgoon & Burgoon, 2001; Burgoon & Hale, 1988). Research has provided empirical support for EVT in a variety of contexts as noted by Clor-Proell (2009), including business settings (e.g., Hodge et al., 2006). In the current context, EVT would predict that after a company has communicated a CSR focus, investors will have an expectation of superior CSR performance from the firm, and when this expectation is violated by the revelation of a CSR-related failure, investors will penalize the firm.

Based on attribution theory and EVT, we hypothesize both a limitation to the documented insurance effect and a potential backfire effect. Specifically, we test for two patterns indicative of a limited insurance effect: (i) whether CSR-focused firms are viewed more favorably than traditional firms following ordinary failures, but not following CSR-related failures; and (ii) whether CSR firms suffer more negative reactions for a CSR failure than for an ordinary failure, while a traditional firm experiences equivalent investor judgments across the two failure types. In addition, we investigate the potential backfire effect by testing whether investment judgments are more negative for a CSR firm than for a traditional firm in the case of a CSR-related failure. Therefore, we test the following three hypotheses, which are visually depicted in Fig. 1.

H1a (Limited Insurance): Following an ordinary product failure, investors will react less negatively to a CSR-focused firm than to a traditional firm, and this insurance benefit of a CSR firm relative to a traditional firm will not be observed following a CSR-related product failure.

H1b (Loss of Insurance): For a CSR-focused firm, investors' reaction to a CSR-related product failure will be significantly more negative than to an ordinary product failure, whereas investors' reactions will not differ between failure types for a traditionally-focused firm.

H2 (Backfire): Investors' reactions to a CSR-related product failure will be significantly more negative for a CSR firm than for a traditionally focused firm.

The Mediating Effect of Reputation

Consumers, creditors, employees, and other stakeholders value CSR (e.g., Chambers et al., 1998; Chernev & Blair, 2015; Guiral, 2012; Joireman et al., 2015; Glavas & Piderit, 2009; Lev et al., 2010; Roberts, 1992; Spicer & Lambdin, 2012; Yoon et al., 2006). Given that CSR is seen as beneficial, and that prior research has established a reciprocal relationship between CSR engagement and corporate reputations (e.g., Simnett et al., 2009; Vilanova et al., 2009; Wu, 2006; Yoon et al., 2006), we posit that the predicted insurance and backfire effects occur via investors' perceptions of a firm's reputation and its management's reputation. Therefore, for each experimental condition, we measure and test whether reputational assessments are part of the cognitive process underlying investors' judgments.

In the case of an ordinary failure, the insurance effect literature demonstrates that investors react less negatively when the firm has disclosed a CSR focus (e.g., Christensen, 2016; Godfrey et al., 2008; Minor & Morgan, 2012; Zahller et al., 2015). This dampening of investors' negative reactions is suggested by Godfrey et al. (2008) to be a consequence of investors giving management and the firm as a whole the "benefit of the doubt," presumably due to it having built a superior reputation as a CSR-engaged company. Thus, the effect on investment judgments predicted by the insurance effect is likely the result of the investors' reputation-related assessments of the firm, and possibly their view of management as well. Such reputational effects are not expected for traditionally focused firms.

Similarly, we reason that in the case of the hypothesized backfire effect, the negative effect of a CSR failure on a CSR firm occurs as a result of damage to the reputation of the firm and its management. This is consistent with attribution theory and EVT, as well as with literature citing the need for CSR-focused firms to maintain their reputations (Bebbington et al., 2008; Russo, 2010) and the fragile nature of corporate reputations in general (Herbig & Milewicz, 1993). Again, such reputational effects are not expected for traditional firms.

This discussion suggests a moderated-mediation effect such that the mediating role of reputation will be more significant for CSR firms than for traditionally focused firms. Moreover, it is possible that the insurance and backfire effects may be manifestations of investors adjusting their assessment of management, but not necessarily of the firm overall. In the case of the insurance effect, investors may give the "benefit of the doubt" to the company as a whole based on the firm's *history* of

CSR engagement as a signal that the corporation is truly CSR-focused. However, investors may not give this same benefit of the doubt to the *current* management team during the time of an ordinary failure. Indeed, investors may blame management for the *current* failure and may push for new leadership. Similarly, the hypothesized backfire effect predicts that investors react severely to a CSR failure within a CSR firm, but this negative reaction could either be a manifestation of a loss of faith in the *current* management team, or a loss of belief in the firm's overall disposition, or both. Hence, it is possible that investors' assessments of management and/*or* of the firm as a whole are the reputational effects that mediate the impact of the failure on investment intentions. Therefore, we propose one hypothesis for the effect of management reputation, and another for the effect of firm reputation.

H3a (Moderated Mediation – Management Reputation): Perceived management reputation will mediate the effect of failure type on investment judgments more significantly for CSR firms than for traditional firms.

H3b (Moderated Mediation – Firm Reputation): Perceived firm reputation will mediate the effect of failure type on investment judgments more significantly for CSR firms than for traditional firms.

METHOD

Participants

The research instrument was administered to 286 online MBA students from an AACSB-accredited regional public US university.[11] Prior literature supports the selection of graduate business students as subjects, and research has established that MBA students serve as a reasonable proxy for nonprofessional investors when the difficulty of the experimental task is low (e.g., see Clor-Proell et al., 2014; Elliott et al., 2007, 2011, 2014, 2017; Hodge et al., 2010; Libby et al., 2002). An email inviting students to participate in the online "study of businessperson decision-making" was sent to the sections of two online MBA accounting classes that had distinct enrollees (i.e., no participant was enrolled in both of the classes).[12] In return for their completion of the survey on the Qualtrics platform, participants were awarded a small amount of extra credit. Of the 286 participants, eight individuals did not complete the questionnaire and were not included in the final sample.[13] Table 1 provides an overview of the demographics of the 278 subjects who were included the final sample.

Fewer of the respondents in the final sample were female (87 of 278 subjects, 31%). The average subject had significant work experience (approximately 13.5 years), was about 35 years old, and had typically taken about three accounting courses and three finance courses. A majority of the participants (78.1%) had experience investing and nearly all (93.2%) said they planned to invest in the future.[14]

Table 1. Background Information on Participants.

Panel A: Continuous Variables ($n = 275$[a])		
Variables	Mean	SD
Age	35.10	7.07
Number of accounting classes completed	3.11	2.68
Number of finance classes completed	2.70	2.25
Years of work experience	13.46	7.20
Panel B: Discrete Variables ($n = 278$)		
Variables	Number	Percentage
Gender		
Female	87	31.3%
Male	191	68.7%
Previous Experience Investing		
Yes	217	78.1%
No	61	21.9%
Plan to Actively Invest in the Future		
Yes	259	93.2%
No	19	6.8%

Note: This table presents the background information for our participants.

[a]Three subjects chose not to answer the questions related to the continuous variable questions, which were the last four questions in the instrument; these subjects were included in the sample since they responded to all items related to the dependent and mediation measures.

Experimental Design

The experiment utilizes a 2×2 between-subjects design, manipulating the firm's focus (*firm type*: CSR or traditional) and whether or not the product failure was closely related to corporate responsibility (*failure type*: CSR or ordinary). Participants were randomly assigned to one of the four experimental conditions resulting from the manipulation of firm type and failure type.

Predicted Results

Fig. 2 depicts the hypothesized relationships of the study. First, the predicted direct effect of the *firm type X failure type* interaction on investment judgments is portrayed. The interaction demonstrates that the effect of product failures (CSR or ordinary) on investment judgments (the dependent variable) depends upon whether the firm is CSR focused or traditionally focused (the moderator). Next, two possible mediating variables are explored as potential mechanisms connecting the *firm type X failure type* interaction to investment judgments. This results in the moderated-mediation model that links the two manipulated variables (*firm type* and *failure type*) to two mediating variables (*perceived management reputation* and *perceived firm reputation*), which in turn influence the dependent variable (investment judgments).

Main Moderation Model (Hypotheses 1a, 1b, and 2)

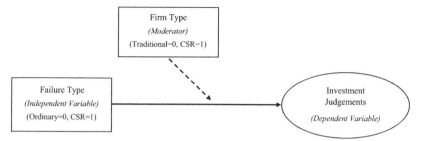

Moderated-Mediation Model (Hypotheses 3a and 3b)

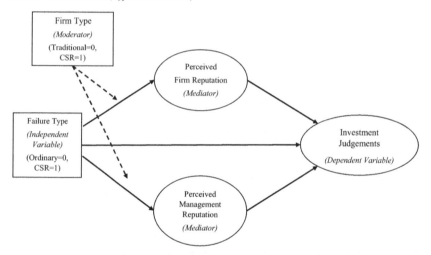

Fig. 2. Depiction of Main Moderation Model and Moderated-Mediation Model. *Note:* Fig. 2 depicts the hypothesized relationships of the study in the form of the moderation model implied by *H1a*, *H1b*, and *H2*, as well as the moderated-mediation model that will be used to test *H3a* and *H3b*. The first model displays the prediction that the direct effect of product failures (CSR or ordinary) on investment judgments depends upon the firm's focus (CSR or traditional). The second model portrays two possible mediating variables (i.e., *perceived management reputation* and *perceived firm reputation*) which are explored as potential mechanisms connecting the *firm type* X *failure type* interaction to investment judgments.

Research Instrument

The instrument provided information about a fictitious firm ("Temp-Perfect") that designs and manufactures heating, ventilation, and air conditioning (HVAC) units. The brief company background and summary of financial information were based on real firms in the HVAC business, and were designed to be noncontroversial and to indicate that the firm is relatively well-performing.

An excerpt from the fictitious company's website was then displayed, which varied the firm's disclosed commitment to CSR as the first manipulation. Next, an announcement from Bloomberg describing a product failure that was either CSR-related or product reliability-related was presented. In both cases, the product involved was a furnace. Following the firm and the furnace failure descriptions, the instrument posed questions related to the dependent measure, the mediating variables, and participant demographics. The following sections describe the independent, mediating, and dependent variables used to test the hypotheses.

Independent Variables

Firm type was manipulated at two levels (CSR vs. Traditional).[15] The CSR firm description included brief quotes from the company's mission statement and website, saying, "...we believe that by investing in our employees, communities, suppliers and the environment, Temp-Perfect will continue to grow and provide quality products to our customers in a socially responsible manner." The CSR firm treatment also explicitly mentions the firm's "annual Corporate Social Responsibility Report" and cites several environmental certifications its products have earned, demonstrating that the firm is engaged in CSR reporting as well as having a history of commendable product CSR performance.[16] In contrast, the traditional firm description makes no mention of social responsibility, sustainability, or the environment, focusing instead on product reliability and affordability. The two firm descriptions (which constitute the firm type manipulations) are based on excerpts from real HVAC company websites, are similar in tone and length (178 words and 175 words), and use similar phrasing and structure (see Appendix A). The HVAC industry was selected since company performance in this sector has clear environmental implications, but it is not controversial (like the oil industry) and is not likely to be considered a luxury-product-industry by US investors.[17]

Failure type was manipulated at two levels (CSR vs. Ordinary). In the ordinary failure treatment, the furnace is experiencing breakdowns during the warranty period that are expected to cost the firm between $2 and $3 million to rectify. In the CSR failure treatment, the furnace is not meeting its advertised energy efficiency and CO_2 emissions standards and the estimated cost to remedy the problem is $2 to $3 million.[18] Thus, the description of the two failure types clearly states the identical expected dollar value of the financial impact on the firm.

Both of the firm types and both of the failure types share consequences for consumers, who are clearly vital stakeholders to any firm and may be considered key constituents in a CSR-focused strategy. However, it is doubtful that the degree of CSR-relatedness would be considered equivalent between the firm and failure type manipulations because the implications for consumers are present in all conditions, but the CSR treatments add environmental commitment in the CSR-focused firm treatment and environmental performance in the CSR-related failure treatment. Manipulation checks (reported in Table 2) reinforce this argument: participants in the CSR firm or CSR failure conditions rated those treatments as significantly more related to CSR than did the participants who assessed the relation to CSR of the traditional firm or ordinary failure conditions.[19]

Dependent Variable

After reading about the furnace problem, survey participants were asked to provide their assessments of management's competency and credibility; to assess the impact that the furnace failure would have on management's reputation; as well as to indicate their feelings toward the firm. Participants were also queried about their personal investment judgments in two questions: one regarding the firm's attractiveness as an investment and the other asking the likelihood that the respondent would consider Temp-Perfect as an investment. Since the reputation-related measures are hypothesized to be the mediating variables through which the manipulations will affect investment judgments (the dependent measure), the investment-related questions were asked first. This sequencing of the questions avoids priming the participants to consider reputational effects before indicating their investment judgments. In addition, the order in which the two investment-related questions were presented was randomized across participants.

Similar to Elliott et al. (2017), two questions were used to gauge the investment assessments of participants: "Based on the information provided, how likely would you be to consider Temp-Perfect as a potential investment?" and "Based on the information provided, how attractive do you think Temp-Perfect is as a potential investment?," recorded using 11-point Likert scales with the endpoints labeled "Not at All Likely (Attractive)" and "Very Likely (Attractive)." Responses were highly correlated ($r = 0.814$, $p < 0.001$). A simple average of the responses was used to form the investment judgment dependent measure (*InvAvg*), since a composite measure can be more reliable than a single item (Gliem & Gliem, 2003), canceling out measurement error in the individual scores (Nunnally & Bernstein, 1994).[20] Cronbach's Alpha for the combined measure was 0.896, supporting the internal reliability of the investment dependent measure (Nunnally, 1978).

Mediating Variables

Principal component analysis (PCA) was used to derive the measure of perceived management reputation from four questions capturing respondents' views of management. The first two questions asked participants to assess how the product failure would affect management's reputation, both measured on 11-point Likert scales: (i) "To what extent will Temp-Perfect management's reputation be negatively impacted in light of the problem with its furnace?" with endpoints labeled "Not at All Impacted" and "Very Negatively Impacted," and (ii) "I think that the problem with Temp-Perfect's furnace will have little impact on management's reputation" with endpoints labeled "Strongly Disagree" and "Strongly Agree." The former was reverse coded for the analyses since for the other three questions, higher values indicate more favorable views of management. The next two questions asked participants for their rating of management's credibility and competency on 7-point Likert scales with endpoints labeled "Not at All Credible (Competent)" to "Very Credible (Competent)." Correlations between the four questions were all greater than 0.5 and statistically significant at the 0.01 level. Cronbach's Alpha was 0.867, above the threshold of 0.70 suggested for a scale to demonstrate sufficient internal reliability (Nunnally, 1978). The PCA revealed a single component with an eigenvalue greater than one. This component accounted for 72% of the variance among the four questions, exceeding the threshold of 50% suggested by Fornell and Larcker (1981). This extracted component is utilized as the measure for perceived management reputation.

Perceived firm reputation was assessed using the RepTrak™ Pulse measure developed by Ponzi et al. (2011) in conjunction with the Reputation Institute. According to Vidaver-Cohen and Brønn (2015), the "Reputation Institute's widely recognized measures have been rigorously tested and used successfully for nearly a decade of large-scale global research" (p. 54). The validity of the RepTrak™ Pulse scale as a short form measure of "corporate reputation" has been supported in later studies (Agarwal et al., 2015; Fombrun et al., 2015), and a number of articles have employed the measure (e.g., Deephouse & Jaskiewicz, 2013). The scale consists of four questions (see Appendix B). In our study, the correlations between the four questions were all greater than 0.7 and statistically significant at the 0.01 level. Cronbach's Alpha was 0.930, supporting the internal reliability of the measure (Nunnally, 1978). Factor analysis confirmed that only one component had an eigenvalue greater than one, accounting for 83% of the variance among the four items, and each item's loading for this component was greater than 0.8. This factor derived using the RepTrak™ Pulse scale is utilized as the measure for perceived firm reputation.

As described in the discussion of *H3a* and *H3b*, it is possible that investors' assessments of management and/or of the firm are the reputational effects that mediate the impact of the failure on investment intentions. To allow for the possibility that the hypothesized backfire and insurance effects occur through changes in how investors view management, or the firm, but not *necessarily* both, we proposed two separate hypotheses and utilize separate measures for testing the effect of management reputation and of firm reputation. However, if all of the items that relate to management and firm reputation assessments are included in a principal components analysis, only one factor is extracted (with an Eigenvalue of 5.420, accounting for 67.74% of the variance among the items). We conduct our mediation analysis using the separate management and firm reputation assessments, but we also use the single, combined measure of reputation in an untabulated rendition of the meditation analysis (see footnote 29).

RESULTS

Manipulation Checks

Six questions were asked at the end of the instrument to verify that the manipulations were successful in eliciting the intended interpretation by participants.[21] Table 2 displays the tests comparing the mean responses across treatments for firm type (CSR versus Traditional) and failure type (CSR versus Ordinary).

In Panel A, the results are reported for the four items used to assess our manipulation of firm type. Participants were asked whether they agreed (11) or disagreed (1) with the following statements, using an 11-point Likert scale: "Based on Temp-Perfect's stated mission, I feel the firm expressed a focus on corporate social responsibility (CSR)" and "Based on Temp-Perfect's stated mission, I feel the firm expressed a focus on a traditional business strategy." Mean responses for the CSR firm versus traditional treatments differ significantly and in the appropriate direction for both the first item (means of 8.50 versus 6.26, respectively; $p < 0.001$) and the second item (6.09 versus 7.54, respectively; $p < 0.001$). In addition to these items, two questions were also posed to further test the firm type manipulation using 11-point Likert scales: "Before you read about the furnace problem, to what extent did you feel that Temp-Perfect was committed to CSR?," with endpoints labeled "Very Committed to CSR" (11)/"Not at All Committed to CSR" (1), and "Without considering the furnace problem, how important is CSR to Temp-Perfect's strategy?," with endpoints labeled "Very Important" (11)/"Not at All Important" (1).[22] For both questions, mean responses were significantly higher in the CSR firm condition than in the traditional firm condition (means for the first question = 9.15 versus 7.32, respectively, $p < 0.001$; and means for the second question = 9.11 versus 7.20, respectively, $p < 0.001$). Thus, the results overall support a successful manipulation of firm type.

In Panel B, the results are presented for the two items used to assess our manipulation of failure type. Using an 11-point Likert scale, participants reported whether they strongly agreed (11) or strongly disagreed (1) with the following statements: "I believe the furnace problem was more related to the Temp-Perfect's failure to ensure the environmental performance of the furnace than to the reliability of the furnace" and "I believe the furnace problem is more related to the product's reliability than to anything related to its Corporate Social Responsibility." Mean responses differ significantly and in the expected direction for the CSR failure versus ordinary failure treatments for both the first item (means of 7.60 versus 4.71, respectively; $p < 0.001$) and the second item (8.46 versus 5.90, respectively; $p < 0.001$). This indicates that the manipulation of failure type was also successful.

Tests of Hypotheses

The analysis of variance presented in Table 3 illustrates the effects of firm and failure treatments on investment judgments. Investment judgment means are reported in Panel A of Table 3, and follow the pattern predicted in Fig. 1. Panel B reveals a marginally significant effect of the *firm type X failure type* interaction on

Table 2. Results of Interpretation Check Tests for Firm and Failure Type Manipulations.

Panel A: Treatment Means (Standard Deviations) and Tests for Interpretation Checks of Firm Type Manipulation

	Traditional Firm Treatment ($n = 139$)	CSR Firm Treatment ($n = 139$)	t-Statistic for Test of Difference in Means
Firm focused on CSR	6.26	8.50	7.913***
	(2.48)	(2.24)	
Firm focused on traditional business strategy[a]	7.54	6.09	−5.39***
	(2.12)	(2.37)	
Commitment to CSR before failure[a]	7.32	9.15	7.22***
	(2.37)	(1.83)	
Importance of CSR to strategy[a]	7.20	9.11	7.36***
	(2.49)	(1.79)	

Panel B: Treatment Means (Standard Deviations) and Tests for Interpretation Checks of Failure Type Manipulation

	Ordinary Failure Treatment ($n = 142$)	CSR Firm Treatment ($n = 136$)	t-Statistic for Test of Difference in Means
Environmental performance related failure	4.71	7.60	10.27***
	(2.42)	(2.55)	
Reliability related failure[a]	8.46	5.90	−9.00***
	(2.06)	(2.67)	

Notes: *$p < 0.10$, **$p < 0.05$, ***$p < 0.01$, two-tailed.
This table presents the means and standard deviations by treatment for the six interpretation check items (measured on eleven-point scales), as well as reporting the results for t-tests of the mean responses across treatments to assess the success of the firm type and failure type manipulations.
[a]For these variables, equal variances were not assumed for means tests, as prescribed by Levene's test.
Variable Descriptions:
Firm Focused on CSR: After reading the explanation distinguishing traditional versus CSR-focused firms, respondents were asked whether they agreed (11) or disagreed (1) with the following statement using a Likert scale: "Based on Temp-Perfect's stated mission, I feel the firm expressed a focus on corporate social responsibility (CSR)."

Firm Focused on Traditional Business Strategy: After reading the explanation distinguishing traditional versus CSR-focused firms, respondents were asked whether they agreed (11) or disagreed (1) with the following statement using a Likert scale: "Based on Temp-Perfect's stated mission, I feel the firm expressed a focus on a traditional business strategy."

Commitment to CSR before Failure: After reading the explanation distinguishing traditional versus CSR-focused firms, respondents were asked, "Before you read about the furnace problem, to what extent did you feel that Temp-Perfect was committed to CSR?," responding on an 11-point Likert scale with endpoints labeled "Very Committed to CSR" (11) or "Not at All Committed to CSR" (1).

Importance of CSR to Strategy: After reading the explanation distinguishing traditional versus CSR-focused firms, respondents were asked, "Without considering the furnace problem, how important is CSR to Temp-Perfect's strategy?," responding on an 11-point Likert scale with endpoints labeled "Very Important" (11) or "Not at All Important" (1).

Environmental Performance Failure: Respondents were asked whether they strongly agreed (11) or strongly disagreed (1) with the following statement using a Likert scale: "I believe the furnace problem was more related to the Temp-Perfect's failure to ensure the environmental performance of the furnace than to the reliability of the furnace."

Reliability Related Failure: Respondents were asked whether they strongly agreed (11) or strongly disagreed (1) with the following statement using a Likert scale: "I believe the furnace problem is more related to the product's reliability than to anything related to its Corporate Social Responsibility."

Table 3. Test of *H1a*, *H1b*, and *H2*.

Panel A: Cell Means (Standard Deviation) for the Investment Judgment Dependent Measure

| | Firm Type | | |
Failure Type	CSR Firm	Traditional Firm	Total
Ordinary failure	7.00	6.51	6.754
	(1.53)	(2.22)	(1.92)
	$n = 70$	$n = 72$	$n = 142$
CSR failure	6.16	6.52	6.34
	(2.16)	(2.00)	(2.08)
	$n = 69$	$n = 67$	$n = 136$
Total	6.58	6.52	
	(1.91)	(2.11)	
	$n = 139$	$n = 139$	

Panel B: ANOVA Testing the Effect of Firm Type X Failure Type on Average Investment Judgment

Source	Type III Sum of Squares	df	Mean Square	F	Sig.
Firm type	0.3	1	0.263	0.1	0.797
Failure type	12.0	1	12.022	3.0	0.083
Firm type X Failure type	12.5	1	12.518	3.2	0.077
Error	1088.9	274	4.494		
Corrected total	1113.8	277			

Panel C: Planned Comparisons

	df	F	Sig.[a]	Related Hypothesis
Effect of firm type in the ordinary failure condition[b]	1	2.11	0.074	*H1a*
Effect of firm type in the CSR failure condition[c]	1	1.13	0.145	*H1a & H2*
Effect of failure type in the traditional firm condition[d]	1	0.98	0.490	*H1b*
Effect of failure type in the CSR firm condition[e]	1	6.18	0.007	*H1b*

Note: Table 3 presents the main experimental results. Panel A presents the ANOVA results. Panel B displays the cell means for each condition. Panel C reports the results of planned comparisons, which are used to test *H1a*, *H1b*, and *H2*. Descriptions of each planned comparison test (corresponding to the superscripts in Panel C) are as follows:
[a]*p*-values for the planned comparisons are one-tailed, conforming to the directional hypotheses. (*p*-values for the ANOVA test are two-tailed.)
[b]Measures the insurance effect predicted in *H1a* (i.e., relative to a traditional firm, the CSR firm is protected by its prior disclosure of its commitment to CSR in the event of an ordinary failure).
[c]Measures both the limitation of the insurance effect predicted in *H1a* (i.e., the CSR firm is not protected by its prior disclosure of its commitment to CSR in the case of a CSR failure, resulting in the CSR firm no longer being judged more favorably compared to a traditional firm), as well as the backfire effect predicted in *H2* (i.e., that a CSR firm will be judged more harshly than a traditional firm in the event of a CSR failure).
[d]Measures the equivalence of the reactions to the two failure types for a traditional firm, predicted in *H1b*.
[e]Measures the difference in reactions to the two failure types for a CSR firm predicted in *H1b* (i.e., the limited insurance effect will produce significantly different investor reactions for a CSR firm when the failure is an ordinary failure compared to a CSR failure).

the investment judgments ($F = 3.15$, $p = 0.077$). The nature of this interaction effect is examined in Panel C using planned comparisons that employ Fisher's LSD test to assess our hypotheses.[23,24] Fig. 3 displays the investment judgment means for the four treatment conditions.

Testing for the Limitation of the Insurance Effect

H1a (Limited Insurance). The insurance effect predicts that when the information presented depicts the firm as having a CSR focus, investors' assessments of the firm as a potential investment following an ordinary failure will be *more favorable* than when no information about the CSR activities of the firm is provided (as in the traditional firm treatment). *H1a* posits that the insurance effect documented in prior literature will be present in the case of an ordinary

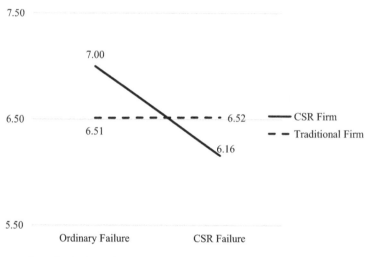

Fig. 3. Depiction of Cell Means. *Note:* Fig. 3 displays the investment judgment means for the four treatment conditions. The data conforms to the well-documented insurance benefit of a CSR focus: the investment judgment mean for the CSR firm is higher than for the traditional firm in the event of an ordinary failure. The diagram also implies that the insurance effect is not observed in the case of a CSR failure: the investment judgment mean for the CSR firm is no longer higher than the mean for the traditional firm in the event of a CSR failure. Furthermore, while the reaction across the two types of failures appears to be equivalent for a traditional firm (6.51 and 6.52), the reactions to the two types of failures appear to differ dramatically for a CSR firm (7.00 versus 6.16), suggesting a more negative reaction in the case of a CSR failure for the CSR firm relative to the traditionally-focused firm. Finally, in the case of a CSR failure, the mean judgment is harsher (6.16) for a CSR firm than for a traditional firm (6.52), suggesting there may be a backfire effect.

product failure, and that this insurance will not be observed following a CSR failure. The pattern of the means depicted in Fig. 4 is consistent with *H1a*.

As shown in Panel A of Table 3, in the case of an ordinary product failure, the mean for the CSR firm is 7.00 (s.d. = 1.53) compared to 6.51 (s.d. = 2.22) for the traditional firm. This difference is marginally significant ($F = 2.11$; $p = 0.074$) as shown in the first planned comparison reported in Panel C of Table 3. Thus, the previously documented insurance effect is replicated in our study. In contrast, as demonstrated by the second planned comparison in Panel C of Table 3, in the case of a CSR failure, the difference in investment judgment between the traditional firm (mean = 6.52, s.d. = 2.00) and the CSR firm (mean = 6.16, s.d. = 2.16) is no longer significant ($F = 1.13$, $p = 0.145$). Here the CSR firm appears to no longer benefit from the insurance effect. These results support the limitation of the insurance effect predicted in *H1a*.

H1b (Loss of Insurance). To provide further evidence of the limitation of the insurance effect, *H1b* predicts that in the CSR firm condition, investor reactions will be significantly more negative following a CSR failure than following an ordinary failure (indicating the insurance benefit is "lost" when the failure is related to CSR), while in the traditional firm condition, investor reactions will not differ between the two failure types. As shown in Panel C of Table 3, the fourth planned comparison indicates that investors had a significantly ($F = 6.18$, $p = 0.007$) more negative reaction to a CSR failure (mean = 6.16, s.d. = 2.16) than to an ordinary failure (mean = 7.00, s.d. = 1.53) when the firm had disclosed a CSR focus. In contrast, the third planned comparison in Panel C of Table 3 shows that the two types of failures do not elicit statistically different reactions for a traditional firm ($F = 0.98$, $p = 0.490$).[25] This pattern of results again supports the limitation of insurance – specifically, the loss of the insurance benefit when a CSR failure is considered, as predicted in *H1b*.

Participants were also asked how surprised they were by the furnace-related failure. Consistent with attribution theory and EVT, untabulated results indicate that investors were significantly more surprised when a CSR firm experienced a CSR failure compared to an ordinary failure ($p = 0.047$, one-tailed).[26,27] In contrast, there was no significant difference in the degree of surprise between failure types for Traditional firms ($p = 0.495$). Thus, this additional test provides further evidence that our theoretical foundation in attribution theory and EVT is supported by the experimental results.

Testing for the Backfire Effect

The second hypothesis posits that when a CSR firm experiences a CSR-related failure, it may not only suffer the loss of the insurance effect (as predicted in *H1a* and *H1b*), but it may also experience a backfire effect, wherein the CSR firm is actually judged as a *less* attractive investment than the traditional firm (*H2*). As shown in Panel A of Table 3, in the case of a CSR-related failure, the mean investment judgment for the CSR firm (6.16, s.d. = 2.16) is in fact lower than the mean for a traditional firm (6.52, s.d. = 2.00). However, this difference is not statistically significant ($F = 1.13$; $p = 0.145$), as shown in the second planned comparison in Panel C of Table 3. Thus, *H2* is not supported.

One possible explanation for the insignificance of the backfire effect is suggested by earlier research regarding reputational loss: Claeys and Cauberghe (2015) find that "consumers are reluctant to change their initial [favorable] attitude toward an organization and therefore attribute less responsibility for a crisis to organizations with a favorable pre-crisis reputation" (p. 64). While we find some evidence that a CSR failure does result in some reevaluation of a firm that has disclosed a CSR-focus (resulting in a loss of the insurance effect, supported in tests of *H1a* and *H1b*), it appears that this reevaluation is not extreme enough to cause investment assessments of a CSR-focused firm to be worse than the assessments of a traditional firm, even following CSR-related failures.

Mediation Analyses
We examine whether perceptions of management's reputation (*H3a*) or of the firm's reputation (*H3b*) mediate the effect of failure type on investment judgments, conditional on the type of firm (see Fig. 2). Treatment means for the two reputation measures are presented in Table 4. The pattern in both panels is consistent with the predicted insurance, limitation of insurance, and backfire effects, respectively: an ordinary failure experienced by the CSR-focused firms elicits the highest mean assessment of both management and the firm as a whole; a CSR-related failure within a CSR firm produces the lowest mean assessment, while the means for a traditional firm are similar (almost equivalent) across the ordinary and CSR-related failures.[28]

Hayes' (2013) Process Model 7 was estimated to examine the proposed indirect effects, using the bootstrap test of Preacher and Hayes (2004) – also see Preacher et al. (2007) – to calculate the 95% confidence intervals, as recommended by Zhao et al. (2010).[29] The results of the moderated-mediation test are visually summarized in Fig. 4 and are presented in Table 5.

H3a (Moderated Mediation – Management Reputation). The first mediation hypothesis predicts that investors' perceptions of management's reputation will mediate the effect of failure type on investment judgments more significantly for CSR firms than for traditional firms. Estimating the model depicted in Fig. 2 using Hayes' (2013) Process Model 7 (with bootstrapping) reveals that the *firm type* by *failure type* interaction significantly ($p = 0.033$) predicts perceptions of management's reputation (see Panel A of Table 5 and path a_1 in Fig. 4), which in turn predicts investment judgments ($p = 0.001$; see Panel B of Table 5 and path b_1 in Fig. 4). Furthermore, the results reveal a significant moderated mediation index in relation to perceived management reputation (Table 5, Panel D: 95% confidence interval of -0.655 to -0.021). Specifically, the indirect effect of failure type, via perceived management reputation, was stronger and significant in the CSR firm condition (Table 5, Panel C: conditional indirect effect = -0.205, SE = 0.117, 95% confidence interval of -0.512 to -0.035), but weaker and not significant in the traditional firm condition (Table 5, Panel C: conditional indirect effect = 0.031, SE = 0.085, 95% confidence interval of -0.105–0.249). Thus, the results indicate that the type of failure influences investment judgments through

Table 4. Cell Means for Reputation Measures.

Panel A: Cell Means (Standard Deviations) for Perceived Management Reputation

| | Firm Type | | |
Failure Type	CSR Firm	Traditional Firm	Total
Ordinary failure	0.19	0.00	0.09
	(0.73)	(1.08)	(0.92)
	$n = 70$	$n = 72$	$n = 142$
CSR failure	−0.26	0.07	−0.10
	(1.19)	(0.90)	(1.07)
	$n = 69$	$n = 67$	$n = 136$
Total	−0.03	0.03	
	(1.01)	(1.00)	
	$n = 139$	$n = 139$	

Panel B: Cell Means (Standard Deviations) for Perceived Firm Reputation

| | Firm Type | | |
Failure Type	CSR Firm	Traditional Firm	Total
Ordinary failure	0.32	0.09	0.19
	(0.79)	(1.06)	(0.94)
	$n = 70$	$n = 72$	$n = 142$
CSR failure	−0.32	−0.08	−0.20
	(1.12)	(0.90)	(1.02)
	$n = 69$	$n = 67$	$n = 136$
Total	0.00	0.00	
	(1.02)	(0.98)	
	$n = 139$	$n = 139$	

Note: Table 4 presents the cell means for the proposed mediators (i.e., management reputation and firm reputation). Panel A reports the means and standard deviations for the Perceived Management Reputation variable (which was constructed using principal component analysis) across the experimental conditions. Panel B displays the cell means for the Perceived Firm Reputation factor (which was derived from the RepTrak™ Pulse scale).

investors' perception of management's reputation more significantly for CSR firms than for traditional firms.[30] This pattern of results supports *H3a*.

H3b (Moderated Mediation – Firm Reputation). The second mediation hypothesis predicts that investors' perceptions of the firm's reputation will mediate the effect of failure type on investment judgments more significantly for CSR firms than for traditional firms. The estimation of Hayes' (2013) Process Model 7 demonstrates the *firm type* by *failure type* interaction significantly predicts perceptions of the firm's overall reputation ($p = 0.036$ in Panel A of Table 5; represented by path a_2 in Fig. 4), which in turn predicts investment judgments ($p < 0.001$ in Panel B of Table 5; represented by path b_2 in Fig. 4). The results also reveal a significant moderated mediation index in regards to perceived firm reputation (Table 5, Panel D: confidence interval of −1.068 to −0.050).

Results for Main Moderation Model (Hypotheses 1a, 1b, and 2)

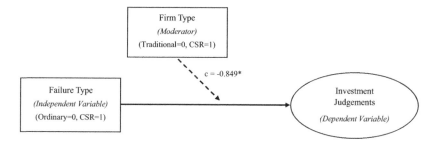

Results for Moderated-Mediation Model (Hypotheses 3a and 3b) using Hayes' Process Model 7

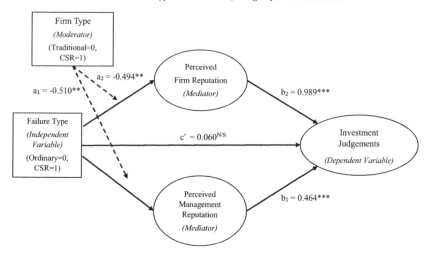

Fig. 4. Depiction of Results for Main Moderation Model and Moderated-Mediation Model. Note: $*p < 0.10$, $**p < 0.05$, $***p < 0.01$, two-tailed. Fig. 4 depicts the result for the moderation model related to *H1a*, *H1b*, and *H2*, as well as the results of the moderated-mediation model corresponding to *H3a* and *H3b*. First, the prediction that the direct effect of product failures (CSR or ordinary) on investment judgments depends upon the firm's focus (CSR or traditional) is supported by the significant interaction effect (path c). In the second model portrayed, the results support both mediation *H3a* and *H3b* (paths a_1 and b_1, as well as paths a_2 and b_2 are all significant), indicating that *perceived firm reputation* and *perceived management reputation* are mechanisms connecting the *firm type X failure type* interaction to investment judgments.

Specifically, the indirect effect of failure type, via perceived firm reputation, was stronger and significant in the CSR firm condition (Table 5, Panel C: conditional indirect effect = -0.632, SE = 0.199, 95% confidence interval of -1.078 to $-$

80 *CSR as Insurance*

Table 5. Process Results of Moderated-Mediation Model Test.

Panel A: Summary Results of the Effect of the Firm Type X Failure Type Interaction on the Proposed Mediator Variables

Dependent Variable: *Perceived Management Reputation*
Model Significance: $p = 0.002$

	Effect	*t-stat*	*p Value*	*Lower CI*	*Upper CI*
Firm type X Failure type	−0.510	0.033	0.033	−0.978	−0.041

Dependent Variable: *Perceived Firm Reputation*
Model Significance: $p = 0.063$

	Effect	*t-stat*	*p Value*	*Lower CI*	*Upper CI*
Firm type X Failure type	−0.494	−2.105	0.036	−0.956	−0.032

Panel B: Summary Results for the Moderated-Mediation Model

Dependent Variable: *InvAvg.*
Model Significance: $p < 0.000$

	Effect	*t-stat*	*p Value*	*Lower CI*	*Upper CI*
Perceived management reputation	0.464	3.455	0.001	0.200	0.728
Perceived firm reputation	0.989	7.255	0.000	0.721	1.258
Failure type (direct effect)	0.060	0.330	0.742	−0.297	0.416

Panel C: Conditional Indirect Effect(s) of Failure Type on Investment Judgments Depending on Firm Type

Mediator	*Firm Type*	*Effect*	*SE*	*Lower CI*	*Upper CI*
Perceived management reputation	Traditional	0.031	0.085	−0.105	0.249
	CSR-focused	−0.205	0.117	−0.512	−0.035

Mediator	*Firm Type*	*Effect*	*SE*	*Lower CI*	*Upper CI*
Perceived firm reputation	Traditional	−0.143	0.165	−0.469	0.175
	CSR-focused	−0.632	0.199	−1.078	−0.298

Panel D: Index of Moderated Mediation

Mediator	*Index*	*SE*	*Lower CI*	*Upper CI*
Perceived management reputation	−0.237	0.153	−0.655	−0.021
Perceived firm reputation	−0.489	0.254	−1.068	−0.050

Note: Table 5 reports the detailed results from testing the moderated-mediation model predicted in *H3a* and *H3b*. Hayes' Process Model 7 with bootstrapping was used to estimate the model. Panel A summarizes results showing that the firm type X failure type interaction significantly predicts perceived management reputation and perceived firm reputation. Panel B displays results for the full moderated-mediation model, demonstrating that both perceived management reputation and perceived firm reputation significantly predict investment judgments and fully mediate the direct effect of failure type, which is no longer significant. Panel C demonstrates that the indirect effect of failure type via each of the mediators is stronger and significant in the CSR firm condition, but weaker and not significant in the traditional firm condition. This is supported by the significant moderated mediation indices reported for both mediators in Panel D. Together, the results presented in this table reveal that *H3a* and *H3b* are both supported: the type of failure influences investment judgments through investors' perceptions of management's reputation and of the firm's reputation, more significantly for CSR firms than for traditional firms.

0.298), but weaker and not significant in the traditional firm condition (Table 5, Panel C: conditional indirect effect $= -0.143$, SE $= 0.165$, 95% confidence interval of -0.469 to 0.175). Therefore, the results indicate that perceived firm's reputation mediates the effect of failure type on investment judgments more significantly for CSR firms than for traditional firms.[31] This pattern of results supports *H3b*.

Since both assessments of management and of the firm overall mediate the *firm type* by *failure type* interaction, it appears that there are systemic reputational effects following a CSR-related failure experienced by a CSR firm.[32] This finding speaks to the fragility of reputation building, and to the importance of carefully monitoring a firm's CSR activities and performance, since both the firm as a whole and the *current* management team would suffer reputational damage if a CSR failure occurs after disclosure of a commitment to CSR.

Supplemental Analyses

Since managerial and corporate reputations arguably affect the firm's future revenues, we also tested our hypotheses using ratings of expected future sales as the dependent variable in place of investment judgments. In these supplemental analyses, we again find support for the hypotheses. The insurance effect is observed for CSR firms in the case of an ordinary failure (i.e., CSR firms suffer lower penalties than traditional firms), as demonstrated by the cell means reported in Panel A of Table 6, and by the first planned comparison reported in Panel C of Table 6 ($p = 0.058$). While reactions to failure types are equivalent for traditional firms, the two types of failures elicit different responses for a CSR firm, indicating that the insurance effect is limited to ordinary failures (see the third and fourth planned comparisons of Table 6, Panel C: $p = 0.184$ and $p = 0.022$, respectively). In the case of a CSR failure, the insurance effect is lost – indeed, using expected future sales as the dependent variable actually reveals a marginally significant backfire effect, with CSR firms experiencing greater penalties than traditional firms for a CSR failure (see the cell means reported in Panel A of Table 6, as well as the second planned comparison in Panel C of Table 6: $p = 0.088$). Thus, the pattern of the means is identical to the pattern observed when using investment judgments as the dependent variable, but now *H2* is also marginally significant.

Table 7 replicates the moderated-mediation model used to test *H3a* and *H3b*, except that assessments of future sales is used in place of investment judgments as the dependent measure. The results again support both hypotheses: the *firm type* X *failure type* interaction influences reputation-related assessments of management and of the firm overall (per Table 7 Panel A, both p-values < 0.05), which in turn affect future sales expectations (see Panel B of Table 7, both reputation measures' p-values < 0.001) more significantly for CSR-focused firms (according to Panel C of Table 7, where the confidence interval for each reputation measure includes zero for the traditional firm but excludes zero in the case of a CSR firm). Therefore, the results are robust when either investment judgments or assessments of expected future sales are considered – with the exception that the proposed

Table 6. Supplemental Analysis: Expectations of Future Sales as an Alternative Dependent Measure.

Panel A: Cell Means (Standard Deviation) for Expectation of Future Sales			
	Firm Type		
Failure Type	CSR Firm	Traditional Firm	Total
Ordinary failure	6.50	5.92	6.20
	(1.78)	(2.46)	(2.17)
	$n = 70$	$n = 72$	$n = 142$
CSR failure	5.74	6.25	5.99
	(2.35)	(2.16)	(2.26)
	$n = 69$	$n = 67$	$n = 136$
Total	6.12	6.08	
	(2.11)	(2.32)	
	$n = 139$	$n = 139$	

Panel B: ANOVA testing the effect of Firm Type X Failure Type on Average Investment Judgment

Source	Type III Sum of Squares	df	Mean Square	F	Sig.
Firm type	0.31	1	0.082	0.0	0.897
Failure type	3.1	1	3.119	0.6	0.424
Firm type X Failure type	20.9	1	20.931	4.3	0.039
Error	1331.0	274	4.858		
Corrected total	1355.2	277			

Panel C: ANOVA testing the effect of Firm Type X Failure Type on Average Investment Judgment

	df	F	Sig.[a]	Related Hypothesis
Effect of firm type in the ordinary failure condition[b]	1	2.49	0.058	*H1a*
Effect of firm type in the CSR failure condition[c]	1	1.85	0.088	*H1a* & *H2*
Effect of failure type in the traditional firm condition[d]	1	0.81	0.184	*H1b*
Effect of failure type in the CSR firm condition[e]	1	4.14	0.022	*H1b*

Note: Table 6 presents the supplemental analysis that investigates the hypotheses using expectations of future sales as an alternative dependent variable. Panel A represents the ANOVA results. Panel B displays the cell means for each condition. Panel C reports the results of planned comparisons, which relate to *H1a*, *H1b*, and *H2*. Descriptions of each planned comparison test (corresponding to the superscripts in Panel C) are as follows:

[a]P-values for the planned comparisons are one-tailed, conforming to the directional hypotheses. (P-values for the ANOVA test are two-tailed.)

[b]Measures the insurance effect predicted in *H1a* (i.e., relative to a traditional firm, the CSR firm is protected by its prior disclosure of its commitment to CSR in the event of an ordinary failure).

[c]Measures both the limitation of the insurance effect predicted in *H1a* (i.e., the CSR firm is not protected by its prior disclosure of its commitment to CSR in the case of a CSR failure, resulting in the CSR firm no longer being judged more favorably compared to a traditional firm), as well as the backfire effect predicted in *H2* (i.e., that a CSR firm will be judged more harshly than a traditional firm in the event of a CSR failure).

[d]Measures the equivalence of the reactions to the two failure types for a traditional firm, predicted in *H1b*.

[e]Measures the difference in reactions to the two failure types for a CSR firm predicted in *H1b* (i.e., the limited insurance effect will produce significantly different investor reactions for a CSR firm when the failure is an ordinary failure compared to a CSR failure).

L. EMILY HICKMAN AND BERNARD WONG-ON-WING

Table 7. Supplemental Analysis: Moderated-Mediation Model Test Using Expectations of Future Sales as the Dependent Measure.

Panel A: Summary Results of the Effect of the Firm Type X Failure Type Interaction on the Proposed Mediator Variables

Dependent Variable: *Perceived Management Reputation*
Model Significance: $p = 0.002$

	Effect	*t-stat*	*p Value*	*Lower CI*	*Upper CI*
Firm type X Failure type	−0.510	0.033	0.033	−0.978	−0.041

Dependent Variable: *Perceived Firm Reputation*
Model Significance: $p = 0.063$

	Effect	*t-stat*	*p Value*	*Lower CI*	*Upper CI*
Firm type X Failure type	−0.494	−2.105	0.036	−0.956	−0.032

Panel B: Summary Results for the Moderated-Mediation Model

Dependent Variable: *InvAvg.*
Model Significance: $p < 0.000$

	Effect	*t-stat*	*p Value*	*Lower CI*	*Upper CI*
Perceived management reputation	0.694	4.368	0.000	0.381	1.007
Perceived firm reputation	0.787	4.879	0.000	0.469	1.104
Failure type (direct effect)	0.227	1.062	0.289	−0.194	0.649

Panel C: Conditional Indirect Effect(s) of Failure Type on Investment Judgments Depending on Firm Type

Mediator	*Firm Type*	*Effect*	*SE*	*Lower CI*	*Upper CI*
Perceived management reputation	Traditional	0.047	0.124	−0.173	0.321
	CSR-focused	−0.307	0.154	−0.645	−0.056

Mediator	*Firm Type*	*Effect*	*SE*	*Lower CI*	*Upper CI*
Perceived Firm Reputation	Traditional	−0.144	0.138	−0.408	0.146
	CSR-focused	−0.503	0.187	−0.910	−0.194

Panel D: Index of Moderated Mediation

Mediator	*Index*	*SE*	*Lower CI*	*Upper CI*
Perceived management reputation	−0.354	0.213	−0.847	−0.014
Perceived firm reputation	−0.389	0.218	−0.867	−0.023

Note: Table 7 reports the results from testing the moderated-mediation model predicted in *H3a* and *H3b*, now using the expectation of future sales as the dependent measure. Hayes' Process Model 7 with bootstrapping was used to estimate the model. Panel A summarizes results showing that the *firm type X failure type* interaction significantly predicts *perceived management reputation* and *perceived firm reputation* (note that this is the same result as was presented in Panel A of Table 5, since the dependent variable is not part of the analysis in this first step of the test). Panel B displays results for the full moderated-mediation model, demonstrating that both *perceived management reputation* and *perceived firm reputation* significantly predict assessments of the firm's future sales prospects and fully mediate the direct effect of *failure type,* which is no longer significant. Panel C demonstrates that the indirect effect of *failure type* via each of the mediators is stronger and significant in the CSR firm condition, but weaker and not significant in the traditional firm condition. This is supported by the significant moderated mediation indices reported for both mediators in Panel D. Together, the results presented in this table reveal that *H3a* and *H3b* are both supported when considering expectations of future sales as an alternative dependent measure.

84

DISCUSSION AND CONCLUSIONS

The pressure for firms to focus on CSR has been growing in recent years, with disclosures of particular aspects of social and environmental performance already mandatory in several European countries (e.g., Dawkins & Lewis, 2003; Joyner & Payne, 2002; KPMG, 2020; Laszlo & Zhexembayeva, 2011). In addition to responding to mounting pressures for social responsibility, firms may choose to disclose their commitment to CSR in order to reap the benefits of CSR reporting, which include a lower cost of equity capital (Dhaliwal et al., 2011), a superior workforce (Greening & Turban, 2000; Kitzmueller & Shimshack, 2012), increased sales (Lev et al., 2010), and, presumably, the ability to attract socially responsible investors. More recent research (e.g., Christensen, 2016; Shiu & Yang, 2017; Zahller et al., 2015) suggests that CSR-focused firms can also benefit from the insurance effect in the case of adverse events, while Krüger (2015) shows that CSR actions may be valued by investors when employed to offset prior CSR-related "Concerns."

This study extends our understanding of the effects of firms' disclosed CSR commitment to firm-level failures that are related to CSR. First, we found confirmation of the previously documented insurance effect when the failure is not strongly related to CSR: in the case of an ordinary product failure, having a CSR focus can help protect a firm from the negative consequences of the firm-level failure. Drawing on attribution theory and EVT, we predicted that when the failure is related to CSR, the insurance effect will not apply (*H1a–H2b*) and the disclosed CSR focus may instead backfire, causing CSR-focused firms to suffer greater penalties than traditional firms (*H2*).

Our results support the hypothesized limitation to the insurance effect. First, compared to a traditional firm, the CSR firm benefits from *less* negative investor reactions following an ordinary failure. However, investor judgments are equivalent for CSR and traditional firms following a CSR-related failure (*H1a*). These results provide evidence that CSR's insurance effect is *limited* – it does not protect CSR-focused firms from the consequences of *CSR-related* failures. Moreover, our results indicate that while a traditional firm experiences equivalent reactions to both types of failures, a CSR-focused firm suffers more negative investor reactions in the case of a CSR-related failure compared to an ordinary failure. This finding again supports the predicted limitation of the insurance effect, as the insurance benefit is "lost" when the failure is related to CSR (*H1b*). Investor judgments are shown to be less favorable (i.e., harsher) for CSR firms than traditional firms in the case of a CSR failure, which is directionally consistent with the proposed backfire effect. However, the difference is not statistically significant ($p = 0.145$). Thus, the hypothesized backfire effect lacks conclusive support (*H2*).[33]

Overall, these results have implications for business practice; namely, that firms disclosing a focus on CSR should realize that the protective shield of goodwill (i.e., the "insurance") derived from their CSR strategy is not effective when the company's failure appears to conflict with the firm's socially responsible message. Furthermore, the directional evidence presented here suggests that utilizing a CSR-as-insurance strategy could possibly "backfire" on a firm that is not diligent in protecting the positive CSR reputation that it has cultivated. Our study, therefore, shines a light on an unanticipated consequence of CSR disclosure: the heightened importance for CSR-oriented firms to manage their CSR-related risks.

Utilizing a moderated-mediation model, we also find that investors' perceptions of management and firm reputations mediate the effect of failure type on investment judgments for CSR firms. The results suggest that in the case of an ordinary failure, disclosure of a CSR-focus can offer protection for the reputation of both management and the firm overall. However, following a failure that is related to CSR, reputations suffer, leading to lower investment intention judgments for CSR-focused firms. Firm and managerial reputation perceptions appear to be a prism through which investors gauge their judgment of the firm as a potential investment in light of the firm's disclosed CSR commitment and the nature of a negative firm-specific event experienced by the company.

Limitations and Future Research

Our study has several limitations as well as opportunities for future research. The instrument was designed to be realistic, basing the fictitious company's financial information, background information, and CSR-related disclosures on those of real firms in the HVAC business. However, like all experiments, ours is still artificial given that it was conducted in a laboratory setting rather than a complex "real world" situation.

Additionally, the manipulation for the CSR-related failure was largely focused on environmental performance, which is just one aspect of CSR. Although Rockness and Williams (1988) found that socially responsible mutual fund managers mentioned environmental performance most frequently when describing the filters used to select firms for inclusion in their funds, and Freedman and Stagliano (2008) report that "the market values environmental disclosure information," it is possible that manipulating other aspects related to CSR in the CSR failure treatment could influence the results. Indeed, Qiu et al. (2016) provide evidence that social disclosures are associated with higher market expectations. Thus, it is possible that social performance failures may lead to more or less extreme effects than environmental failures having similar direct financial consequences. Future experimental or archival studies could explore the relative magnitude of penalties across failures that correspond to the varied aspects of social responsibility.

Future studies could also explore whether some types of CSR failures are seen as having longer term effects than others. Another avenue for research would be to investigate whether the backfire effect we hypothesized has a significant impact beyond some "tipping point" – perhaps the relative severity or frequency of a CSR-related failure determines whether investors assess greater penalties on CSR-committed firms than on firms without a perceived CSR strategy.

Finally, in our experiment, the CSR-focused firm treatment includes two *distinct* aspects of CSR engagement: CSR reporting and CSR performance.[34] While these are separate and not interchangeable facets of CSR engagement, we included both in the treatment in order to enhance the strength and realism of our manipulation since many firms seeking to build a reputation for CSR publish CSR reports *and* seek certifications for products to showcase their CSR performance successes. Moreover, firms that distinguish themselves through their CSR performance as well as by producing CSR reports are likely to be viewed as CSR-focused (which was the intent of the manipulation). Since this design choice precludes the examination of CSR reporting and CSR performance separately, future research could investigate the two independently to test whether the limited insurance effect and a pattern consistent with the backfire effect are present for each distinct aspect of CSR engagement.

ACKNOWLEDGMENTS

We would like to thank Khondkar Karim (Editor) and an anonymous reviewer for *Advances in Accounting Behavioral Research* for their insightful comments, Steven Salterio for his helpful suggestions, as well as participants of the 2018 AAA Accounting, Behavior, and Organizations Research Conference, the 2018 AAA Southwest Region Meeting, and the AAA Annual Meeting for their input.

NOTES

1. For ease of reference, firms that have disclosed a focus on CSR will be referred to as "CSR-focused firms" or "CSR firms," while firms that have not explicitly sought to build a reputation for social and environmental practices will be referred to as "traditional firms." Similarly, failures that directly relate to the broad social impacts or environmental impacts of the firm's products will be referred to as "CSR-related failures" or "CSR failures," while failures that are not strongly tied to social or environmental performance will be referred to as "ordinary failures." We recognize that all firms and all failures may relate to CSR to some degree (see the discussion in the *Independent Variables* section), but we use dichotomous language in this study for the sake of clarity.

2. It is important to note that the true intent of a firm's management cannot be observed. According to attribution theory, the disposition of an actor is inferred by the observer from the behavior of the actor (Jones & Davis, 1965; Kelley, 1973). Consequently, in the current context, investors' expectations are formed on the basis of their perception of a firm's commitment to CSR, which is itself based on observable management behavior (e.g., disclosure of commitment to CSR). We discuss this further in the next section.

3. The results of two pilot studies foreshadowed (but were not affected by) the Volkswagen and Chipotle incidents, which occurred after the initial data collection. These two pilot studies produced similar results and conclusions as the present study, with the exception that the hypothesized backfire effect was statistically significant in both pilot studies.

4. It is interesting to note that following the 2015 e-coli outbreak, Chipotle shareholders submitted a proposal to require the firm to publish an annual sustainability report

(www.bizjournals.com/denver/news/2016/03/25/chipotle-board-nixing-idea-of-sustainabili-ty.html). Though the proposal did not pass, Chipotle began publishing a CSR report in the following year. While this formal disclosure of CSR activities was likely prompted by the CSR failure, Chipotle would be considered to have displayed a CSR-focused strategy prior to the failure given the disclosures made on its website and in its advertising materials.

5. Participants rated the firm's attractiveness as an investment and indicated the likelihood they would consider the firm as a potential investment, each on an 11-point Likert-type scale; the average of these two responses is used as the dependent variable. See section *3.4.2 Dependent Variable* for further discussion.

6. KLD ratings refers to the Kinder, Lydenberg, Domini Research & Analytics ratings, which have transitioned into MSCI's Environmental, Social, and Governance (ESG) data.

7. One possible explanation for the unexpected negative effect of positive CSR events is that the Strengths and Concerns listed in KLD do not necessarily correspond to a firm's overall reputation for, or disclosed commitment to, CSR. For example, Fig. 1 of Krüger (2015) shows a KLD *Concern* for Apple, Inc. stemming from employee lawsuits, while the same KLD report cites a *Strength* for Apple as a top-50 employer of the disabled (p. 29). Thus, Apple exhibits both contemporaneous CSR Concerns and Strengths. Consequently, whether the company has established (in investors' minds) an overall CSR-focus is unclear. Indeed, several studies have cast doubt upon the construct validity of the KLD scores, questioning whether the KLD reliably identifies "good CSR" companies and cautioning against netting or summing the Concerns and Strengths (Bouten et al., 2017; Chatterji et al., 2009; Mattingly & Berman, 2006; Saadaoui & Soobaroyen, 2018; Sharfman, 1996).

8. Hahn and Kühnen (2013) and Brooks and Oikonomou (2018) provide comprehensive discussions of CSR-related benefits.

9. Further discussion of disingenuous CSR engagement or reporting is provided by Schaltegger and Burritt (2010) and Gray (2010), among others.

10. As discussed in the *Independent Variables* section, we recognize that all product failures are related to CSR to some extent since they have consequences for consumers. However, we assert that failures involving product performance will not be viewed as being strongly tied to CSR (i.e., they will be considered "ordinary" failures), while failures involving environmental or social consequences, beyond the impact on consumers, will be viewed as directly related to CSR. Our manipulation checks support this assertion. Thus, Minor and Morgan (2012) do not investigate "CSR failures," leaving open the question of whether the insurance effect may be limited and whether there may be a backfire effect in cases of CSR-related failures.

11. The study was reviewed by the university's institutional review board and received exempt status.

12. The research topic and research questions were not described in this recruitment email; rather, the email merely invited the students to participate in a "study of businessperson decision-making."

13. Three other participants who completed the survey except for demographic questions were included in the sample.

14. Results are robust to excluding subjects who stated they did not plan to actively invest in the future.

15. The traditional firm treatment creates the control conditions in the experiment, providing a benchmark to which responses for the CSR firm may be compared. This design allows for a test of the insurance effect (in the case of an ordinary failure), a test of the hypothesized limitation to the insurance effect (in the case of a CSR-related failure), and a test of the backfire effect (in the case of a CSR failure), all of which predict differing reactions to the two types of failures based on the firm type treatment.

16. The certifications cited in the CSR-firm manipulation are modeled after those listed for an actual firm in the HVAC industry. Such certifications can be a key part of how firms seek to build a CSR-focused reputation (Fombrun, 2005; Miles et al., 1997). We recognize that the CSR-firm treatment describes a firm that both produces CSR reports as well as has

a history of commendable environmental performance. Future research could separate the disclosure and performance aspects to test their effects independently.

17. Torelli et al. (2011) find that consumers respond negatively to the communication of CSR activities when the firm/product is associated with a luxury brand. Hence, we selected an industry whose products are unlikely to be considered a luxury product by U.S. investors in order to avoid such an effect.

18. The instrument's wording implied that the firm would not have accrued for the full cost of the furnace breakdowns since they were "excessive." In addition, responses to the two failure types were equivalent in the traditional firm conditions ($p = 0.490$ in the third planned comparison in Panel C of Table 3), alleviating the concern that respondents believe that the firm has already accrued for this warranty expense and that this belief affects their reactions to the two failure types.

19. The result (reported in Panel C of Table 3) that the well-documented insurance effect was present in the ordinary failure condition of our study provides further evidence that participants interpreted the CSR and non-CSR manipulations as intended.

20. Using either of the two investment assessments separately produced similar results and inferences.

21. The questions were presented to participants in a randomized order.

22. The wording of these two check questions requests that participants judge the firm's CSR-focus without considering the furnace problem. This is necessary in order to check whether the firm type manipulations were successful, independent of the failure type manipulation.

23. Two demographic characteristics were significantly correlated with the dependent variable at the 0.01 level: number of accounting classes taken ($r = 0.121$, $p < 0.01$) and gender ($r = 0.200$, $p < 0.01$). Including either demographic characteristic as a covariate in the analysis of variance produced statistically and inferentially similar results.

24. Since contrast coding would not allow us to test all three hypotheses, we considered Rothman (1990) and Saville (1990) in deciding to use planned comparisons. Specifically, following the significant ANOVA result, we tested our hypotheses using planned comparisons that employed Fisher's LSD test, the results of which are presented in Panel C of Table 3. It is critical to recognize that these are indeed planned comparisons rather than post-hoc tests, and that these are not orthogonal comparisons. It is also important to note that we do not conduct all possible comparisons – rather, we only conduct the comparisons that test our hypotheses.

25. This result also provides some assurance that the failure manipulations were successfully designed to be fundamentally equal before considering the impact of a firm's CSR focus.

26. Attribution Theory predicts that a CSR failure experienced by a CSR-focused firm represents out-of-role behavior, which leads observers to conclude that earlier CSR activities were disingenuous and that the firm's true disposition is not CSR-focused. The Attribution Theory based logic requires that participants viewed the firm as being committed to CSR prior to the furnace failure. Responses to the third manipulation check (reported in Table 2) demonstrate that participants considering the CSR-focused firm did in fact feel that the company was strongly committed to CSR before the failure (mean of 9.15 on an 11-point scale with 11 being "Very Committed to CSR"). (Additionally, the fourth manipulation check question in Table 2 demonstrated that participants in the CSR-focused firm condition felt that CSR was of great importance to the firm's underlying strategy (mean of 9.11 on an 11-point scale with 11 being "Very Important.") Thus, the precondition for the attribution-based argument appears to have been met.

27. Expectancy Violations Theory predicts that after a company has publicly disclosed a CSR focus, investors form an expectation of superior CSR performance from the firm, and if this expectation is violated by a CSR failure, negative reactions can be anticipated from shareholders.

28. In untabulated analysis, the cell means for each individual reputation-related item display this same pattern, demonstrating the general consistency in perceptions of firm and management reputation.

29. In place of Baron and Kenny's (1986) procedure, Spencer et al. (2005) and Zhao et al. (2010) recommend the Preacher and Hayes (2004) bootstrap test of the indirect effect, particularly because it is often more powerful than Sobel's test (which assumes a normally distributed indirect effect).

30. Of the demographic characteristics, only gender was significantly correlated with the measure of perceived management's reputation ($r = 0.174, p < 0.01$). Including gender as a covariate in the moderated-mediation analysis produced statistically and inferentially similar results.

31. None of the demographic characteristics were significantly correlated (all p-values > 0.10) with the measure of perceived firm reputation.

32. Indeed, in untabulated analyses, considering all the firm and management reputation-related items simultaneously reveals a single factor; when this factor is used, the means follow the pattern displayed in Table 4 and the mediation results are significant in the same manner as for the separate firm and management measures (as reported in Table 5). Hence, conclusions drawn would hold if a single, combined measure was used.

33. Using an alternative dependent measure – expectations of future sales – provides further support for *H1a* and *H1b*, and results in a marginally significant test of *H2* ($p = 0.088$), suggesting the backfire effect may warrant further investigation in future research.

34. We would like to thank an anonymous reviewer for highlighting this design choice and the need to emphasize that CSR reporting and CSR performance are not synonymous, even though both were included in our CSR-focused firm treatment.

REFERENCES

Adams, C. A., & Larrinaga-González, C. (2007). Engaging with organisations in pursuit of improved sustainability accounting and performance. *Accounting, Auditing & Accountability Journal, 20*(3), 333–355.

Agarwal, J., Osiyevskyy, O., & Feldman, P. M. (2015). Corporate reputation measurement: Alternative factor structures, nomological validity, and organizational outcomes. *Journal of Business Ethics, 130*(2), 485–506.

Baron, R. M., & Kenny, D. A. (1986). The moderator–mediator variable distinction in social psychological research: Conceptual, strategic, and statistical considerations. *Journal of Personality and Social Psychology, 51*(6), 1173–1182.

Bebbington, J., Larrinaga, C., & Moneva, J. M. (2008). Corporate social reporting and reputation risk management. *Accounting, Auditing & Accountability Journal, 21*(3), 337–361.

Bouten, L., Cho, C. H., Michelon, G., & Roberts, R. W. (2017). CSR performance proxies in large-sample studies: "Umbrella advocates", construct clarity and the "validity police". *SSRN Electronic Journal.* https://doi.org/10.2139/ssrn.3107182

Brammer, S., & Pavelin, S. (2005). Corporate reputation and an insurance motivation for corporate social investment. *The Journal of Corporate Citizenship, 20*, 39–51.

Brooks, C., & Oikonomou, I. (2018). The effects of environmental, social and governance disclosures and performance on firm value: A review of the literature in accounting and finance. *The British Accounting Review, 50*(1), 1–15.

Brown, T. J., & Dacin, P. A. (1997). The company and the product: Corporate associations and consumer product responses. *Journal of Marketing, 61*(1), 68–84.

Brown-Liburd, H., & Zamora, V. L. (2015). The role of corporate social responsibility (CSR) assurance in investors' judgments when managerial pay is explicitly tied to CSR performance. *Auditing: A Journal of Practice & Theory, 34*(1), 75–96.

Burgoon, J. K., & Burgoon, M. (2001). Expectancy theories. In W. P. Robinson & H. Giles (Eds.), *The new handbook of language and social psychology* (pp. 79–99). John Wiley and Sons, Ltd.

Burgoon, J. K., & Hale, J. L. (1988). Nonverbal expectancy violations: Model elaboration and application to immediacy behaviors. *Communication Monographs, 55*, 58–79.

Chambers, E., Foulon, M., Jones, H., Hankin, S., & Michaels, E. (1998). The war for talent. *McKinsey Quarterly, 3*, 44–57.

Chatterji, A. K., Levine, D. I., & Toffel, M. W. (2009). How well do social ratings actually measure corporate social responsibility? *Journal of Economics and Management Strategy, 18*(1), 125–169.

Cheng, M. M., Green, W. J., & Ko, J. C. W. (2015). The impact of strategic relevance and assurance of sustainability indicators on investors' decisions. *Auditing: A Journal of Practice & Theory, 34*(1), 131–162.

Chernev, A., & Blair, S. (2015). Doing well by doing good: The benevolent halo of corporate social responsibility. *Journal of Consumer Research, 41*(6), 1412–1425.

Cho, C. H., Roberts, R. W., & Patten, D. M. (2010). The language of US corporate environmental disclosure. *Accounting, Organizations and Society, 35*(4), 431–443.

Christensen, D. (2016). Corporate accountability reporting and high-profile misconduct. *The Accounting Review, 91*(2), 377–399.

Chung, J., & Cho, C. H. (2018). Current trends within social and environmental accounting research: A literature review. *Accounting Perspectives, 17*(2), 207–239.

Claeys, A. S., & Cauberghe, V. (2015). The role of a favorable pre-crisis reputation in protecting organizations during crises. *Public Relations Review, 41*(1), 64–71.

Clor-Proell, S. M. (2009). The effects of expected and actual accounting choices on judgments and decisions. *The Accounting Review, 84*(5), 1465–1493.

Clor-Proell, S. M., Proell, C. A., & Warfield, T. D. (2014). The effects of presentation salience and measurement subjectivity on nonprofessional investors' fair value judgments. *Contemporary Accounting Research, 31*(1), 45–66.

Dawkins, J., & Lewis, S. (2003). CSR in stakeholder expectations: And their implication for company strategy. *Journal of Business Ethics, 44*(2), 185–193.

De Roeck, K., & Delobbe, N. (2012). Do environmental CSR initiatives serve organizations' legitimacy in the oil industry? Exploring employees' reactions through organizational identification theory. *Journal of Business Ethics, 110*(4), 397–412.

Deephouse, D. L., & Jaskiewicz, P. (2013). Do family firms have better reputations than non-family firms? An integration of socioemotional wealth and social identity theories. *Journal of Management Studies, 50*(3), 337–360.

Dhaliwal, D., Li, O., Tsang, A., & Yang, Y. (2011). Voluntary nonfinancial disclosure and the cost of equity capital: The initiation of corporate social responsibility reporting. *The Accounting Review, 86*(1), 59–100.

Elliott, W. B., Grant, S. M., & Rennekamp, K. M. (2017). How disclosure features of corporate social responsibility reports interact with investor numeracy to influence investor judgments. *Contemporary Accounting Research, 34*(3), 1596–1621.

Elliott, W. B., Hobson, J. L., & Jackson, K. E. (2011). Disaggregating management forecasts to reduce investors' susceptibility to earnings fixation. *The Accounting Review, 86*(1), 185–208.

Elliott, W. B., Hodge, F. D., Kennedy, J. J., & Pronk, M. (2007). Are MBA students a good proxy for nonprofessional investors? *The Accounting Review, 82*(1), 139–168.

Elliott, W. B., Jackson, K. E., Peecher, M. E., & White, B. J. (2014). The unintended effect of corporate social responsibility performance on investors' estimates of fundamental value. *The Accounting Review, 89*(1), 275–302.

Fombrun, C. J. (2005). A world of reputation research, analysis and thinking—Building corporate reputation through CSR initiatives: Evolving standards. *Corporate Reputation Review, 8*(1), 7–12.

Fombrun, C. J., Ponzi, L. J., & Newburry, W. (2015). Stakeholder tracking and analysis: The RepTrak® system for measuring corporate reputation. *Corporate Reputation Review, 18*(1), 3–24.

Fornell, C., & Larcker, D. F. (1981). Evaluating structural equation models with unobservable variables and measurement error. *Journal of Marketing Research, 18*(1), 39–50.

Freedman, M., & Stagliano, A. J. (2008). Accounting disclosures of toxics release inventory for 2002. *Accounting and the Public Interest, 8*(1), 21–38.

Glassman, J. K. (2012, May). 5 mutual funds for socially responsible investors. *Kiplinger Online.* http://www.kiplinger.com/article/investing/T041-C016-S001-5-mutual-funds-for-socially-responsible-investors.html

Glavas, A., & Piderit, S. K. (2009). How does doing good matter? Effects of corporate citizenship on employees. *Journal of Corporate Citizenship,* (36), 51–70.

Gliem, J. A., & Gliem, R. R. (2003). Calculating, interpreting, and reporting Cronbach's alpha reliability coefficient for Likert-type scales. In Midwest Research-to-Practice Conference in Adult, Continuing, and Community Education, Columbus, Ohio.

Global Affairs Canada. (2021). *Responsible business conduct abroad.* Government of Canada. http://www.international.gc.ca/trade-agreements-accords-commerciaux/topics-domaines/other-autre/csr-rse.aspx?lang=eng

Godfrey, P. C., Merrill, C. B., & Hansen, J. M. (2008). The relationship between corporate social responsibility and shareholder value: An empirical test of the risk management hypothesis. *Strategic Management Journal, 30,* 425–445.

Gray, R. (2010). Is accounting for sustainability actually accounting for sustainability… and how would we know? An exploration of narratives of organisations and the planet. *Accounting, Organizations and Society, 35*(1), 47–62.

Gray, R., Dey, C., Owen, D., Evans, R., & Zadek, S. (1997). Struggling with the praxis of social accounting stakeholders, accountability, audits and procedures. *Accounting, Auditing & Accountability Journal, 10*(3), 325–364.

Greening, D. W., & Turban, D. B. (2000). Corporate social responsibility as a competitive advantage in attracting a quality workforce. *Business & Society, 39*(3), 254–280.

Guiral, A. (2012). Corporate social performance, innovation intensity, and financial performance: Evidence from lending decisions. *Behavioral Research in Accounting, 24*(2), 65–85.

Hahn, R., & Kühnen, M. (2013). Determinants of sustainability reporting: A review of results, trends, theory, and opportunities in an expanding field of research. *Journal of Cleaner Production, 59,* 5–21.

Hayes, A. F. (2013). Mediation, moderation, and conditional process analysis. In *Introduction to mediation, moderation, and conditional process analysis: A regression-based approach* (pp. 1–20). Guilford Publications.

Helper, L. (2015). Volkswagen and the dark side of corporate sustainability. *GreenBiz.* http://www.greenbiz.com/article/volkswagen-and-dark-side-of-corporate-sustainability?utm_medium=email&utm_source=e-news&utm_campaign=greenbuzz&mkt_tok=3RkMMJWWfF9wsRouuqXIZKXonjHpfsX96O4oT%2Frn28M3109ad%2BrmPBy32oUAWp8na%2BqWCgseOrQ8kl0JV86%2FRc0RrKAbH0ShTA3%2BkqjbYZlndekgjJk%3D

Herbig, P., & Milewicz, J. (1993). The relationship of reputation and credibility to brand success. *Journal of Consumer Marketing, 10*(3), 18–24.

Hickman, L. E., & Cote, J. (2019). CSR reporting and assurance legitimacy: A client–assuror dyad investigation. *Journal of Applied Accounting Research, 20*(4), 372–393.

Hodge, F., Hopkins, P., & Pratt, J. (2006). Management reporting incentives and classification credibility: The effects of reporting discretion and reputation. *Accounting, Organizations and Society, 31*(7), 623–634.

Hodge, F., Hopkins, P., & Wood, D. (2010). The effects of financial statement information proximity and feedback on cash flow forecasts. *Contemporary Accounting Research, 27*(1), 101–133.

Joireman, J., Smith, D., Liu, R., & Arthurs, J. (2015). It's all good: Corporate social responsibility reduces negative and promotes positive responses to service failures among value-aligned customers. *Journal of Public Policy and Marketing, 34*(1), 32–49.

Jones, E. E., & Davis, K. E. (1965). From acts to dispositions. In *Advances in experimental social psychology* (Vol. 2, pp. 219–266). Academic Press.

Jones, G. H., Jones, B. H., & Little, P. (2000). Reputation as reservoir: Buffering against loss in times of economic crisis. *Corporate Reputation Review, 3*(1), 21–29.

Joyner, B. E., & Payne, D. (2002). Evolution and implementation: A study of values, business ethics and corporate social responsibility. *Journal of Business Ethics, 41*(4), 297–311.

Kelley, H. (1973). The processes of causal attribution. *American Psychologist, 28*(2), 107–128.

Kitzmueller, M., & Shimshack, J. (2012). Economic perspectives on corporate social responsibility. *Journal of Economic Literature, 50*(1), 51–84.

KPMG. (2020). *The time has come – The KPMG survey of sustainability reporting 2020.* KPMG IMPACT. https://assets.kpmg/content/dam/kpmg/xx/pdf/2020/11/the-time-has-come.pdf

Krüger, P. (2015). Corporate goodness and shareholder wealth. *Journal of Financial Economics, 115*(2), 304–329.

Larrinaga-González, C., Carrasco-Fenech, F., Caro-González, F. J., Correa-Ruíz, C., & Páez-Sandubete, J. M. (2001). The role of environmental accounting in organizational change – An exploration of Spanish companies. *Accounting, Auditing & Accountability Journal, 14*(2), 213–239.

Laszlo, C., & Zhexembayeva, N. (2011). *Embedded sustainability – The next big competitive advantage.* Greenleaf Publishing.

Lev, B., Petrovits, C., & Radhakrishnan, S. (2010). Is doing good good for you? Yes, charitable contributions enhance revenue growth. *Strategic Management Journal, 31*(2), 182–200.

Li, Y., Gong, M., Zhang, X. Y., & Koh, L. (2018). The impact of environmental, social, and governance disclosure on firm value: The role of CEO power. *The British Accounting Review, 50*(1), 60–75.

Libby, R., Bloomfield, R., & Nelson, M. W. (2002). Experimental research in financial accounting. *Accounting, Organizations and Society, 27,* 775–810.

Mattingly, J. E., & Berman, S. L. (2006). Measurement of corporate social action: Discovering taxonomy in the Kinder Lydenburg Domini ratings data. *Business & Society, 45*(1), 20–46.

Merkl-Davies, D. M., & Brennan, N. M. (2007). Discretionary disclosure strategies in corporate narratives: Incremental information or impression management? *Journal of Accounting Literature, 26,* 116–194.

Miles, M. P., Munilla, L. S., & Russell, G. R. (1997). Marketing and environmental registration/certification: What industrial marketers should understand about ISO 14000. *Industrial Marketing Management, 26*(4), 363–370.

Minor, D., & Morgan, J. (2012). CSR as reputation insurance: Primum non nocere. *California Management Review, 53*(3), 40–59.

Miralles-Quirós, M. M., & Miralles-Quirós, J. L. (2017). Improving diversification opportunities for socially responsible investors. *Journal of Business Ethics, 140*(2), 339–351.

Newman, G. E., Gorlin, M., & Dhar, R. (2014). When going green backfires: How firm intentions shape the evaluation of socially beneficial product enhancements. *Journal of Consumer Research, 41*(3), 823–839.

Nunnally, J. (1978). *Psychometric methods* (pp. 464–465). McGraw-Hill.

Nunnally, J. C., & Bernstein, I. H. (1994). *Psychometric theory* (3rd ed.). McCraw-Hill.

Peloza, J. (2006). Using corporate social responsibility as insurance for financial performance. *California Management Review, 48*(2), 52–72.

Ponzi, L. J., Fombrun, C. J., & Gardberg, N. A. (2011). RepTrak™ pulse: Conceptualizing and validating a short-form measure of corporate reputation. *Corporate Reputation Review, 14*(1), 15–35.

Preacher, K. J., & Hayes, A. F. (2004). SPSS and SAS procedures for estimating indirect effects in simple mediation models. *Behavior Research Methods, Instruments, & Computers, 36,* 717–731.

Preacher, K. J., Rucker, D. D., & Hayes, A. F. (2007). Assessing moderated mediation hypotheses: Theory, methods, and prescriptions. *Multivariate Behavioral Research, 42,* 185–227.

Qiu, Y., Shaukat, A., & Tharyan, R. (2016). Environmental and social disclosures: Link with corporate financial performance. *The British Accounting Review, 48*(1), 102–116.

Roberts, R. (1992). Determinants of corporate social responsibility disclosure: An application of stakeholder theory. *Accounting, Organizations and Society, 17*(6), 595–612.

Rockness, J., & Williams, P. F. (1988). A descriptive study of social responsibility mutual funds. *Accounting, Organizations and Society, 13*(4), 397–411.

Rothman, K. J. (1990). No adjustments are needed for multiple comparisons. *Epidemiology, 1*(1), 43–46.

Russo, M. (2010). *Companies on a mission: Entrepreneurial strategies for growing sustainably, responsibly, and profitably.* Stanford University Press.

Saadaoui, K., & Soobaroyen, T. (2018). An analysis of the methodologies adopted by CSR rating agencies. *Sustainability Accounting, Management and Policy Journal, 9*(1), 43–62.

Saville, D. J. (1990). Multiple comparison procedures: The practical solution. *The American Statistician, 44*(2), 174–180.

Schaltegger, S., & Burritt, R. L. (2010). Sustainability accounting for companies: Catchphrase or decision support for business leaders? *Journal of World Business, 45*(4), 375–384.

Sen, S., & Bhattacharya, C. B. (2001). Does doing good always lead to doing better? Consumer reactions to corporate social responsibility. *Journal of Marketing Research, 38*(2), 225–243.

Sharfman, M. (1996). The construct validity of the Kinder, Lydenberg & Domini social performance ratings data. *Journal of Business Ethics, 15*(3), 287–296.

Shiu, Y. M., & Yang, S. L. (2017). Does engagement in corporate social responsibility provide strategic insurance-like effects? *Strategic Management Journal, 38*(2), 455–470.

Simnett, R., Vanstraelen, A., & Chua, W. F. (2009). Assurance on sustainability reports: An international comparison. *The Accounting Review, 84*(3), 937–967.

Spencer, S. J., Zanna, M. P., & Fong, G. T. (2005). Establishing a causal chain: Why experiments are often more effective than mediational analyses in examining psychological processes. *Journal of Personality and Social Psychology, 89*(6), 845–851.

Spicer, A., & Lambdin, L. (2012). *Walmart's sustainability journey: Lee Scott's founding vision.* University of Arkansas Case. https://uarkive.uark.edu/xmlui/bitstream/handle/10826/527/Lee%20Scott%27s%20Founding%20Vision.pdf?sequence=1

Story, J., & Neves, P. (2015). When corporate social responsibility (CSR) increases performance: Exploring the role of intrinsic and extrinsic CSR attribution. *Business Ethics: A European Review, 24*(2), 111–124.

Torelli, C. J., Monga, A. B., & Kaikati, A. M. (2011). Doing poorly by doing good: Corporate social responsibility and brand concepts. *Journal of Consumer Research, 38*(5), 948–963.

U.S. SIF. (2016). *U.S. SIF foundation 2016 report on U.S. sustainable, responsible and impact investing trends – Executive summary.* https://www.ussif.org/files/SIF_Trends_16_Executive_Summary(1).pdf

U.S. SIF. (2020). *Sustainable and impact investing – Overview.* https://www.ussif.org//Files/Trends/2020%20Trends%20Report%20Info%20Graphic%20-%20Overview.pdf

Vidaver-Cohen, D., & Brønn, P. S. (2015). Reputation, responsibility, and stakeholder support in Scandinavian firms: A comparative analysis. *Journal of Business Ethics, 127*(1), 49–64.

Vilanova, M., Lozano, J., & Arenas, D. (2009). Exploring the nature of the relationship between CSR and competitiveness. *Journal of Business Ethics, 87*, 57–69.

Wall Street Journal. (2015, December 22). A Chipotle Education: The all-natural evangelists get an E. coli reality check. *WSJ.* http://www.wsj.com/articles/a-chipotle-education-1450829240

Wang, Q., Dou, J., & Jia, S. (2016). A meta-analytic review of corporate social responsibility and corporate financial performance: The moderating effect of contextual factors. *Business & Society, 55*(8), 1083–1121.

Werther, W., & Chandler, D. (2005). Strategic corporate social responsibility as global brand insurance. *Business Horizons, 48*(4), 317–324.

Wu, M. (2006). Corporate social performance, corporate financial performance, and firm size: A meta analysis. *Journal of American Academy of Business, 8*(1), 163–171.

Yoon, Y., Gürhan-Canli, Z., & Schwarz, N. (2006). The effect of corporate social responsibility (CSR) activities on companies with bad reputations. *Journal of Consumer Psychology, 16*(4), 377–390.

Zahller, K., Arnold, V., & Roberts, R. W. (2015). Using CSR disclosure to develop social resilience to exogenous shocks: A test of investor perceptions. *Behavioral Research in Accounting, 27*(2), 155–177.

Zhao, X., Lynch, J. G., & Chen, Q. (2010). Reconsidering Baron and Kenny: Myths and truths about mediation analysis. *Journal of Consumer Research, 37*(2), 197–206.

APPENDIX A

EXCERPTS FROM RESEARCH INSTRUMENT

The following general background information was presented at the beginning of the "Company Background" section and was identical for all participants:

COMPANY BACKGROUND

Temp-Perfect is a long-time designer and manufacturer of heating, ventilation, and air conditioning equipment (HVAC), specializing in home and office building sectors of the construction market. Temp-Perfect has been able to distinguish itself for its service to contractors and its innovative features. Research has shown that Temp-Perfect has enjoyed a strong reputation based on word-of-mouth recommendations.

Temp-Perfect has been profitable and its shares have performed well during the recent economic recovery. A summary of the firm's recent financial performance is provided in the table below.

	2013	2014	2015
Net Sales	$258.51 Million	$284.09 Million	$294.94 Million
Net Income	12.59 Million	12.15 Million	13.50 Million
Dividends Per Share	$0.60	$0.72	$0.76
Total Assets	$169.20 Million	$170.57 Million	$169.19 Million
Total Debt	31.90 Million	46.51 Million	38.66 Million
Shares Outstanding	2.11 million shares	2.12 million shares	2.14 million shares
Earnings Per Share	$5.97 per share	$5.73 per share	$6.31 per share
Price Per Share on Dec. 31	$91.63	$88.98	$98.31

The following is the CSR-Focused Firm Treatment:
The following *Mission Statement* is displayed on the company's website:

Our mission is to sustainably build industry-leading, reliable heating and air conditioning products. We believe that by investing in our employees, communities, suppliers, and the environment, Temp-Perfect will continue to grow and provide quality products to our customers in a socially responsible manner.

We take pride in providing a superior indoor atmosphere to our customers in a sustainable and socially responsible manner.

Our products not only make indoor spaces more comfortable, but they also reduce energy use, saving our customers money and minimizing their impact on the environment.

In fact, Temp-Perfect led the industry in the phase-out of ozone-depleting refrigerants and continues such leadership. All of our products are **ENERGY STAR** certified, and our three newest factories received **LEED® Certification**. We also offer air conditioners and heat pumps that achieve **SEER** (Seasonal Energy Efficiency Ratio) ratings of 20, far exceeding the rating of 13 required by U.S. regulations.

For more information about our environmental progress and social programs, please see our annual **Corporate Social Responsibility Report**.

The following is the Traditional Firm Treatment:
The following *Mission Statement* is displayed on the company's website:

Our mission is to build the most reliable and affordable heating and air conditioning products on the market. We believe that by putting our commitment to our customers and to the quality and affordability of our products first, growth and profit are bound to follow.

We take pride in providing superior indoor comfort to our customers at a very affordable price.

Our products not only make indoor spaces more comfortable places to live and work, but they also are backed by our industry-leading five-year warranty, ensuring our customers enjoy the full value of our products.

In addition, all of Temp-Perfect's products are supported by knowledgeable associates who can help you find the perfect air conditioning solution for your home or business and can arrange for quick, hassle-free installation. We continuously build upon our history of proven innovation to improve the comfort of our customers' homes and offices.

For more information about our industry-leading warranty and other product details, please see our **Buyers Guide.**

The following is the Ordinary-Failure Treatment:
Recently, *Bloomberg* reported that according to an independent study, Temp-Perfect's Comfort Plus furnace was breaking down frequently during the 5-year warranty period. Earlier, the company had prominently advertised the performance reliability of its Comfort Plus furnace. Analysts have estimated that to correct the problem, it will cost the firm between $2 million to $3 million.

The following is the CSR-Failure Treatment:
Recently, *Bloomberg* reported that according to an independent study, Temp-Perfect's Eco-Comfort furnace was not meeting the level of energy efficiency and CO_2 emissions indicated on its label. Earlier, the company had prominently advertised the low energy-usage and low emissions features of its Eco-

Comfort furnace. Analysts have estimated that to correct the problem, it will cost the firm between $2 million to $3 million.

APPENDIX B

REPTRAK™ PULSE MEASURE

The four questions – shown below – assess the extent to which participants "feel good" about the firm, trust the firm, admire the firm, and whether the firm has a "good overall reputation."

In light of the furnace problem, please rate the extent to which you agree with each of the following statements:

Temp-Perfect is a company I have a good feeling about.

	1	2	3	4	5	6	7	
Strongly Disagree	○	○	○	○	○	○	○	Strongly Agree

Temp-Perfect is a company that I trust.

	1	2	3	4	5	6	7	
Strongly Disagree	○	○	○	○	○	○	○	Strongly Agree

Temp-Perfect is a company that I admire and respect.

	1	2	3	4	5	6	7	
Strongly Disagree	○	○	○	○	○	○	○	Strongly Agree

Temp-Perfect has a good overall reputation.

	1	2	3	4	5	6	7	
Strongly Disagree	○	○	○	○	○	○	○	Strongly Agree

THE EFFECT OF ACADEMIC PERFORMANCE, INTERNSHIP EXPERIENCE, GENDER, AND BEING A TRANSFER STUDENT ON EARLY JOB ATTAINMENT OF ACCOUNTING GRADUATES

Hossein Nouri[a] and Carolyn M. Previti[b]

[a]*The College of New Jersey, USA*
[b]*Seton Hall University, USA*

ABSTRACT

Increasing one's chances for early job attainment is a major motivation for accounting graduates. Accounting programs are often evaluated by the job attainment rates of their graduates. Therefore, it is important to understand the factors that affect the early job attainment of accounting graduates. This study provides insight into variables that influence job outcomes for accounting graduates. In particular, our results demonstrate that gender, internship experience, grade point average (GPA), and transfer status each significantly impact the early employment of accounting students. Further, the relationships between gender and job attainment, as well as GPA and job attainment, are partially mediated through internship experience. This suggests that gender and GPA not only impact job outcomes directly but also impact job outcomes through their effect on internship attainment. The findings could help accounting programs better prepare, advise, and assist future students in their academic activities, thereby improving students' chances of early accounting job attainment.

Keywords: Job attainment; job offer; GPA; internship; gender; transfer students; accounting students; mediation

---

Advances in Accounting Behavioral Research, Volume 27, 97–113
Copyright © 2024 by Emerald Publishing Limited
All rights of reproduction in any form reserved
ISSN: 1475-1488/doi:10.1108/S1475-148820240000027004

INTRODUCTION

Job outcomes are an important consideration for students and parents evaluating institutions of higher education. According to the Cooperative Institutional Research Program (CIRP) Freshman Survey, over half of incoming college students (54.8%) report that job outcomes are "very important" in their decision to attend a particular university (Stolzenberg et al., 2020).[1] Additionally, from a college or university's perspective, a high job placement rate among graduates reflects positively on the institution and can attract prospective students. Thus, especially in the ever-evolving field of accounting, it is important to understand what traits employers value in new hires so that students, parents, and educators can make informed choices. To this end, we analyze the impact of gender, academic performance as measured by grade point average (GPA), internship experience, and transfer from community colleges on the early job attainment of accounting graduates. We provide evidence of the significant impact of each variable on accounting graduates' early job outcomes, including an unexpected result whereby male students are less likely to obtain early job offers than their female counterparts. We further demonstrate the difficulty transfer students face in securing early job offers, as compared to students who begin their education at the focal college.[2] Our findings yield actionable insights into how accounting programs can best support their students in their job searches.

While prior studies examine these factors in isolation or various other combinations, this study contributes to the literature by combining the analysis of these four factors and focusing specifically on accounting students' initial job outcomes. This provides unique insight into the influence of each variable, holding the others constant, in the case of accounting undergraduates' job attainment. Our investigation is motivated by several observations reported in prior literature: (1) gender can impact job progression (Nasser & Abouchedid, 2003), (2) various fields, including accounting, use GPA as a "key metric" in the hiring process (Brown, 2015; Dinius & Rogow, 1988), (3) employers value internship experience in prospective hires (Low et al., 2016; Rigsby et al., 2013), and (4) transfer from community college can impact academic outcomes (D'Amico et al., 2014; Domingo & Nouri, 2016).[3–5] Using survey data from accounting students during the fall of their senior year at a liberal arts college in the Northeast of the United States of America, our work extends these areas of the literature to provide unique insights into the characteristics that influence accounting students' initial job outcomes.

Notably, we demonstrate that male students of accounting and transfer students are less likely to achieve early job offers as compared to their female and native student counterparts. In supplemental analysis, we document that the relationships between gender and job attainment, and between GPA and job attainment, are partially mediated by internship experience. While gender and GPA each directly affect job outcomes, gender and GPA also affect job outcomes through their relationship with internship experience and the subsequent relationship between internships and job outcomes. We thereby contribute to prior literature addressing traits that students and recruiters consider to be important factors in hiring (Wilson, 2021), and ways in which accounting programs can support their students in their job searches (Wessels & Sumner, 2014). The results of this study can aid college administrators and accounting departments as they advise students on their careers. The findings also can help accounting students better manage their academic and professional activities so that they may secure initial job offers in the accounting field.

The remainder of this paper is organized into four sections. The next section provides the literature review and related hypotheses, followed by the methods and results sections. The last section presents the conclusion, limitations, and practical implications of the findings.

LITERATURE REVIEW AND HYPOTHESES

Early job offers matter to both students and parents, as well as colleges and universities. Accordingly, there exists a stream of literature devoted to understanding those traits that employers value in recent graduates. In addition, the AICPA provides trend reporting on the supply and demand for accounting graduates. In 2020, 52,481 students in the United States graduated with an accounting bachelor's degree. Of these graduates, 16,128, approximately 31%, were hired by CPA firms (AICPA, 2021). The remaining 69% of graduates likely sought out jobs in industry or continued to graduate studies. While the hiring of these accounting graduates into CPA firms has largely been the focus of prior studies, such research limits our understanding of the job market for accounting graduates by excluding over 36,000, or 69%, of these graduates. Our study recognizes the multitude of sectors hiring accounting graduates. We therefore focus on accounting students' job outcomes (the supply side of labor), rather than the traits CPA firms use in their hiring decisions (a limited scope of the demand side).

Even among CPA firms, rather than the broader job market for accounting graduates, the demand for new graduates yields unique challenges. The market for CPA firm new hires is no longer limited to accounting degree holders.[6] As accounting firms have begun to hire more nonaccounting bachelor's graduates, accounting students must now compete with nonaccounting students for jobs that were historically extended only to accounting students (AICPA, 2021). It is therefore increasingly important for colleges and universities' accounting departments, as well as accounting students and their parents, to understand the factors that help students secure early job offers. To this end, we examine the effect of four student traits – GPA, gender, internship experience, and transfer from community college – on early job attainment of accounting graduates.

Grade Point Average

Many professions use GPA as a prescreening criterion when recruiting college graduates. According to Brown (2015), "sectors such as finance, tech, accounting, and engineering still use GPA as a key metric in their initial evaluations of candidates." Reshwan (2016) notes that many employers consider "a strong GPA as an indicator that a potential employee can handle pressure, learns quickly and is motivated to succeed." In the accounting field, GPA has been shown to affect students' ability to secure interviews (Davidson, 1994) as well as internships (Aoki, 2011). Aoki (2011) notes that an overall GPA of 3.3 or higher is generally needed for consideration for internships since high GPAs demonstrate work ethic, dedication, and evidence of technical competence, which are indicators of success on the CPA exam (Violette & Chene, 2008). In addition, Dinius and Rogow's (1988) research concludes that GPA is a defining characteristic used in the hiring process and in recruiting accounting students. The findings of these studies suggest that GPA is an important factor in early job offers, leading to the first hypothesis of the study (stated in alternative form):

H1. Grade Point Average (GPA) has a positive relationship with early job attainment of accounting graduates.

Gender

Gender is also thought to impact job attainment and job advancement. The impact of gender is twofold: gender may directly impact job attainment and progression, while societally reinforced perceptions of women in the workplace may adversely affect women's career aspirations (Nasser & Abouchedid, 2003). In essence, there may be both a direct effect of biases against women and mothers in the workplace on women's careers and an indirect effect of these biases on women's careers, whereby women underestimate their own abilities and potential for career advancement. These lowered aspirations and the documented motherhood penalty in the US lead to lower rates of positive career progression in females as compared to their male counterparts (Danziger & Eden, 2007; Jee et al., 2019; Nasser & Abouchedid, 2003).[7] Nasser and Abouchedid (2003) analyze the job attainment of Lebanese students, concluding that employment rates in the 5-year period following graduation are higher among male graduates. Danziger and Eden's (2007) Israeli study addresses discrimination women face in the workplace, which can create a "self-fulfilling prophecy" in which women face pressure to lower their career aspirations in response to societal expectations. Kübler et al. (2018) examine a nationally representative sample of German firms by presenting short curriculum vitae (CVs) of fictitious applicants for apprenticeship positions to human resource managers. They find that human resource managers provide worse evaluations for women than men, on average, controlling for all attributes of the CV. Further, Anderson et al. (1994) address the potential biases women in the accounting profession face, citing the 1989 Supreme Court case of *Hopkins vs. Price Waterhouse*. The case focuses on gender as well as the impact of appearance and family structure in the creation of bias in the field of public accounting.

Additional experimental research demonstrates gender-based bias in the workplace. González et al. (2019) mailed two sets of fictitious resumes to 1,372 job postings from a broad range of occupations in Spain. For each job opening, four fake applications were sent, which "consisted of two sets of matched CVs, with each set containing a CV from one male and one female with equivalent characteristics. The two sets differed in either candidates' level of skills/qualifications for the job or their parenthood status" (p. 190). They found differences in favor of men, signaling gender bias in recruitment. The bias was reduced when women had higher qualifications but increased when they had children. In another recent study, Kline et al. (2022) sampled 125 entry-level job postings in different geographical areas by 108 of the largest US employers. These researchers mailed over 83,000 applications to these employers. Eight applications with randomized characteristics, in pairs, were sent for each job offer with a gap of one to 2 days between consecutive pairs. About 24% of "applicants" were contacted by firms within 30 days, resulting in 11,114 job contacts. Kline et al. (2022) found that two-digit Standard Industrial Classification (SIC) codes explained roughly half of firm-level variation in contact gaps for gender, indicating that some firms favored male applicants and others favored female applicants, with little geographical dispersion effect. These findings are similar to recent research by Kline and Walters (2021) and by Hangartner et al. (2021), who found that gender discrimination varies bidirectionally across jobs in Mexico and Switzerland, respectively.

On the other hand, Davidson (1994) does not find significant differences in age or gender between those who received an interview for public accounting roles and those who did not. Further, Campbell et al. (2013) fail to find a significant impact of gender on accounting students' academic performance at their large, state university. It is therefore of interest whether gender impacts accounting employment, especially at the onset of one's career. Our setting of early job attainment permits us to separate the longevity effects of gender on job progression and promotion from the impact gender may have on obtaining an initial job offer after graduation. Our related, alternative form hypothesis is stated as follows:

H2. Student gender has a significant effect on early job attainment of accounting graduates.

Transfer From Community College

Being a transfer student from a community college may also affect job outcomes for accounting graduates. Research by Domingo and Nouri (2016) investigates the impact of being a transfer student on academic performance as compared to "native" students, those who begin and complete their education at the same institution.[8] Domingo and Nouri (2016) find that native accounting students outperform transfers in academics. In addition, prior studies show that academic and social integration are strengthened by information networks among students, faculty, and support services for native students (D'Amico et al., 2014; Karp et al., 2010; Lester et al., 2013). Nouri and Domingo (2019), citing Laanan (2007) and Townsend and Wilson (2006), contend that "many community college transfer students experience difficulty adjusting to the academic rigor, campus environment, and competition among students after transfer to a four-year institution" (p. 50). These difficulties may, in turn, hamper a transfer student's early job attainment. The related, alternative form hypothesis is stated as follows:

H3. There is a significant difference between native accounting students and transfer accounting students from a community college on early job attainment.

Internship Experience

With the rise of internships as a means of employers evaluating prospective hires and students evaluating prospective work environments, accounting research has sought to measure the benefits of internships on the job attainment of accounting students (Beard, 1998; Knouse et al., 1999; Oliver et al., 1996). The overwhelming agreement is that internships correlate positively with early job attainment. Oliver et al. (1996) find that employers looked to internship experience as a significant factor in their recruitment of accounting graduates. Beard (1998) focuses on the rise of for-credit internship programs in undergraduate accounting education and the related positive impact on students, universities, and employers. Knouse et al. (1999) highlight the differences in GPA and job attainment of those with internship experience, finding that students who participate in internships have higher GPAs and higher rates of employment than those without internship experience. Further, Cheng et al. (2009) show the effect of work experience and academic performance on employment rates among undergraduates in Australia, finding that related work experience and academic performance positively correlate with employment results. Rigsby et al. (2013) and Low et al. (2016) focus their respective studies on accounting internship experience as a highly valued quality by potential employers, indicating internships have a positive impact on job attainment among accounting graduates. The findings of these studies suggest the following alternative form hypothesis:

H4. Internship experience has a positive effect on early job attainment of accounting graduates.

METHOD AND RESULTS

The data for this study were collected from senior accounting students at a 4-year public liberal arts college in the Northeast of the USA. The college is highly selective and admits students with an average SAT score of 1265 who are in the top 15% of their high school ranking (TCNJ Admissions). The average class size at the institution is 21 and the student-faculty ratio is 13:1 (TCNJ Quick Facts). About 60% of all business students at the college surveyed receive at least one job offer before graduation (Careers and Outcomes). The school's robust accountancy program aimed at positive career outcomes includes a mandatory course in career planning. The course integrates a mock interview, resume critique, and shadowing program into the accounting curriculum. The school attracts recruiting efforts from each of the Big 4 public accounting firms (Deloitte, EY, KPMG, and PwC), regional and local firms, and corporations. Students at the college where the study is conducted mainly participate in internships at public accounting firms during the spring of their junior year and the summer before their senior year. Some students return to campus in the fall of their senior year having secured a job offer. Others interview in the fall semester of their senior year for full-time employment. Students are therefore surveyed about their career outcomes at the end of the fall semester of their senior year. Data were collected from the fall of 2012–2018 for those students graduating in December 2012 through May 2019.

From 2012 through 2018, 395 accounting students were asked to complete a questionnaire at the end of their fall senior year.[9] Two surveys were removed from the sample because of missing information. Descriptive statistics are presented in Table 1.

Of the 393 students, 262, or 66.7%, had received early full-time offers when surveyed at the end of the fall of their senior year. Two hundred fifty-six of the students receiving early job offers had prior internship experience.[10] Average compensation reported by those with job offers was equal to $58,769 and ranged from $41,600 to $70,000.

Two hundred twenty-two, or 56.5%, of the accounting students surveyed were male. This percentage is slightly higher than that of the AICPA's 2019 report, which states that 51% of accounting graduates across the country are male (AICPA, 2019). However, this study spans a 7-year period, whereas the AICPA report covers only the 2017–2018 academic year. From 2012 through 2017, the AICPA statistics indicate a higher percentage of male accounting students as compared to female students. Thus, the higher observed percentage of male students in this study reflects the impact of the years 2012 through 2017's higher national rate of male accounting students. The average GPA of the 393 students surveyed is 3.343, and the average SAT score is 1267. This average SAT score is nearly equivalent to the overall college average of 1265 (TCNJ Admissions).

Transfer students account for 18.3% of the sample. A study published by the American Association of Accounting reports that 40.1% of accounting majors at

Table 1. Descriptive Statistics.

	N	Mean	Std. Deviation
Gender	393	0.435	0.4964
Transfer from community college	393	0.817	0.3873
GPA	393	3.343	0.3477
Internship experience	393	0.651	0.4771
Job offer	393	0.667	0.4720

Note: Gender: 1 = Female, 0 = Male. Transfer from Community College: 1 = Native (Began College Education at Focal College), 0 = Transfer. Internship Experience: 0 = No, 1 = Yes. Job Offer: 0 = No, 1 = Yes.

2-year community colleges intended to transfer to a 4-year college or university, and 16.4% of all accounting majors at 4-year colleges or universities have earned an associate degree at a community college (American Accounting Association, 2010). Therefore, the percentage of transfer students from community colleges in this study is comparable to the average percentage of transfer students in accounting programs nationwide. This comparability of gender breakout and transfer student percentages to the national averages among accounting programs provides some assurance regarding the study's generalizability.

Binomial logistic regression was performed to ascertain the effects of gender, transfer from community college, GPA, and internship experience on the likelihood that students receive an early job offer. The linearity of the continuous variable GPA with respect to the logit of the dependent variable, early job offer, was assessed via the Box and Tidwell (1962) procedure. A Bonferroni correction was applied using all six terms in the model, resulting in statistical significance being accepted when $p < 0.0083$ (Tabachnick & Fidell, 2013). Based on this assessment, our continuous independent variable GPA was found to be linearly related to the logit of the dependent variable, early job offer ($p = 0.377$). There were 10 studentized residuals with values ranging from -2.584 to -5.935 standard deviations, which were kept in the analysis.[11] In addition, the area under the ROC curve was 0.867 (95% CI, 0.831 to 0.904), which is an excellent level of discrimination according to Hosmer et al. (2013). Table 2 presents the correlation matrix for variables in the study.[12]

As shown in Table 2, there is preliminary evidence of univariate relationships between each independent variable and the dependent variable of job outcomes. The results of the logistic regression model show that it is statistically significant, $\chi^2(4) = 165.198$ ($p < 0.001$). The model explains 47.7% (Nagelkerke R^2) of the variance in early job offers and correctly classified 81.7% of cases. Sensitivity is 88.9%, indicating those students who received a job offer and the model correctly identified them. Specificity is 67.2%, showing those students who did not have a job offer and the model correctly identified them. The positive predictive value is 84.42%, meaning that of all students who received an early job offer, 84.42% were correctly predicted. The negative predictive value was 75.21%, meaning that of all students who did not get an early job offer, 75.21% were correctly predicted. Table 3 presents the results of logistic regression analysis.[13]

Table 2. Spearman Rho Correlation Matrix.

	Transfer From Community College	GPA	Internship Experience	Early Job Offer
Gender	0.031	0.133**	0.179**	0.207**
Transfer from community college		0.276**	0.150**	0.251**
GPA			0.362**	0.489**
Internship experience				0.491**

Note: $n = 393.$**$p < 0.01$.

Table 3. Logistic Regression Analysis of Early Job Offer.

Variables	B	S.E.	Wald	df	Sig.	Exp(B)	95% C.I. for EXP(B)	
							Lower	Upper
Gender	0.708	0.286	6.141	1	0.013	2.029	1.160	3.552
Transfer from community college	0.770	0.336	5.242	1	0.022	2.159	1.117	4.173
GPA	2.977	0.472	39.827	1	0.000	19.632	7.788	49.489
Internship experience	1.802	0.275	43.041	1	0.000	6.060	3.537	10.380
Constant	−11.031	1.546	50.937	1	0.000	0.000		

Note: Gender: 1 = Female, 0 = Male. Transfer from Community College: 1 = Native (Began College Education at Focal College), 0 = Transfer. Internship Experience: 0 = No, 1 = Yes. Job Offer: 0 = No, 1 = Yes.

As shown in Table 3, all four predictor variables are statistically significant, permitting us to reject the null hypotheses in favor of the stated alternatives for hypotheses *H1*, *H2*, *H3*, and *H4*. The results indicate that the odds of getting an early job offer are 2.029 times greater for females as opposed to male students, 2.159 times greater for native students than transfer students, and 6.06 times greater for students who have internship experience than those without internship experience. In addition, the findings show that for each one-tenth unit (0.10) increase in GPA, the odds of getting an early job offer increase by a factor of 1.9632. The findings show that by holding GPA constant, the chances of obtaining an early job offer are highest for native female students with internship experience and lowest for male transfer students without internship experience. This finding of male students' difficulty in securing early job offers, as compared to female students, runs contrary to the authors' expectations as informed by prior literature. While we cannot comment on the job progression of male and female students due to scope limitations, our study provides evidence that holding all else constant, female students of accounting do not struggle to secure early job offers as compared to male students, but in fact are more likely to obtain that initial job offer.

Supplemental Analysis

To add to our understanding of how these predictor variables relate to job attainment, we conducted a supplemental path analysis using mediation. Discussion with recently recruited accounting graduates indicates that students can obtain their full-time job offers through internships, lending credence to our mediation of the impact of gender, GPA, and transfer status on job offers through their impact on internships. That is, gender, GPA, and transfer status may both directly impact job offers, and indirectly impact job offers through their relationship with internship experience. In untabulated analysis, we find evidence that supports both the direct and indirect paths of gender and GPA to job offers, and evidence that supports only a direct path from transfer status to job offers. We therefore remove the insignificant path from transfer to internship experience and reanalyze the mediated model. The results are presented in Table 4 and Fig. 1.

Table 4. Mediated Regression Analysis of Early Job Offer.

	B	S.E.	Est./S.E.	p Value
Job Offer On				
GPA	1.697	0.281	6.047	0.000
Gender	0.379	0.158	2.396	0.017
Transfer from community college	0.450	0.181	2.487	0.013
Internship experience	0.963	0.118	8.144	0.000
Internship Experience ON				
GPA	0.336	0.108	3.123	0.002
Gender	0.156	0.074	2.096	0.036
Intercepts				
Internship experience	−0.594	0.356	−1.667	0.096

Note: Gender: 1 = Female, 0 = Male. Transfer from Community College: 1 = Native (Began College Education at Focal College), 0 = Transfer. Internship Experience: 0 = No, 1 = Yes. Job Offer: 0 = No, 1 = Yes.

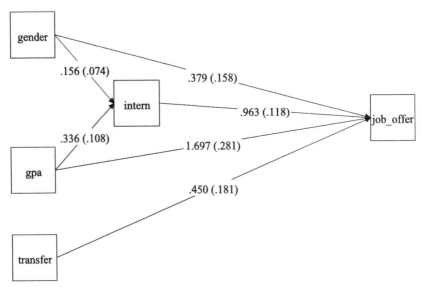

Fig. 1. Mediated Regression Analysis of Early Job Offers. *Note 1:* The above model with mediation was originally run with gender, GPA, and transfer all relating to internships, as well as directly impacting job offers. However, in predicting internships, the coefficient on transfer was insignificant. We therefore removed the insignificant path from transfer to internships and reran the analysis. The model has good fit to the data (an insignificant Chi-Square test of model fit, an RMSEA under 0.05, and a CFI over .95). Parentheses show standard errors for each link. *Note 2:* Gender: 1 = Female, 0 = Male. Transfer from Community College: 1 = Native (Began College Education at Focal College), 0 = Transfer. Internship Experience: 0 = No, 1 = Yes. Job Offer: 0 = No, 1 = Yes.

Not only are female students and those with higher GPAs more likely to obtain job offers, but they are also more likely to obtain internships, which in turn increases their job offer likelihood. Our mediated model fits the data well, with an insignificant value in the Chi-Square test of model fit, a Root Mean Square Error of Approximation (RMSEA) of 0.03, and a Comparative Fix Index (CFI) of 0.995. This analysis provides additional insight into the process by which accounting students obtain job offers, complementing our main findings on the significant impact of GPA, gender, transfer status, and internship experience on job offers. Coupled with our major result regarding GPA, our supplemental analysis indicates that students with higher GPAs are both more likely to obtain internships and more likely to obtain initial job offers than those with lower GPAs. In addition, female students are both more likely to obtain internships and more likely to obtain initial job offers than their male counterparts.

CONCLUSIONS, LIMITATIONS, AND PRACTICAL IMPLICATIONS

This study examines the impact of GPA, internship experience, gender, and transfer status on early job attainment for accounting graduates. The main results indicate that each factor has a significant impact on the early job attainment of accounting students. The findings show that a one tenth of a unit (0.10) increase in GPA increases early job offers by a factor of 1.963. Internship experience is also impactful on the odds of getting an early job offer, as those with internship experience were 6.06 times more likely to obtain an early job offer than those without. The chances of getting an early job offer were 2.16 times greater for native students than transfer students and 2.03 times greater for female than male accounting students. In supplemental analysis, we find evidence that female students and those with higher GPAs are both more likely to obtain job offers and more likely to obtain internships, which in turn increases their chances of obtaining an early job offer.

From a practical standpoint, this study reinforces two commonly held beliefs regarding what factors affect early job attainment of accounting graduates: both GPA and internship experience affect early job offers. Academic performance, as measured by GPA, has long been shown to impact job offers. Coupled with prior research, this study's results reinforce that notion and therefore support the importance of maintaining a high GPA as a means of strengthening one's chances of obtaining an internship and securing early employment in accounting. Therefore, it is recommended that accounting programs and faculty explain the importance of GPA on early job attainment to freshman students. At the same time, faculty and career services professionals should be aware of the potential negative consequences of encouraging students to focus solely on their GPA, as employers consider other factors as well. According to Adams (2015), universities' career services professionals report that many employers use a GPA "floor" in hiring decisions but also acknowledge the potential for consideration of students' other responsibilities and hardships that may impact GPA. Further,

Renshaw (2018) documents that CPAs with lower GPAs have the ability to out-earn CPAs with higher GPAs in the longer term.[14]

In addition, in Roth and Clarke's (1998) meta-analysis of studies that reported salary as the dependent variable, the authors find corrected correlations of 0.20 for grades and starting salary, 0.28 for grades and current salary, and 0.07 for grades and salary growth (1998). Roth et al.'s (1996) meta-analysis shows that the number of years since graduation affects the correlation between GPA and measurement of job performance. These researchers report stronger correlations between GPA and job performance closer to graduation, with correlations weakening as the years since graduation increase. Therefore, while GPA can affect early job attainment, it may not have a significant impact on long-term success or growth. Furthermore, internship experience is impactful in accounting job offers and provides a meaningful opportunity for students to gain exposure to the accounting profession. In fact, Wilson (2021) provides evidence that while 74% of students surveyed consider GPAs to be a deciding factor in obtaining internships, recruiters list personality and fit with the firm as most impactful. Students should view their application criteria through the same holistic lens of recruiters, taking into account a host of attributes that are sought after by employers.

Likewise, the findings of this study indicate that internship experience has a substantial and positive impact on early job outcomes. Students must therefore actively seek out opportunities for internships, and accounting programs, with the help of career services, should seek to increase internship opportunities for their students. As Rigsby et al. (2013) report, internship experience benefits students' job attainment whether or not a job offer is secured through the internship. Pernsteiner (2015) extends this line of reasoning, finding that internships are helpful for accounting students' development of soft skills. Shahid and Nouri (2014) compared the academic performance of interns and non-interns during the internship semester and found that full-time internship students did not perform differently from non-intern students during the concurrent semester, revising beliefs that internship will negatively affect the GPA and course grades during the semester of a full-time internship. For these reasons, it is recommended that accounting students seek out internships, particularly those at firms with which they hope to secure full-time employment.

Apart from reinforcing common beliefs regarding job attainment, the study also contributes actionable insights and avenues for future research regarding transfer status and gender in early job attainment. We find a significant impact of transfer from community college on early job attainment: native students were 216% more likely to obtain early job offers than their transfer student counterparts. This may stem from difficulties in both the social and academic aspects of transferring (Domingo & Nouri, 2016; Karp et al., 2010). These factors may jointly contribute to lower rates of early job offers for students who transfer from a community college. Thus, 4-year institutions should aim to develop more robust relationships with community colleges from which they receive transfer students. In addition, 4-year institutions can develop transition programs to support transfer students academically and socially. These efforts may enhance the continuity of study for transfer students and minimize any negative impact of transferring on job attainment.

Finally, the results of this study indicate that female accounting students receive early job offers at a higher rate than male accounting students. This finding suggests that the previously documented gender-based discrimination women experience in their careers does not manifest in lower initial job attainment among female accounting students. This may be indicative of less hiring biases against women at the early career level. Still, our finding regarding male accounting students' lower likelihood of securing early job offers indicates a need to further explore these gender-based differences in internship and early job outcomes. Kline et al. (2022) observe that women are being contacted more than men for job offers at firms with more female managers. They report that when recruiting is centralized (callback from the same phone number), firms favor female applicants. At the institution where this study was conducted, the majority of the firms' recruiting representatives were female. A potential explanation for our finding may be that the firms' recruiting group's gender can affect the internship and job offers of accounting students (Kline et al., 2022). Another possible cause of this lower rate of early job attainment among male students may relate to differences in interviewing or soft skills, not effectively seeking internships, or other considerations that our research design is unable to capture. In this study, 57.7% of male students received internships compared to 74.9% of female students, which affected job offers for female students. Within the scope of this study, it is recommended that accounting programs and faculty advise all students early on about the importance of those variables that reflect students' active involvement in their educational careers, including having higher GPAs and internship experience, as such variables significantly affect job offers. Future studies can further explore this unexpected finding regarding gender[15] and job offers in order to best advise male accounting students in their early job attainment process.

The findings of this study are subject to several limitations. As the study focuses on the job outcomes of students at one college, it is possible that the results do not generalize to institutions of higher education that differ significantly from that of this study. We stress, however, that the percentage of transfer students and male and female students at the focal college are similar to the national averages among accounting programs. This provides some reassurance regarding potential generalizability. Still, future studies can be conducted at other universities with different student demographics to provide further evidence that the results are not limited to the focal college. Second, the findings of this study may not generalize to accounting graduates with a master's degree, as the data analyzed were from a 4-year liberal arts college offering undergraduate degrees in accounting. Third, the survey approach also has limitations, such as the use of self-reported measures.

Fourth, problems of omitted variables may exist. For example, race was not included in this study, as students were predominately white/Caucasian. Data on first-generation college students were also not obtained in the course of this study but may be impactful for early job offers. In addition, other factors may contribute to early job offers, such as communication and interpersonal skills (Moncada & Sanders, 1999) as well as technological knowledge (Cooper et al., 2019). Future studies can include a broader set of factors affecting the early job attainment of accounting students.

Finally, although this study finds that GPA affects early job offers for accounting students, this effect may be firm-specific. That is, the impact of GPA on job offers may be stronger at larger public accounting firms that attract and seek out top performers. The majority of accounting students at the studied college receive employment in large public accounting firms rather than at regional or local firms. In addition, Aoki (2011) further notes that while GPA is important for a public accounting internship and job offer, it is not the only factor. Other traits that public accounting firms consider include time management skills and involvement and leadership outside of the classroom. Future studies may, therefore, test the hypothesis that students with lower GPAs who secure early employment do so with regional and local accounting firms or have other activities and capabilities that increase their chances of obtaining internships and job offers.

ACKNOWLEDGMENTS

We would like to thank Tony Curatola, David Gefen, Ferhat Zengul (discussant), and participants at the 2020 AAA Annual Meeting for their comments on an earlier draft of this paper. We also gratefully acknowledge the feedback provided by an anonymous reviewer and Khondkar Karim.

NOTES

1. The Higher Education Institute at UCLA's CIRP Freshman Survey provides insights into incoming college students' characteristics and motivations for attending college. Academic reputation was the only reason with a higher rate of agreement among respondents, with 63.2% as compared to 54.8% for job outcomes (Stolzenberg et al., 2020).

2. In keeping with prior literature regarding transfer students, we refer to these students who began their studies at the focal college as "native" students.

3. Nasser and Abouchedid (2003) focus on Lebanese students' job attainment, concluding that employment rates over a 5-year period following graduation are higher among male graduates. This Lebanese study, however, does not specifically address accounting graduates.

4. Dinius and Rogow (1988) analyze GPA in conjunction with quality of university attended, professionalism, personality, and participation in organizations, but do not consider transfer status or gender.

5. While prior research on students who transfer from community college considers academic outcomes (D'Amico et al., 2014; Domingo & Nouri, 2016), our work is unique in providing insights into job attainment.

6. Graduates with degrees in nonaccounting business disciplines, computer science, and math make up 23%, 6%, and 3% of CPA firm new hires in 2020, respectively.

7. The motherhood penalty refers to the discrepancies in pay between mothers and fathers in the workplace, as well as between mothers and women without children.

8. In keeping with prior literature regarding transfer students, we define the term native students to mean those students who began, and were on track to complete, their studies at

the focal college. This is in contrast to transfer students, who we define as students who transferred to the focal college from a community college.

9. To properly evaluate internships and provide advice to students, the department of accounting asks all senior accounting students complete a questionnaire at the end of Fall semester of their senior year (response rate of 100%). No IRB approval was needed for this since the information is used for advice and helping students.

10. Interpreting the means of the dichotomous variables as reported in Table 1, Gender's mean of 0.435 indicates that 43.5% of surveyed students are women (Gender: $1 =$ Female, $0 =$ Male). The mean of 0.817 for the Transfer variable can be interpreted to mean that 81.7% of students surveyed began their higher education journey at the focal college (Transfer:1 $=$ Native, 0 $=$ Transfer). For internship experience, a mean of 0.651 indicates that 65.1% of students reported having prior internship experience (Internship Experience: $1 =$ Internship, $0 =$ No internship). Lastly, the mean of 0.667 on job offer is interpreted to mean that 66.7% of students obtained an early job offer (Job Offer: $1 =$ Early job offer, $0 =$ No early job offer).

11. We checked these outliers and did not find any concern. For example, the highest outlier (-5.935) was related to a native female student with GPA of 3.80 who did not have internship experience and did not receive an early job offer. This could be due to other factors such as communication skills that are not examined in this study.

12. There is no evidence of multicollinearity among the independent variables, as Variance Inflation Factors (VIFs) fall well under the commonly accepted benchmark of 10.

13. We also ran logistic regression with six dummy variables for different years the questionnaires were gathered. None of them were significant and the significance of all other variables were not affected. Therefore, these year dummy variables were not included in the results presented in this paper.

14. Renshaw (2018) defines low GPAs as those falling below or equal to 3.25, and high GPAs as exceeding 3.25. In Renshaw's sample, 21% of surveyed CPAs report GPAs under or equal to 3.25, and 79% report GPAs over 3.25.

15. "The authors recognize the limitations associated with measuring gender as a binary variable."

REFERENCES

Adams, S. (2015). Do employers care about college grades? https://www.forbes.com/sites/susanadams/2015/07/08/do-employers-care-about-college-grades/?sh=7deb27ba4b07

AICPA 2019 Accounting Graduates Supply and Demand Report. (2019). https://www.aicpa.org/content/dam/aicpa/interestareas/accountingeducation/newsandpublications/downloadabledocuments/2019-trends-report.pdf

AICPA 2021 Accounting Graduates Supply and Demand Report. (2022). https://www.aicpa.org/professional-insights/download/2021-trends-report

American Accounting Association. (2010). *Accounting in community colleges: Who teaches, who studies?* Report prepared by David W. Leslie. The College of William and Mary. http://aaahq.org/Portals/0/documents/resources/FacultyTrends_2Year.pdf

Anderson, J. C., Johnson, E. N., & Reckers, P. M. J. (1994). Perceived effects of gender, family structure, and physical appearance on career progression in public accounting: A research note. *Accounting, Organizations and Society, 19*(6), 483–491.

Aoki, J. H. (2011). *How to navigate public accounting recruitment.* Undergraduate Honors Capstone Project, Utah State University. https://digitalcommons.usu.edu/cgi/viewcontent.cgi?article=1106&context=honors

Beard, D. F. (1998). The status of internships/cooperative education experiences in accounting education. *Journal of Accounting Education, 16*(3/4), 507–516.

Box, G. E. P., & Tidwell, P. W. (1962). Transformation of the independent variables. *Technometrics, 4,* 531–550.

Brown, L. (2015). Does college GPA matter when looking for a job? https://www.noodle.com/articles/does-college-gpa-matter-when-looking-for-a-job

Campbell, A., Choo, F., Lindsay, D. H., & Tan, K. B. (2013). Accounting student characteristics from 2005–2010 archival transcript data. *The Journal of Education for Business, 88*, 70–75.

Careers and Outcomes. (n.d.). http://business.tcnj.edu/academics/careers-and-outcomes/

Cheng, M., Kang, H., Roebuck, P., & Simnett, R. (2009). The employment landscape for accounting graduates and work experience relevance. *Australian Accounting Review, 19*(4), 342–351.

Cooper, L. A., Holderness, D. K., Jr., Sorensen, T. L., & Wood, D. A. (2019). Robotic process automation in public accounting. *Accounting Horizons, 33*(4), 15–35.

D'Amico, M. M., Dika, S. L., Elling, T. W., Algozzine, B., & Ginn, D. J. (2014). Early integration and other outcomes for community college transfer students. *Research in Higher Education, 55*(4), 370–399.

Danziger, N., & Eden, Y. (2007). Gender-related differences in the occupational aspirations and career-style preferences of accounting students. *Career Development International, 12*(2), 129–149.

Davidson, R. A. (1994). Use of perceptions in employee selection by accounting firms. *Revue Canadienne des Sciences de l'Administration; Montreal, 11*(4), 331–338.

Dinius, S. H., & Rogow, R. B. (1988). Application of the Delphi method in identifying characteristics big eight firms seek in entry-level accountants. *Journal of Accounting Education, 6*, 83–101.

Domingo, M. S., & Nouri, H. (2016). How do transfer students in accounting compare academically to "native" students? *Global Perspectives on Accounting Education, 13*, 21–35.

González, M. J., Cortina, C., & Rodríguez, J. (2019). The role of gender stereotypes in hiring: A field experiment. *European Sociological Review, 35*(2), 187–204.

Hangartner, D., Kopp, D., & Siegenthaler, M. (2021). Monitoring hiring discrimination through online recruitment platforms. *Nature, 589*(2021), 572–576.

Hosmer, D. W., Jr., Lemeshow, S., & Sturdivant, R. X. (2013). *Applied logistic regression* (3rd ed.). Wiley.

Jee, E., Misra, J., & Murray-Close, M. (2019). Motherhood penalties in the U.S., 1986–2014. *Journal of Marriage and Family, 81*, 434–449.

Karp, M. M., Hughes, K. L., & O'Gara, L. (2010). An exploration of Tinto's integration framework for community college students. *Journal of College Student Retention: Research, Theory & Practice, 12*(1), 69–86.

Kline, P., Rose, E. K., & Walters, C. R. (2022). Systemic discrimination among large U.S. employers. *Quarterly Journal of Economics, 137*(4), 1963–2036.

Kline, P., & Walters, C. R. (2021). Reasonable doubt: Experimental detection of job-level employment discrimination. *Econometrica, 89*(2021), 765–792.

Knouse, S. B., Tanner, J. R., & Harris, E. W. (1999). The relation of college internships, college performance, and subsequent job opportunity. *Journal of Employment Counseling, 36*(1), 35–44.

Kübler, D., Schmid, J., & Stüber, R. (2018). Gender discrimination in hiring across occupations: A nationally-representative vignette study. *Labour Economics, 55*(December), 215–229.

Lester, J., Leonard, J. B., & Mathias, D. (2013). Transfer student engagement: Blurring of social and academic engagement. *Community College Review, 41*(3), 202–222.

Low, M., Botes, V., Dela Rue, D., & Allen, J. (2016). Accounting employers' expectations – The ideal accounting graduates. *e-Journal of Business Education & Scholarship of Teaching, 10*(1), 36–57.

Moncada, S. M., & Sanders, J. C. (1999). Perceptions in the recruiting process. *The CPA Journal, 69*(1), 38–41.

Nasser, R., & Abouchedid, K. (2003). Occupational attainment through Lebanon's higher education: Using individual, societal, structural and gender factors as predictors. *Career Development International, 8*(7), 328–338.

Nouri, H., & Domingo, M. S. (2019). Gender and performance in accounting courses during and after shock periods. *Advances in Accounting Education: Teaching and Curriculum Innovations, 23*, 47–66.

Oliver, T. W., Que, A. L., Farinacci, C. S., & Garland, B. C. (1996). Employer preferences for the background of entry-level accountants: Degree, certification, verification, internship, and experience. *The Journal of Education for Business, 72*(2), 82–86.

Pernsteiner, A. J. (2015). The value of an accounting internship: What do accounting students really gain? *Academy of Educational Leadership Journal, 19*(3), 223–233.

Renshaw, Q. (2018). *GPA & other factors that influence earnings and success among CPAs.* https://digitalcommons.csbsju.edu/cgi/viewcontent.cgi?article=1002&context=ur_cscday

Reshwan, R. (2016). Does GPA matter when applying for a job? https://money.usnews.com/money/blogs/outside-voices-careers/articles/2016-04-26/does-gpa-matter-when-applying-for-a-job

Rigsby, J. T., Addy, N., Herring, C., & Polledo, D. (2013). An examination of internships and job opportunities. *Journal of Applied Business Research, 29*(4), 1131–1143.

Roth, P. L., BeVier, C. A., Switzer, F. S., III., & Schippmann, J. S. (1996). Meta-analyzing the relationship between grades and job performance. *Journal of Applied Psychology, 81*(5), 548–556.

Roth, P. L., & Clarke, R. L. (1998). Meta-analyzing the relation between grades and salary. *Journal of Vocational Behavior, 53*, 386–400.

Shahid, A., & Nouri, H. (2014). Full-time accounting internships and concurrent academic performance of full-time students. *Journal of Social and Behavioral Sciences, 44*(1), 1–20.

Stolzenberg, E. B., Aragon, M. C., Romo, E., Couch, V., McLennan, D., Eagan, M. K., & Kang, N. (2020). *The American freshman: National norms fall 2019.* Higher Education Research Institute, UCLA. https://www.heri.ucla.edu/monographs/TheAmericanFreshman2019.pdf

Tabachnick, B. G., & Fidell, L. S. (2013). *Using multivariate statistics* (6th ed.). Pearson.

The College of New Jersey (TCNJ) Admissions. (2022). Undergraduate admissions: First-year applicants. https://admissions.tcnj.edu/applications/first-year-applicants/#requirements

The College of New Jersey (TCNJ) Quick Facts. (2022). https://tcnj.edu/about/quick-facts/

Violette, G., & Chene, D. (2008). What local and regional accounting firms look for in new hires. *The CPA Journal, 78*(12), 66–68.

Wessels, S. B., & Sumner, D. F. (2014). Integrating career development into the accounting curriculum. *American Journal of Business Education, 7*(1), 21–30.

Wilson, B. (2021). What students and recruiters report regarding public accounting internships. *Journal of Higher Education Theory and Practice, 21*(2), 25–31.

THE ASSOCIATION BETWEEN BUDGETARY PARTICIPATION WITH COMPETITIVE ADVANTAGE: A SEQUENTIAL MEDIATION MODEL

Sophia Su, Kevin Baird and Nuraddeen Nuhu

Macquarie University, Australia

ABSTRACT

This study examines the sequential mediating role of employee organisational commitment (EOC) and innovation on the relationship between budgetary participation and competitive advantage. Data were collected from a mail survey questionnaire of 86 Australian organisations with PROCESS applied to analyse the data. The study's findings make a significant contribution to the budgetary participation and behavioural management literature and practice. Specifically, the study provides a theoretical insight into the role of an important employee behavioural factor, EOC and innovation in mediating the relationship between budgetary participation and competitive advantage. In particular, the findings inform practitioners that budgetary participation influences the EOC of employees and subsequently influence competitive advantage through exploratory innovation.

Keywords: Budgetary participation; employee organisational commitment; competitive advantage; exploratory innovation; exploitative innovation

INTRODUCTION

Budgeting is considered to be an important tool for promoting intended behaviour, with the process in which budgets are developed considered to be a crucial tool in fostering such behaviour (Abernethy & Brownell, 1999). Budgetary participation is an important element of the budget-setting process (Chong & Chong, 2002), as it is found to induce subordinates to accept and commit to their budget goals (Chong & Chong, 2002; Merchant, 1981). While there is extensive research on budgetary participation and its effects, such studies predominately focus on the effect of budgetary participation on various aspects of managerial/ job performance (e.g. Chong & Chong, 2002; Douglas & Wier, 2000; Heath & Brown, 2007; Kren, 1992; Marginson & Ogden, 2005; Murray, 1990). Accordingly, this study contributes to the literature by examining the effect of budgetary participation on a business unit level outcome, competitive advantage. Specifically, we examine the association between budgetary participation and competitive advantage and consider the mediating paths through which this relationship transpires.

Competitive advantage here refers to the level of success of organisations relative to their competitors (Schilke, 2014) with organisations attempting to achieve a competitive edge through producing higher quality products (Agus & Hassan, 2011), introducing new processes (Al-Omiri, 2012; Duh et al., 2012) and/ or management innovations (Barney, 1991; Hamel, 2006; Lin et al., 2016; Mol & Birkinshaw, 2006, 2009; Volberda et al., 2013; Zhang et al., 2019). Our focus on the association between budgetary participation and competitive advantage is crucial given budgets represent the integral process through which organisations allocate their limited resources towards innovation initiatives, thereby attempting to achieve competitive advantage. Furthermore, in line with the employee behaviour literature which emphasises the importance of human capital (Raffer, 2018; Uddin & Arif, 2016), it is expected that budgetary participation will influence employee behaviour with higher (lower) levels of budgetary participation leading to more (less) satisfied employees, thereby enhancing (inhibiting) the ability of organisations to achieve competitive advantage. Accordingly, we aim to contribute to the employee behaviour literature by examining the influence of budgetary participation on the ability of an organisation to achieve competitive advantage.

In examining this relationship, we also aim to contribute to the research examining the mediating factors which influence the effect of budgetary participation on organisational outcomes. In particular, in a similar vein to previous studies which have considered the role of mediating variables (Covaleski et al., 2006; Venkatesh & Blaskovich, 2012) such as the role of budget goal commitment and job-related information (Chong & Chong, 2002), role ambiguity (Jermias & Yigit, 2013), information and environmental volatility (Kren, 1992), budget goal difficulty (Chong & Tak-Wing, 2003), broad scope management accounting systems (Cheng, 2012) and intrinsic and extrinsic motivation (Zainuddin & Zainal, 2012) on the relationship between budgetary participation and managerial/job performance, we aim to examine the intervening mechanisms through which budgetary participation leads to competitive advantage. We consider two mediating factors here, an individual level employee behavioural factor, employee organisational commitment (EOC) and a business unit level outcome, innovation (exploitative and exploratory), incorporating a sequential mediation model in which the effect of budgetary participation on competitive advantage is hypothesised to transpire via EOC and innovation.

EOC here refers to 'an employees' identification with the organisation's goals and values; their willingness to exert a great effort on behalf of the organisation;

and their intention to stay with the organisation (Porter et al., 1974; Su et al., 2009, p. 2494).[1] Our focus on the mediating role of EOC is pertinent given Covaleski et al.'s (2006) and Venkatesh and Blaskovich's (2012) claim that the impact of budgetary participation on performance outcomes occurs via human capital, that is, employee's mental state and behaviour. In particular, we expect that the level of budgetary participation will influence the level of EOC of employees with higher (lower) budgetary participation resulting in higher (lower) EOC. For instance, in line with social identity theory, it is expected that employees will be more likely to feel a stronger sense of belongingness and be more likely to identify with their organisation (Brammer et al., 2007) when they participate in setting their budget targets, that is, higher budgetary participation (Oluwalope & Sunday, 2017). Accordingly, budgetary participation has the potential to facilitate higher EOC, as participation in the budgetary process develops employees' positive emotional feelings towards their organisation (Winata & Mia, 2005).

In addition, it is argued that EOC is a potential driver of outcomes as more committed employees will work harder, subsequently leading to better performance (Yahya et al., 2008). Therefore, in line with Damanpour and Schneider (2006) who emphasise the significant role of employees in building capacity for change and innovation, we examine the subsequent influence of EOC on our second mediator, innovation. Innovation here refers to the extent to which organisations are successful in respect to 'experimentation with new alternatives', referred to as exploratory innovation, and the 'refinement and extension of existing competencies', referred to as exploitative innovation (March, 1991, p. 85). The inclusion of innovation as a mediator is pertinent given more committed employees (i.e. EOC) will exhibit more innovative behaviour as the positive emotional feelings such employees have towards their organisations motivates them to be more creative (Winata & Mia, 2005). Furthermore, as innovation is considered to be a crucial source of competitive advantage (Damanpour & Schneider, 2006; Elenkov & Manev, 2005), it is important to examine the influence of innovation, as a mediator through which the effect of EOC on competitive advantage transpires.

Hence, as depicted in Fig. 1, the objective of this study is to examine the sequential mediating role of EOC and innovation on the relationship between budgetary participation and competitive advantage. The study's findings make a significant contribution to the budgetary participation and behavioural management literature and practice. Specifically, the study provides a theoretical insight into the role of an important employee behavioural factor, EOC and innovation in mediating the relationship between budgetary participation and competitive advantage. In particular, the findings inform practitioners that budgetary participation influences the EOC of employees which subsequently influences competitive advantage through exploratory innovation.

The remainder of the paper is organised as follows. The next section provides an overview of the key constructs and develops the hypotheses. The following section reports the research methodology employed in the study and discusses the measurement of the variables. Section four then presents the empirical findings of

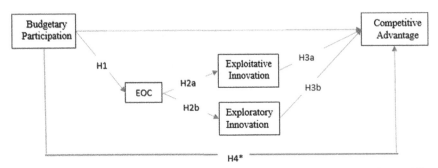

*H4 refers to the indirect effect of budgetary participation on competitive advantage through sequential mediating variables EOC and exploitative and exploratory innovation.

Fig. 1. The Overall Model.

the study, and the final section presents the discussion, conclusion and the limitations of the study.

LITERATURE REVIEW AND HYPOTHESES DEVELOPMENT

Budgetary Participation

Budgetary participation refers to 'a process in which a manager is involved with, and has influence on, the determination of his or her budget (Ndiwalana, 2009, p. 13; Parkinson & Taggar, 2000) with the extent of budgetary participation referring to the extent to which managers are involved in setting the budget' (Subramaniam & Mia, 2001). Budgetary participation can reduce information asymmetry (Jermias & Yigit, 2013) and result in improved communication and understanding between superiors and subordinates (Ebdon & Franklin, 2006; Jermias & Yigit, 2013; Ni et al., 2009). There is extensive research examining the influence of budgetary participation (Nouri & Parker, 1998; Yuen, 2007). However, the majority of previous studies have focused on the impact of budgetary participation on managerial/job performance with less focus on the impact of budgetary participation on other important business unit level outcomes such as competitive advantage, and little emphasis placed on examining how the effect of budgetary participation on competitive advantage transpires. Accordingly, as previously discussed, this study examines the impact of budgetary participation on competitive advantage, and the mediating role of EOC and innovation on this relationship.

The following section will discuss the association between budgetary participation and EOC (*H1*). This is then followed by a discussion of the association between EOC with both exploitative (*H2a*) and exploratory innovation (*H2b*), and the association between exploitative and exploratory innovation with competitive advantage (*H3a* and *H3b*). Finally, the indirect effect of budgetary participation on competitive advantage through the sequential mediating variables, EOC and exploratory and exploitative innovation, (*H4a* and *H4b*) will be discussed.

The Association Between Budgetary Participation and Employee Organisational Commitment

Participative budgeting is an important accounting-based planning and control process (Subramaniam et al., 2002) which can lead to positive job-related outcomes through greater information exchange, better coordination of activities and increased employee involvement (Govindarajan, 1986; Mia, 1989). However, while the majority of studies focus on the direct link between budgetary participation and the achievement of outcomes, we argue that such relationships are mediated by the influence of budgetary participation on employees' behavioural attitudes, specifically their EOC. Accordingly, relying on Kanter's (1977) theory of organisational empowerment and social identity theory, we theorise the association between budgetary participation and EOC.

First, in line with Kanter's (1977) theory of organisational empowerment, participation evokes a sense of empowerment. Hence, when employees are involved in the budget setting process, they will have greater opportunity to make decisions and to become ego-involved in their work (Subramaniam et al., 2002), with such involvement strengthening their feelings of being in charge (Chong & Chong, 2002). While previous studies suggest that such involvement can strengthen employees' identification with and motivation to achieve budget goals (Chong & Chong, 2002; Ndiwalana, 2009; Shields & Shields, 1998) and/or organisational goals (Lowe, 2012), in addition to enhancing motivation participation in strategic planning can also influence affective commitment to the organisation (Freeman, 1989; Shields & Shields, 1998). Specifically, it is expected that through budgetary participation, employees will feel more satisfied and committed to their organisation (Laschinger et al., 2001).

Similarly, in line with social identity theory, it is argued that employees' involvement in the budgetary setting process will result in them feeling a stronger sense of self-identification with and commitment to their organisation. For instance, the opportunity to express opinions and be involved in decision-making can enhance employees' sense of belonging (Brown et al., 2007). Wong-On-Wing et al. (2010) also maintain that budgetary participation influences employees' feeling of belongingness and increases their identification with their organisation. Hence, as employees feel a strong sense of belonging, it is expected that they will be more committed to serving their organisation (Cohen, 2007; Selvina & Yuliansyah, 2015).

In line with the above discussion, we hypothesise that budgetary participation will be positively associated with EOC.

H1. Budgetary participation is positively associated with the level of employee organisational commitment.

The Association Between Employee Organisational Commitment and Business Unit Innovation

While budgetary participation can enhance innovation (Bessant, 1982; Lyons, 1971), as discussed in the last section, we argue that this occurs due to the influence of budgetary participation on EOC, with the commitment of employees, in turn influencing innovation. We maintain that EOC will influence innovation (both exploratory and exploitative innovation) within business units for a number of reasons. First, on a more general level, budgets 'contribute to knowledge creation and innovation through the generation of the affective commitment necessary for employees to be willing to share their knowledge' (Camelo-Ordaz et al., 2011, p. 1442). Specifically, given knowledge sharing is essential for innovation (see Camelo-Ordaz et al., 2011), we argue that innovation will be more successful when employees are committed to their organisation and its goals (Hislop, 2003; Nonaka et al., 2001; Takeuchi, 2001; Thompson & Heron, 2006) as they will be more likely to share knowledge in respect to innovations amongst employees.

Secondly, in line with social exchange theory which maintains that the recipient of benefits will feel obliged to reciprocate the favour to the provider of such benefits (Eisenberger et al., 1990), as employees who are provided with the opportunity to participate in budgets will be more committed to the organisation, they are more likely to share their knowledge to facilitate the initiation of new ideas and/or devote their efforts to innovations. This argument is supported in the literature with Iverson (1996) reporting a positive association between affective commitment and the level of support for and acceptance of organisational change (Ng et al., 2010) and evidence that employees' sense of being valued and supported was found to be associated with the level of innovation (Eisenberger et al., 1990).

Hence, EOC is expected to facilitate innovation, both exploitative and exploratory innovation. In respect to exploitative innovation, consistent with self-identification theory, employees with higher EOC are more likely to identify with the goals and values of their organisation, and to exert effort towards the achievement of such goals (Porter et al., 1974; Su et al., 2009). Accordingly, employees with higher EOC are more likely to engage, contribute and support organisational actions and projects aimed at improving existing operations, that is, exploitative innovation (March, 1991). Similarly, as employees with higher EOC pursue endeavours that benefit and improve their organisation (Cook & Wall, 1980; Lee et al., 2006) and which boost the reputation of their organisation (Tirelli & Goh, 2015), they will be more likely to be involved in creative endeavours designed to improve the quality of the products and services of their organisation, that is, exploitative innovation (Bedford, 2015).

EOC is also expected to promote exploratory innovation, that is, developing new product/service capabilities (Bedford, 2015), as committed employees have a stronger desire to engage in continuous learning, upskilling and keeping up with competitive changes and development in their industries (Cegarra-Navarro et al., 2020). Hence, as employees with higher EOC are more concerned with the ability of their organisations to attain competitiveness in the marketplace (Cook & Wall, 1980), such employees will be more likely to partake in actions and projects involving new products/services (i.e. exploratory innovation) in an attempt to promote the competitiveness of their organisation.

Hence, as discussed, it is expected that innovation (both exploitative and exploratory) will be higher in business units when EOC is higher. Therefore, we hypothesise that EOC will be positively associated with exploitative and exploratory innovation.

H2a. Employee organisational commitment is positively associated with exploitative innovation.

H2b. Employee organisational commitment is positively associated with exploratory innovation.

The Association Between Innovation and Competitive Advantage

Many authors maintain that innovation is essential for competitive advantage (Chen et al., 2009; Chen & Tsou, 2007; Forsman, 2013; Garcia-Morales et al., 2007; Weerawardena & Sullivan-Mort, 2001; Zollo & Winter, 2002) with Chen et al. (2009, p. 154) stating that 'innovation is a key source of competitive advantage in the era of [the] knowledge economy (Daghfous, 2004; Prajogo & Ahmed, 2006)'. Successful innovation can make external imitation more difficult and allow firms to sustain their advantages better (Garcia-Morales et al., 2007). Similarly, Roberts and Amit (2003) state that the development of competitive advantage is positively associated with an organisation's innovative activity.

In line with the resources-based theory which indicates that having unique competencies enables an organisation to gain competitive advantage (Henri, 2006), the enhancement of existing competencies (i.e. exploitative innovation) (Bedford, 2015) enables an organisation to fare better than its competitors, that is, competitive advantage. Specifically, exploitative innovation, which involves implementing incremental improvements and modifications to products and/or services (Bedford, 2015) will yield positive outcomes such as an increased market share and/or higher returns on sales, thereby resulting in increased competitive advantage. Similarly, given the focus of exploratory innovation on experimentation and developing new processes or products (Bedford, 2015), exploratory innovation will position an organisation as a leader in its industry in respect to initiating and implementing change, thereby providing it with a competitive edge. Specifically, as organisations aspire to develop and implement new processes and/ or products and/or services and strive to be the first in the market, consistent with the RBV, exploratory innovation can provide an organisation with a strategic advantage over competitors through an improved market share and a higher return on sales, due to their increased ability to adapt and promptly meet the changing demands of consumers (Verma et al., 2001).

We therefore hypothesise that both exploitative and exploratory innovations will be positively associated with competitive advantage.

H3a. Exploitative innovation is positively associated with competitive advantage.
H3b. Exploratory innovation is positively associated with competitive advantage.

The Mediating Effect of Employee Organisational Commitment and Innovation on the Association Between Budgetary Participation and Competitive Advantage

Based on the preceding discussion and hypotheses relating to the positive effect of budgetary participation on EOC (*H1*), the subsequent positive effect of EOC on both exploitative and exploratory innovation (*H2a* and *H2b*), and in turn the subsequent positive effect of both exploitative and exploratory innovation on competitive advantage (*H3a* and *H3b*), it is inferred that the effect of budgetary participation on competitive advantage will transpire sequentially first through EOC and then innovation. This sequential mediation is theoretically grounded in the literature supporting these relationships. For instance, while budgeting is generally considered to be a tool that promotes intended behaviours (Abernethy & Brownell, 1999), budgetary participation (Chong & Chong, 2002) was also found to induce subordinates to accept and commit to their organisations' goals (Chong & Chong, 2002; Merchant, 1981), as the involvement of employees in budgeting enhances and increases their commitment to their organisations. Subsequently, as employees with higher commitment to their organisations identify with the goals and values of their organisations, and are more willing to exert effort on behalf of their organisations (Su et al., 2009), such employees will partake in and support activities that would improve existing (i.e. exploitative innovation) and/or develop new (i.e. exploratory innovation) capabilities and competencies (Bedford, 2015). Consequently, consistent with the resource-based theory, the resulting innovative endeavours would enable an organisation to perform better than competitors (Henri, 2006), leading to increased competitive advantage.

Accordingly, we hypothesise that:

H4a. The effect of budgetary participation on competitive advantage is sequentially mediated by employee organisational commitment and exploitative innovation.

H4b. The effect of budgetary participation on competitive advantage is sequentially mediated by employee organisational commitment and exploratory innovation.

METHOD

Sample Selection and Data Collection

Data were collected by distributing a survey questionnaire to a random sample of 475 general managers of Australian organisations identified in the OneSource Database (2017).[2] The business unit was chosen as the unit of analysis as the extent of budgetary participation, innovation and competitive advantage may differ between different business units within an organisation. General managers were selected as

SOPHIA SU ET AL.

they have sufficient knowledge about the extent of budgetary participation, innovation and competitive advantage within their business units. As previously mentioned, the focus on budgetary participation and EOC is at the individual level (i.e. the general manager) with the impact of these behavioural-related variables in respect to the level of innovation and competitive advantage assessed at the business unit level.

To improve the response rate, Dillman's (2007) tailored design method was employed in regard to the development of questions and the personalisation of the distribution procedures. A total of 86 completed questionnaires were returned (18.1%) with 49 (10.3%) questionnaires returned following the initial mail-out, and a further 37 (7.8%) received following the follow-up-mail-out. Non-response bias tests were conducted by comparing each of the independent and the dependent variables for early and late responders. The results revealed that there were no significant differences for any of the variables, thereby enabling us to conclude that non-response bias was not a problem (Roberts, 1999). Common method bias was also tested by conducting Harman's (1967) single factor test. The results showed that the highest Eigenvalue value was less than 50% (16.7%) indicating that common method bias was not considered to be a problem (Podsakoff et al., 2003).

Variable Measurement

The survey items for budgetary participation, EOC, innovation and competitive advantage were all scored using five-point scales. The results of principal component-based exploratory factor analysis and the Cronbach's (1951) alpha statistics assessing the internal reliability of each variable are provided in Table 1, with the descriptive statistics provided in Table 2.

Budgetary Participation

Budgetary participation was measured using an adapted version of Milani's (1975) six-item instrument. General managers were asked to indicate the extent to which they agreed with each item using anchors of '1 = Not at all' and '5 = To a great extent'. Item 3 ('targets incorporated in my budget are difficult to achieve') was removed due to a low factor loading.[3] The results of the exploratory factor analysis show that the remaining five-items loaded on one dimension with the individual item loadings of these five items all above 0.60 (see Table 1). The Cronbach's (1951) alpha for the scale is 0.78 which exceeds the cut-off point of 0.70 (Nunnally, 1978).

Employee Organisational Commitment

While Meyer and Allen (1997) classify EOC into three components, namely affective, continuance and normative commitment, this study only focuses on affective commitment as both continuance and normative commitment are beyond the control of management (Su et al., 2009). Specifically, this study applies Cook and Wall's (1980) nine-item scale to measure the level of EOC with

Table 1. Principal Component Factor Analyses and Cronbach's Alpha Scores for the Latent Variables.

Factors and Cronbach's Alpha Scores ($n = 86$)	Cronbach's Alpha	Factor Loadings
Panel A: Budgetary Participation	0.78	
I am involved in setting all portions of my budget (item 1)		0.67
The reasoning provided by my supervisor when budget revisions are made is very logical (item 2)		0.73
I have a high amount of influence on the final budget (item 4)		0.85
My contribution to the budget is very important (item 5)		0.80
When the budget is being set, my supervisor seeks my requests, opinions and/or suggestions very frequently (item 6)		0.64
Panel B: EOC	0.77	
I am quite proud to be able to tell people who it is I work for (item 1)		0.74
I sometimes feel like leaving this employment for good (item 2)		0.72
I feel that I am a part of the organisation (item 5)		0.85
In my work I like to feel I am applying some effort not just for myself but for the organisation as well (item 6)		0.66
The offer of a small increase in remuneration by another employer would not seriously make me think of changing my job (item 7)		0.66
I am determined to make a contribution for the good of my organisation (item 9)		0.77
Panel C: Innovation		
Exploratory Innovation	0.91	
Being first to market with new products/services (item 2)		0.77
Developing new generation product/service capabilities (item 3)		0.84
Introducing new product/service frequently (item 4)		0.87
Experimenting with new products/services (item 5)		0.77
Opening up new product/service markets (item 9)		0.70
Exploitative Innovation	0.87	
Improving quality of existing products/services (item 6)		0.85
Implementing frequent, but incremental, modifications to existing products/services (item 7)		0.89
Improving efficiency in the provision of existing products/services (item 8)		0.80
Increasing economies of scale in existing product/service markets (item 10)		0.69
Panel D: Competitive Advantage	0.90	
We have gained strategic advantages over our competitors (item 1)		0.75
We have a large market share (item 2)		0.64
Overall, we are more successful than our major competitors (item 3)		0.80
Our earnings before interest and taxes (EBIT) is continuously above industry average (item 4)		0.91
Our return on investment (ROI) is continuously above industry average (item 5)		0.91
Our return on sales (ROS) is continuously above industry average (item 6)		0.88

Table 2. Descriptive Statistics ($n = 86$).

Variable	Mean	SD	Theoretical Range	Actual Range
Budgetary participation	4.16	0.70	1.00–5.00	1.20–5.00
EOC	4.31	0.70	1.00–5.00	1.67–5.00
Exploratory innovation	3.03	0.90	1.00–5.00	1.00–5.00
Exploitative innovation	3.61	0.77	1.00–5.00	1.50–5.00
Competitive advantage	3.05	0.85	1.00–5.00	1.00–5.00
lnSize	4.77	1.56	NA	1.10–8.01
Tenure	11.12	9.51	NA	0.75–35.00
Strategy	2.45	1.14	1.00–5.00	1.00–5.00

general managers asked to indicate the extent to which they agreed with each item using anchors of '1 = Strongly disagree' and '5 = Strongly agree'. Three items ('I sometimes feel like leaving this employment for good'; 'I am not willing to put myself out just to help the organisation'; and 'I would not advise a close friend to join my organisation') were removed as a result of low factor loadings. The exploratory factor analysis supported the use of the remaining six items which loaded on the one dimension and had factor loadings above 0.60 (see Table 1). The Cronbach's (1951) alpha for the scale is 0.77.

Innovation

A ten-item measure of innovation was adapted from Bedford (2015), who developed the scale based on He and Wong (2004) and Jansen et al. (2006). General managers were asked to indicate the extent to which their business unit had been successful in respect to each item using anchors of '1 = Very unsuccessful' and '5 = Very successful'. The exploratory factor analysis revealed that nine of the ten items loaded on two dimensions.[4] In line with Bedford (2015) the first dimension, including items 2, 3, 4, 5 and 9, represents exploratory innovation, while the second dimension, including items 6, 7, 8 and 10, represents exploitative innovation (see Table 1). The Cronbach's (1951) alphas were 0.91 for exploratory innovation and 0.87 for exploitative innovation indicating satisfactory reliability.

Competitive Advantage

Competitive advantage was measured using Schilke's (2014) six-item instrument. General managers were asked to indicate whether they agreed with each item in respect to their business unit's performance, with anchors of '1 = Strongly disagree' and '5 = Strongly agree'. The results of the exploratory factor analysis suggest that the six-item scale is one dimensional, with all of the factor loadings above 0.60 (see Table 1). The Cronbach's (1951) alpha for the scale is 0.90.

Control Variables

Three control variables, size, tenure and strategy, were included in the model to control for their potential effect on the dependent variables (i.e. EOC, exploitative innovation, exploratory innovation and competitive advantage). First, organisational size was chosen as a potential factor that can enhance employees' commitment as larger organisations are expected to be able to offer more career development and promotion opportunities (Su et al., 2009). Similarly, larger organisations are more likely to have more resources to facilitate innovation (Mol & Birkinshaw, 2009) and hence, develop stronger competitive advantage (Urbancova, 2013). Size was measured using the natural log of the number of employees.

Secondly, tenure was chosen as it was expected that employees who had worked for their organisation for a longer period would be more committed to their organisation (Brimeyer et al., 2010). In addition, according to attraction-selection-attrition (ASA) theory employees with longer tenure manage to survive the early attrition process (Schneider et al., 1995) and are expected to be high achievers and more innovative (Liu et al., 2016), thereby leading to higher organisational innovation and competitive advantage. Tenure was measured based on the number of years respondents had worked in their organisation.

Thirdly, strategy was chosen as organisations with a prospector strategy are more innovative and actively look for potential or emerging opportunities (Silva et al., 2010). Accordingly, they are expected to exhibit a higher level of innovation and competitive advantage compared to those who focus more on a defender strategy. In addition, Park (2015) argues that organisations with a prospector strategy value creative ideas and knowledge and hence, employees in those organisations are presented with more opportunities to participate in decision making, leading to a higher level of commitment to their organisation.

Strategy was measured using Miles and Snow's (1978) typology of defender and prospector with respondents given descriptions for both strategies. Organisations with a defender strategy are expected to operate 'in a relatively stable product or service area; offer a more limited range of goods and/or services than its competitors, attempts to protect its domain by offering higher quality, superior goods and/or service, lower prices, and so forth; and are not often at the forefront of developments in the industry'. Organisations with a prospector strategy are expected to operate 'within a broad product-market domain that undergoes periodic redefinition; values being "first in" in new product (goods and/or service) areas even if not all of these efforts prove to be highly profitable; and may not maintain market strength in all of the areas they enter'. Respondents were asked to indicate the extent to which these descriptions describe their business unit using anchors of '1 = Type 1' and '5 = Type 2', with higher (lower) scores indicating a tendency towards a prospector (defender) strategy.

RESULTS

Table 1 provides the results of the preliminary assessments of the reliability and dimensionality of all of the multi-item constructs (i.e. exploratory factor analysis and Cronbach's (1951) alpha scores). Consistent with the Cronbach's (1951) alpha scores provided in Table 1, the composite reliability scores for all of the latent variables were above 0.7 (see Table 3), demonstrating satisfactory reliability.

The convergent validity of the measurement model was assessed by examining each construct's average variance extracted (AVE). Table 3 reveals that the AVEs for all of the constructs in the model were higher than 0.5, suggesting acceptable convergent validity (Chin, 1998). Discriminant validity was assessed by comparing the square roots of each construct's AVE to the correlations between other constructs. The diagonal values in Table 3 report the square roots of the AVEs with the other values reporting the correlation coefficients. The square roots of the AVEs were all higher than the respective correlations between the constructs, indicating acceptable discriminant validity (Chin, 1998).

PROCESS, an SPSS add-on macro developed by Hayes (2013), was used to analyse the data.[5] PROCESS employs ordinary least squares regression to estimate the parameters of each equation which is considered to be a common practice in observed variable path analysis (Hayes et al., 2017). One of the advantages of PROCESS is that 'it simplifies the implementation of mediation, moderation, and conditional process analysis with observed (i.e. "manifest") variables' (Hayes et al., 2017, p. 77). Given that there are two sequential mediating variables included in this study PROCESS is considered to be appropriate (i.e. budgetary participation influences competitive advantage through EOC and innovation success). Specifically, Model 1 was selected to test the hypothesised model depicted in Fig. 1 using 5,000 bootstrap samples and at 95% confidence interval. Table 4 Model 1 reveals that budgetary participation is positively associated with the level of EOC ($\beta = 0.505, p = 0.000$), thereby supporting *H1*.

Table 3. Composite Reliability, Average Variance Extracted (AVE), Discriminant Validity and Correlations ($n = 86$).

Latent Construct	Composite Reliability	AVE	Correlation and Square Root of AVE				
			BP	EOC	INNO1	INNO2	CA
Budgetary participation (BP)	0.86	0.55	**0.74**				
EOC	0.87	0.54	0.57	**0.73**			
Exploratory innovation (INNO1)	0.93	0.73	0.12	0.31	**0.85**		
Exploitative innovation (INNO2)	0.91	0.73	0.40	0.48	0.60	**0.85**	
Competitive advantage (CA)	0.92	0.67	0.26	0.48	0.53	0.51	**0.82**

Note: NB The diagonal figures in bold represent the square root of the AVE values.

Table 4. The Association Between Budgetary Participation, EOC, Innovation and Competitive Advantage.

Independent Variables	Model 1 (DV: EOC)		Model 2 (DV: Exploitative Innovation)		Model 3 (DV: Exploratory Innovation)		Model 4 (DV: Competitive Advantage)	
	Co-efficient	p Value	Co-efficient	p Value	Co-efficient	p Value	Co-efficient	p Value
Budgetary participation	0.505	0.000**	0.148	0.230	−0.102	0.507	0.069	0.626
EOC	–	–	0.403	0.002**	0.409	0.011*	0.076	0.614
Exploitative innovation	–	–	–	–			0.255	0.095
Exploratory innovation	–	–	–	–			0.292	0.012*
Control Variables								
Size	0.046	0.240	−0.060	0.173	−0.073	0.191	0.031	0.540
Tenure	0.015	0.032*	0.008	0.284	0.003	0.771	0.005	0.583
Strategy	0.017	0.763	0.082	0.190	0.274	0.001**	0.048	0.524
F-value	10.255		5.975		4.614		5.085	
p Value	0.000		0.000		0.001		0.000	
R^2	0.339		0.274		0.226		0.316	

Note: N.B. DV denotes dependent variable; EOC denotes employee organisational commitment. **significant at 1% significance level; **significant at 5% significance level.

In regard to the control variables, only tenure is found to be positively significantly associated with the level of EOC ($\beta = 0.015$, $p = 0.032$).

Table 4 Model 2 provides support for *H2a* with a significant positive association found between the level of EOC and exploitative innovation ($\beta = 0.403$, $p = 0.002$). *H2b* is also supported with Table 4 Model 3 showing a significant positive association between the level of EOC and exploratory innovation ($\beta = 0.409$, $p = 0.011$). Strategy is the only control variable found to be positively significantly associated with innovation, specifically, exploratory innovation ($\beta = 0.274$, $p = 0.001$).

Table 4 Model 4 indicates that while exploratory innovation is significantly positively associated with competitive advantage ($\beta = 0.292$, $p = 0.012$), there is no significant association between exploitative innovation and competitive advantage ($\beta = 0.255$, $p = 0.095$). Hence, while *H3b* is supported, *H3a* is not supported. No control variables were found to be significantly associated with competitive advantage.

Finally, as the confidence interval (CI) [lower level of 0.001 and upper level of 0.163] does not cross zero, Table 5 shows that budgetary participation is indirectly positively associated with competitive advantage with this association sequentially mediated through EOC and exploratory innovation. Therefore, *H4b* is supported. However, as the indirect effect of budgetary participation on

Table 5. The Sequential Mediating Effect of EOC and Innovation on the Association Between Budgetary Participation and Competitive Advantage.

Indirect Paths	Lower Level (95% CI)	Upper Level (95 CI)
Budgetary participation → EOC → Exploitative innovation → Competitive advantage	−0.027	0.163
Budgetary participation → EOC → Exploratory innovation → Competitive advantage	0.001	0.163

competitive advantage through EOC and exploitative innovation is not significant (i.e. the lower level and upper level Cis cross zero), *H4a* is not supported.[6]

DISCUSSION AND CONCLUSIONS

This study aimed to improve our understanding of the sequential mediating role of EOC and innovation in translating budgetary participation into a business unit level outcome, specifically competitive advantage. A theoretical model was developed and PROCESS was applied to test the model using the data collected from a survey questionnaire of 86 Australian organisations.

The results generally confirm the hypothesised associations. Indeed, participation in the budgeting process significantly enhances the level of EOC, which in turn significantly improves both exploratory and exploitative innovation with exploratory innovation subsequently enhancing business unit's competitive advantage. The association between budgetary participation and the level of EOC confirms Shields and Shields' (1998) proposition that the process of participating in budgeting will allow employees to 'experience self-respect and feelings of equality arising from the opportunity to express his or her values' (p. 59), thereby improving their morale. Shields and Shields (1998) also posit that the increasing level of morale can subsequently reduce employees' resistance to change and enhance their adaptability, which is in line with our findings of a positive association between the level of EOC and innovation.

In addition, while the level of EOC positively influences both exploratory and exploitative innovations, only exploratory innovation subsequently leads to competitive advantage. Such findings are plausible with Lengnick-Hall (1992) arguing that innovations which are more difficult to imitate are more likely to facilitate the development of sustainable competitive advantage. Specifically, while exploitative innovations mainly focus on improving existing products, markets and technologies, which can be easily imitated by other organisations, exploratory innovations focus on the creation of new products, markets and technologies, and hence are more difficult to duplicate.

The study contributes to the literature in several ways. First, it provides a new theoretical insight into the association between budgetary participation and desirable business unit level outcomes by investigating the mediating role played by the level of EOC and innovation. In doing so it contributes to the psychology-based budgeting research which suggests that budgeting affects mental states, which subsequently influence performance (Covaleski et al., 2006). Secondly, the study extends the mediation line of budgeting research by assessing two mediators simultaneously and in sequence, with the results suggesting that the effect of budgetary participation on competitive advantage is enacted through the sequential mediating effect of EOC and exploratory innovation. Further, while previous studies examining the mediating role of variables on the impact of budgetary participation have focused on managerial/job performance, this study focused on a different but equally important outcome variable, competitive advantage, which is considered to be essential for long term organisational success (Mundra et al., 2011) and survival (Kronborg & Thomsen, 2009).

The study also has important implications for practice. Specifically, the findings provide practitioners with an insight into the important and sequential role of EOC and innovation as the mediators of the relationship between budgetary participation and competitive advantage. First, our findings demonstrate the importance of EOC in understanding the influence of budgetary participation on desirable business unit level outcomes. Specifically, it is not budgetary participation itself that enhances innovation, but its positive impact on EOC which in turn enhances innovation. Consequently, organisations should not only focus on promoting employees' participation in the budgeting process but also understand and manage the psychological effect of the budgeting process on employees' commitment to their organisation. Hence, top management should endeavour to introduce strategies that can be applied to enhance employees' commitment to their organisation including caring about their well-being and valuing their contributions to the organisation; providing appropriate training and promotional opportunities, and offering stable continuous employment. In addition, given that EOC can enhance sustainable competitive advantage through the enhancement of exploratory innovation, management should endeavour to encourage exploratory innovative activities such as searching for new and emerging markets, developing new products and introducing new technologies.

The study is subject to the usual limitations of the survey method including the inability to assert casual relationships, and hence future studies may look to apply alternative research methods to provide a richer understanding of the hypothesised associations. In addition, while EOC and innovation have been identified as important factors that mediate the association between budgetary participation and competitive advantage, future studies could investigate how other possible mediating variables such as job satisfaction and/or job-related stress may influence this association. Finally, as the study compares variables at multiple levels, it fails to consider the time-lag usually warranted to observe the impact of individual level actions on aggregated outcomes, that is, innovation and competitive advantage. While we maintain that the significant observed findings negate this limitation somewhat, as the level of budgetary participation within organisations may be stagnant over time, future studies may utilise a cross sectional approach to explore these relationships.

NOTES

1. This definition defines EOC from both the attitudinal and behavioural perspectives and has been widely used in the literature (Foote & Seipel, 2005; Metcalfe & Dick, 2002; Su et al., 2013; Su et al., 2009; Varona, 1996).

2. It is an aggregated database which provides contact details of companies, executives, industries, etc.

3. A cut-off point of 0.6 was used in all of the factor analyses conducted in the study (MacCallum et al., 2001).

4. Item 1 'Developing low cost products/services' was removed due to a low factor loading.

5. The results were also re-assessed using PLS, with similar results identified.

6. PROCESS also tested additional three indirect paths (i.e. Budgetary participation → EOC → Competitive advantage; Budgetary participation → Exploitative innovation → Competitive advantage; Budgetary participation → Exploratory innovation → Competitive advantage) with none of them found to be significant.

REFERENCES

Abernethy, M. A., & Brownell, P. (1999). The role of budgets in organizations facing strategic change: An exploratory study. *Accounting, Organizations and Society, 24*(3), 189–204.

Agus, A., & Hassan, Z. (2011). Enhancing production performance and customer performance through total quality management (TQM): Strategies for competitive advantage. Procardia-social and behavioral science. *The Proceedings of 7th International Strategic Management Conference, 24*, 1650–1662.

Al-Omiri, M. A. (2012). The factors influencing the adoption of total quality management with emphasis on innovative/strategic management accounting techniques: Evidence from Saudi Arabia. *International Journal of Customer Relationship Marketing and Management, 3*(3), 33–54.

Barney, J. (1991). Firm resources and sustained competitive advantage. *Journal of Management, 17*(1), 99–120.

Bedford, D. S. (2015). Management control systems across different modes of innovation: Implications for firm performance. *Management Accounting Research, 28*, 12–30.

Bessant, J. R. (1982). Influential factors in manufacturing innovation. *Research Policy, 11*, 117–132.

Brammer, S., Millington, A., & Rayton, B. (2007). The contribution of corporate social responsibility to organizational commitment. *International Journal of Human Resource Management, 18*(10), 1701–1719.

Brimeyer, T. M., Perrucci, R., & Wadsworth, S. M. (2010). Age, tenure, resources for control, and organizational commitment. *Social Science Quarterly, 91*(2), 511–530.

Brown, S., Squire, B., & Blackmon, K. (2007). The contribution of manufacturing strategy involvement and alignment to world-class manufacturing performance. *International Journal of Operations & Production Management, 27*(3), 282–302.

Camelo-Ordaz, C., García-Cruz, J., Sousa-Ginel, E., & Valle-Cabrera, R. (2011). The influence of human resource management on knowledge sharing and innovation in Spain: The mediating role of affective commitment. *International Journal of Human Resource Management, 22*(7), 1442–1463.

Cegarra-Navarro, J.-G., Wensley, A. K., Martinez-Martinez, A., & García-Pérez, A. (2020). Linking organisational commitment with continuous learning through peripheral vision and procedural memory. *European Management Journal, 38*(6), 874–883.

Chen, Y.-S., Lin, M.-J. J., & Chang, C.-H. (2009). The positive effects of relationship learning and absorptive capacity on innovation performance and competitive advantage in industrial markets. *Industrial Marketing Management, 38*, 152–158.

Chen, J. S., & Tsou, H. T. (2007). Information technology and adoption for service innovation practices and competitive advantage: The case of financial firms. *Information Research, 12*(3), 314–336.

Cheng, M.-T. (2012). The joint effect of budgetary participation and broad-scope management accounting systems on management performance. *Asian Review of Accounting, 20*(3), 184–197.

Chin, W. W. (1998). The partial least squares approach to structural equation modelling. *Modern Methods for Business Research, 295*, 295–336.

Chong, V. K., & Chong, K. M. (2002). Budget goal commitment and informational effects of budget participation on performance: A structural equation modelling approach. *Behavioral Research in Accounting, 14*, 65–86.

Chong, V. K., & Tak-Wing, S. L. (2003). Testing a model of the motivational role of budgetary participation on job performance: A goal setting theory analysis. *Asian Review of Accounting, 11*(1), 1–17.

Cohen, A. (2007). Commitment before and after: An evaluation and reconceptualization of organizational commitment. *Human Resource Management Review, 17*(3), 336–354.

Cook, J., & Wall, T. (1980). New work attitude measures of trust, organizational commitment and personal need non-fulfillment. *Journal of Occupational Psychology, 53*, 39–52.

Covaleski, M., Evans, J. H., Luft, J. L., & Shields, M. D. (2006). Budgeting research: Three theoretical perspectives and criteria for selective integration. *Handbooks of Management Accounting Research, 2*, 587–624.

Cronbach, L. J. (1951). Coefficient alpha and the internal structure of tests. *Psychometrika, 16*, 297–334.

Daghfous, A. (2004). Absorptive capacity and the implementation of knowledge-intensive best practices. S.A.M. *Advanced Management Journal, 69*(2), 21–27.

Damanpour, F., & Schneider, M. (2006). Phases of the adoption of innovation in organizations: Effects of environment, organization and top managers. *British Journal of Management, 17*, 215–236.

Dillman, D. A. (2007). *Mail and internet surveys: The tailored design method* (2nd ed.). John Wiley and Sons.

Douglas, P. C., & Wier, B. (2000). Integrating ethical dimensions into a model of budgetary slack creation. *Journal of Business Ethics, 28*(3), 267–277.

Duh, R. R., Hsu, A. W., & Huang, P. W. (2012). Determinants and performance effect of TQM practices: An integrated model approach. *Total Quality Management and Business Excellence, 23*(5/6), 689–701.

Ebdon, C., & Franklin, A. L. (2006). Citizen participation in budgeting theory. *Public Administration Review, 66*(3), 437–447.

Eisenberger, R., Fasolo, P., & Davis-LaMastro, V. (1990). Perceived organizational support and employee diligence, commitment, and innovation. *Journal of Applied Psychology, 75*(1), 51–59.

Elenkov, D. S., & Manev, I. M. (2005). Top management leadership and influence on innovation: The role of sociocultural context. *Journal of Management, 31*(3), 381–402.

Foote, D. A., & Seipel, S. J. (2005). Employee commitment and organizational policies. *Management Decision, 43*, 203–219.

Forsman, H. (2013). Environmental innovations as a source of competitive advantage or vice versa. *Business Strategy and the Environment, 22*, 306–320.

Freeman, E. B. (1989). Effectiveness of strategic planning: A multidimensional view. *Academy of Management Proceedings, 1*, 12–16.

Garcia-Morales, V. J., Ruiz-Moreno, A., & Llorens-Montes, F. J. (2007). Effects of technology absorptive capacity and technology proactivity on organizational learning, innovation and performance: An empirical examination. *Technology Analysis and Strategic Management, 19*(4), 527–558.

Govindarajan, V. (1986). Impact of participation in the budgetary process on managerial attitude and performance: Universalistic and contingency perspectives. *Decision Sciences, 17*(4), 496–516.

Hamel, G. (2006). The why, what, and how of management innovation. *Harvard Business Review, 84*(2), 72–84.

Harman, H. (1967). *Modern factor analysis*. University of Chicago Press.

Hayes, A. (2013). *Introduction to mediation, moderation, and conditional process analysis: A regression-based approach*. Guilford Press.

Hayes, A. F., Montoya, A. K., & Rockwood, N. J. (2017). The analysis of mechanisms and their contingencies: Process versus structural equation modeling. *Australasian Marketing Journal*, *25*(1), 76–81.

He, Z. L., & Wong, P. K. (2004). Exploration vs. exploitation: An empirical test of the ambidexterity hypothesis. *Organization Science*, *15*, 481–494.

Heath, R. S., & Brown, J. F. (2007). A re-examination of the effect of job-relevant information on the budgetary participation-job performance relation during an age of employee empowerment. *Journal of Applied Business Research*, *23*(1), 111–124.

Henri, J. F. (2006). Management control systems and strategy: A resource-based perspective. *Accounting, Organizations and Society*, *31*(6), 529–558.

Hislop, D. (2003). Linking human resource management and knowledge management via commitment: A review and research agenda. *Employee Relations*, *25*, 182–202.

Iverson, R. D. (1996). Employee acceptance of organizational change: The role of organizational commitment. *International Journal of Human Resource Management*, *7*, 122–149.

Jansen, J. J., Van Den Bosch, F. A., & Volberda, H. W. (2006). Exploratory innovation, exploitative innovation, and performance: Effects of organizational antecedents and environmental moderators. *Management Science*, *52*, 1661–1674.

Jermias, J., & Yigit, F. (2013). Budgetary participation in Turkey: The effects of information asymmetry, goal commitment, and role ambiguity on job satisfaction and performance. *Journal of International Accounting Research*, *12*(1), 29–54.

Kanter, R. M. (1977). *Men and women of the corporation*. Basic Book.

Kren, L. (1992). Budgetary participation and managerial performance: The impact of information and environmental volatility. *The Accounting Review*, *67*(3), 511–526.

Kronborg, D., & Thomsen, S. (2009). Foreign ownership and long-term survival. *Strategic Management Journal*, *30*(2), 207–219.

Laschinger, H., Finegan, J., & Shamian, J. (2001). The impact of workplace empowerment, organizational trust on staff nurses' work satisfaction and organizational commitment. *Health Care Management Review*, *26*(3), 7–23.

Lee, Y., Lee, J., & Lee, Z. (2006). Social influence on technology acceptance behavior: Self-identity theory perspective. *ACM SIGMIS Database: The DATABASE for Advances in Information Systems*, *37*(2–3), 60–75.

Lengnick-Hall, C. A. (1992). Innovation and competitive advantage: What we know and what we need to learn. *Journal of Management*, *18*(2), 399–429.

Lin, H.-F., Su, J.-Q., & Higgins, A. (2016). How dynamic capabilities affect adoption of management innovations. *Journal of Business Research*, *69*(2), 862–876.

Liu, Z., Ge, L., & Peng, W. (2016). How organizational tenure affects innovative behavior? The role of culture difference and status determinants. *Nankai Business Review International*, *7*(1), 99–126.

Lowe, G. (2012). How employee engagement matters for hospital performance. *Healthcare Quarterly*, *15*(2), 29–39.

Lyons, T. F. (1971). Role clarity, need for clarity, satisfaction, tension, and withdrawal. *Organizational Behavior & Human Performance*, *6*, 99–110.

MacCallum, R. C., Widaman, K. F., Preacher, K. J., & Hong, S. (2001). Sample size in factor analysis: The role of model error. *Multivariate Behavioral Research*, *36*, 611–637.

March, J. G. (1991). Exploration and exploitation in organizational learning. *Organization Science*, *2*, 71–87.

Marginson, D., & Ogden, S. (2005). Coping with ambiguity through the budget: The positive effects of budgetary targets on managers' budgeting behaviours. *Accounting, Organizations and Society*, *30*(5), 435–456.

Merchant, K. A. (1981). The design of the corporate budgeting system: Influences on managerial behavior and performance. *The Accounting Review*, *56*(4), 813–829.

Metcalfe, B., & Dick, G. (2002). Is the force still with her? Gender and commitment in the police. *Women in Management Review*, *17*, 392–403.

Meyer, J. P., & Allen, N. J. (1997). *Commitment in the workplace*. Sage.

Mia, L. (1989). The impact of participation in budgeting and job difficulty on managerial performance and work motivation: A research note. *Accounting, Organizations and Society*, *14*, 347–357.

Milani, K. (1975). The relationship of participation in budget-setting to industrial supervisor performance and attitudes: A field study. *The Accounting Review, 50*(2), 274–284.

Miles, R. W., & Snow, C. C. (1978). *Organisational strategy, structure and process.* McGraw Hill.

Mol, M., & Birkinshaw, J. (2006). Against the flow: Reaping the rewards of management innovation. *European Business Forum, 27,* 24–29.

Mol, M. J., & Birkinshaw, J. (2009). The sources of management innovation: When firms introduce new management practices. *Journal of Business Research, 62,* 1269–1280.

Mundra, N., Gulati, K., & Vashisth, R. (2011). Achieving competitive advantage through knowledge management and innovation: Empirical evidences from the Indian IT sector. *The IUP Journal of Knowledge Management, 9*(2), 7–25.

Murray, D. (1990). The performance effects of participative budgeting: An integration of intervening and moderating variables. *Behavioral Research in Accounting, 2*(2), 104–123.

Ndiwalana, J. K. (2009). *Budgeting participation, goal commitment and employee performance.* Master of Science dissertation, Makerere University.

Ng, T. W., Feldman, D. C., & Lam, S. S. (2010). Psychological contract breaches, organizational commitment, and innovation-related behaviors: A latent growth modelling approach. *Journal of Applied Psychology, 95*(4), 744–751.

Ni, F.-Y., Su, C.-C., Chung, S.-H., & Cheng, K.-C. (2009). Budgetary participation's effect on managerial outcomes: Mediating roles of self-efficacy and attitudes toward budgetary decision makers. *NTU Management, 19*(2), 321–347.

Nonaka, I., Toyama, R., & Konno, N. (2001). SECI, BA and leadership: A unified model of dynamic knowledge creation. In I. Nonaka & D. Teece (Eds.), *Managing industrial knowledge: Creation, transfer and utilization.* Sage.

Nouri, H., & Parker, R. J. (1998). The relationship between budget participation and job performance: The roles of budget adequacy and organizational commitment. *Accounting, Organizations and Society, 23*(5), 467–483.

Nunnally, J. C. (1978). *Psychometric theory* (2nd ed.). McGraw-Hill.

Oluwalope, A. A., & Sunday, O. (2017). Impact of budgetary participation and organizational commitment on managerial performance in Nigeria. *Accounting and Finance Research, 6*(3), 48–55.

Park, R. (2015). Employee participation and outcomes: Organizational strategy does matter. *Employee Relations, 37*(5), 604–622.

Parkinson, J., & Taggar, S. (2000). Impact of strategy, human resource management, budgeting and participation on return on assets. *Journal of Human Resource Costing and Accounting, 5*(2), 45–61.

Podsakoff, P. M., MacKenzie, S. B., Lee, J. Y., & Podsakoff, N. P. (2003). Common method biases in behavioral research: A critical review of the literature and recommended remedies. *Journal of Applied Psychology, 88*(5), 879.

Porter, L. W., Steers, R. M., Mowday, R. T., & Boulian, P. V. (1974). Organizational commitment, job satisfaction, and turnover among psychiatric technicians. *Journal of Applied Psychology, 59*(5), 603–609.

Prajogo, D. I., & Ahmed, P. K. (2006). Relationships between innovation stimulus, innovation capacity, and innovation performance. *R & D Management, 36*(5), 499–515.

Raffer, K. (2018). Neoliberalism and globalisation – Justifying policies of redistribution. In *John Hicks: His contributions to economic theory and application.* Routledge.

Roberts, E. S. (1999). In defence of the survey method: An illustration from a study of user information satisfaction. *Accounting and Finance, 39,* 53–79.

Roberts, P. W., & Amit, R. (2003). The dynamics of innovative activity and competitive advantage: The case of Australian retail banking, 1981 to 1995. *Organization Science, 14*(2), 107–122.

Schilke, O. (2014). On the contingent value of dynamic capabilities for competitive advantage: The nonlinear moderating effect of environmental dynamism. *Strategic Management Journal, 35,* 179–203.

Schneider, B., Goldstein, H. W., & Smith, D. B. (1995). The ASA framework: An update. *Personnel Psychology, 48*(4), 747–773.

Selvina, M., & Yuliansyah, Y. (2015). Relationships between budgetary participation and organizational commitment: Mediated by reinforcement contingency. *International Research Journal of Biological Sciences, 8*(2), 69–80.

Shields, J. F., & Shields, M. D. (1998). Antecedents of participative budgeting. *Accounting, Organizations and Society, 23*(1), 49–76.

Silva, N. D., Hutcheson, J., & Wahl, G. D. (2010). Organizational strategy and employee outcomes: A person–organization fit perspective. *Journal of Psychology, 144*(2), 145–161.

Su, S., Baird, K., & Blair, B. (2009). Employee organizational commitment: The influence of cultural and organizational factors in the Australian manufacturing industry. *International Journal of Human Resource Management, 20*(12), 2494–2516.

Su, S., Baird, K., & Blair, B. (2013). Employee organizational commitment in the Australian public sector. *International Journal of Human Resource Management, 24*(2), 243–264.

Subramaniam, N., McManus, L., & Mia, L. (2002). Enhancing hotel managers' organisational commitment: An investigation of the impact of structure, need for achievement and participative budgeting. *Hospitality Management, 21*, 303–320.

Subramaniam, N., & Mia, L. (2001). The relation between decentralised structure, budgetary participation and organisational commitment: The moderating role of managers' value orientation towards innovation. *Accounting, Auditing and Accountability, 14*(1), 12–30.

Takeuchi, H. (2001). Towards a universal management of the concept of knowledge. In I. Nonaka & D. Teece (Eds.), *Managing industrial knowledge: Creation, transfer and utilization* (pp. 315–329). Sage.

Thompson, M., & Heron, M. (2006). Relational quality and innovative performance in R&D based science and technology firms. *Human Resource Management Journal, 16*, 28–47.

Tirelli, A., & Goh, S. C. (2015). The relationship between trust, learning capability, affective organisational commitment and turnover intentions. *International Journal of Human Resources Development and Management, 15*(1), 54–68.

Uddin, R., & Arif, A. (2016). Talent management and organizational performance: An empirical study in retail sector in Sylhet City, Bangladesh. *IOSR Journal of Business and Management, 18*(10), 11–18.

Urbancova, H. (2013). Competitive advantage achievement through innovation and knowledge. *Journal of Competitiveness, 5*(1), 82–96.

Varona, F. (1996). Relationship between communication satisfaction and organizational commitment in three Guatemalan organizations. *Journal of Business Communication, 33*(2), 111–140.

Venkatesh, R., & Blaskovich, J. (2012). The mediating effect of psychological capital on the budget participation-job performance relationship. *Journal of Management Accounting Research, 24*(1), 159–175.

Verma, R., Thompson, G. M., Moore, W. L., & Louviere, J. J. (2001). Effective design of products/services: An approach based on integration of marketing and operations management decisions. *Decision Sciences, 32*(1), 165–194.

Volberda, H., Van Den Bosch, F., & Heij, C. (2013). Management innovation: Management as fertile ground for innovation. *European Management Review, 10*(1), 1–15.

Weerawardena, J., & Sullivan-Mort, G. (2001). Learning, innovation and competitive advantage in not-for-profit aged care marketing: A conceptual model and research propositions. *Journal of Nonprofit & Public Sector Marketing, 9*(3), 53–73.

Winata, L., & Mia, L. (2005). Information technology and the performance effect of managers' participation in budgeting: Evidence from the hotel industry. *International Journal of Hospitality Management, 24*(1), 21–39.

Wong-On-Wing, B., Guo, L., & Lui, G. (2010). Intrinsic and extrinsic motivation and participation in budgeting: Antecedents and consequences. *Behavioral Research in Accounting, 22*(2), 133–153.

Yahya, N. M., Ahmad, N. N., & Fatima, A. H. (2008). Budgetary participation and performance: Some Malaysian evidence. *International Journal of Public Sector Management, 21*(6), 658–673.

Yuen, D. (2007). Antecedents of budgetary participation enhancing employee's job performance. *Managerial Auditing Journal, 22*(5), 512–526.

Zainuddin, S., & Zainal, D. (2012). The impact of intrinsic and extrinsic motivation on job performance in a participative budget setting: A research note. *Journal of Accounting Perspectives, 5*, 48–58.

Zhang, Y., Khan, U., Lee, S., & Salik, M. (2019). The influence of management innovation and technological innovation on organisational performance. A mediating role of sustainability. *Sustainability, 11*, 495–515.

Zollo, M., & Winter, S. G. (2002). Deliberate learning and the evolution of dynamic capabilities. *Organization Science, 13*(3), 339–351.

GOOD JOBS FINDING BAD GUYS: AN EXPLORATION OF THE WORK OF SPECIAL AGENTS OF THE INTERNAL REVENUE SERVICE USING THE JOB CHARACTERISTICS MODEL

Robert A. Warren[a] and Timothy J. Fogarty[b]

[a]*Radford University, USA*
[b]*Case Western Reserve University, USA*

ABSTRACT

The Criminal Investigations unit of the Internal Revenue Service (IRS) is charged with the criminal enforcement of the tax code. Using a grounded theory approach and based on 32 interviews with 28 retired and four active special agents of the IRS, this paper attempts to explore their world. This is structured with the job characteristics model, which evaluates work roles in accordance with the extent that incumbents possess the opportunity to use a variety of skills, exercise autonomy, receive feedback, experience the significance of their work and are able to produce whole results. In general, the interviews suggest that the work of special agents is highly enriched in these terms. Nonetheless, Criminal Investigations itself is challenged as an organization on several fronts.

Keywords: Internal Revenue Service; criminal investigation; special agent; job characteristics; tax enforcement

INTRODUCTION

Tax textbooks and tax instructors provide minimum treatment for the process of tax law enforcement. That which is covered tends to focus on the civil side, dealing with the selection of returns for auditing and the penalties for underpayment. Hardly any acknowledgment is given to the criminal aspects of the tax law. A particularly insightful student might reason that tax evasion might become so willful in motive and so elevated in amount to warrant penalties beyond proper payment plus interest and penalties. However, beyond that point, little systematic information exists that would inform the student about criminal investigations conducted by the Internal Revenue Service (IRS). This lacuna limits the ability to appreciate the workings of the government to protect the integrity of the tax collection process. It also prevents students from considering unique career opportunities.

This paper is motivated by the need of the academic literature to further an understanding of the work lives of those who possess accounting expertise. Whereas the literature has been successful in informing us about the careers of accountants who work for public accounting firms, and to a lesser extent, those who work for corporations, government engagements remain a mystery. Therefore, we start with the need for a factual description of the work done by IRS criminal investigators. A broader motivation comes from the sociology of work wherein we posit the need for a qualitative rendering of this occupation as it is understood by those within it. Organized by the job characteristic model from the management literature, this paper uses insights about the work of criminal investigation that have been collected in interviews with recently retired tax agents. Using the words of these participants, this paper offers an otherwise unavailable perspective about the purpose and reality of criminal tax efforts in the United States. It also offers an opportunity for the reader to contemplate what a good job might be, no matter where it is located.

The balance of the paper is organized into five sections. The first section offers a factual overview of the criminal division of the IRS. The second introduces the job characteristics model. Although this model constituted mainstream management theory, it has not been well represented in the accounting literature. The next section details the conduct of the study with particular attention to data collection. The fourth and longest section of the paper reveals the extent to which the interviewees affirm the five core characteristics of meaningful work. In essence, this material summarizes the nature of the occupation from the vantage point of those that lived it. The final section recapitulates the major findings from this work. This includes parallels to other types of accounting work.

THE ORGANIZATIONAL SETTING

IRS–Criminal Investigation (CI) is the division within the agency responsible for the enforcement of criminal violations of the Internal Revenue Code (IRC). It also enforces the federal statutes that prohibit money laundering and currency structuring. The law enacted by Congress includes criminal sanctions for particularly egregious instances of tax evasion such as a business that keeps the proverbial second set of books, or one that fails to properly withhold and remit employment taxes. However, the fact that any successful criminal activity produces ill-gotten gain that, by not being properly reported as taxable income creates a second criminal offense, brings CI into a more generalized law enforcement effort. Here, proving the commission of a crime is a necessary precursor to the establishment that the tax law has been willfully violated. Between these extremes, the purposeful effort to create false explanations for the acquisition of money from criminal behavior (e.g., money laundering) is also a crime that comes within the domain of CI.

As of September 30, 2021, CI included 2,046 special agents who constitute the backbone of the division (Internal Revenue Service, 2021). They are sworn law enforcement officers with powers similar to those of local police and those agents in parts of the government more closely identified with criminality such as the FBI. In order to fully carry out their duties, special agents are authorized to do many things normally not associated with the tax law, including execute search warrants, make warrant-less arrests, serve subpoenas, seize property, and carry firearms. They also receive basic law enforcement training so that they would be able to aggressively pursue the criminal element. A nontrivial component of the time of special agents is devoted to maintaining their skills and readiness in these domains, such as quarterly firearms training and hand-to-hand defensive fighting practice. Although these individuals often have formal education in accounting, their job with CI takes them into activities not usually associated with that occupation, such as polygraph examination and undercover operations. CI agents are located in field offices across the US since proximity to criminal behavior is essential to its mitigation.

The work of special agents with CI is rarely conducted in an occupational vacuum. The cases that they pursue often begin as referrals from other law enforcement organizations. 23,820 of the 42,394 (56%) cases opened from FY 2010 through FY 2020 came from either the US Attorney's Office or another state or federal law enforcement agency (Austin, 2017; Nimmo, 2021). These are made in recognition of CI's differential possession of financial expertise and its concern for the tax dimensions of larger forms of criminality. Cases investigated by CI often exceed the limitations of administrative resolution, thereby requiring the US Attorney's Office to pursue grand jury indictments. The CI office often lends its human resources to a host of agencies when they are engaged in high-profile high-priority matters such as domestic terrorism. When agents pursue the international aspects of financial crimes, their involvement with other organizations also expands.

In part a reflection of the heavy physical demands of the job, special agents may retire at age 50 with 20 years of service, or at any age after 25 years on the job, but they must retire when they reach 57 years of age unless they are the beneficiaries of a special waiver. These stipulations put heavy pressure on the division to actively hire and train new recruits.

Unfortunately, in recent years, CI has not been very successful in maintaining its size. Although most observers chart a rise in the criminal behaviors that involve tax underpayment, CI has experienced a 13.8% budget decline since 2010 (OECD, 2010; TIGTA, 2011, 2017), and has lost 22% of its special agent workforce, representing a loss of 602 people (Austin, 2017; IRS, 2017a, 2017b). CI has distinctly been affected by the funding reductions that have reduced the size of the more general US income tax collection process (Marr & Murray, 2016; Nessa et al., 2016).

As demanded by the nature of law enforcement, the work of agents is both complex and unpredictable. To some extent, every case is different and evolves on its own terms. Dependent upon the degrees of cooperation or resistance that is discovered, agents often have to use strategies that are unique to the case. Agents often have to be inventive to fashion workarounds that will allow them needed access. Much of the work is interpersonal in nature, requiring interviewing skills. The most productive agents are those that are constantly on the move and rarely at their desks. Agents work in conjunction with a variety of people, but typically not with anyone at CI. This renders them into de facto independent contractors that are only managed in the loosest sense. Their performance is also difficult to evaluate because federal law forbids IRS personnel from being evaluated based on statistics or investigative outcomes.

In sum, special agents who work for CI have jobs that both resemble others in the accounting field and are *sui generis*. They deploy detailed knowledge of the tax code and they are valued by others for their possession of this expertise. Their work tends not to be limited to office environments and spreadsheets, but instead offers plentiful interactions with those that subscribe to a different set of values. By treading upon the darker side of the street, they work in ways that most of their accounting peers only see in the movies.

THE JOB CHARACTERISTICS MODEL

How individual jobs are designed and prescribed is believed to have consequence for the various ways that their possessors perform. Here, performance should be understood in a broad sense that transcends technical accomplishment and reaches the aspiration to persist and excel in the work. The job characteristics model (Hackman & Lawler, 1971) specified that jobs that possessed five specific attributes were likely to yield the most positive results for both organization and individuals. These are skill variety, autonomy, feedback, task identity, and task significance. This articulation spawned a large degree of academic work in measurement and design, and prompted corporations to actively consider job enrichment programs. Collectively, the theory, and this corporate response, could be seen as a humanistic reaction against scientific management and other efforts to rigorously mechanize human activity that many believed contributed to alienation, apathy, and poor-quality output.

Good jobs first allowed people to develop and practice a variety of skills. The essence of humanity should not be reduced to the repetition of one act but should instead engage the person as a problem solver capable of bringing a variety of consequential efforts to whatever issue is at hand.

Whereas the assembly line organized and systematized labor into collective efforts, the job characteristics model extols the value of personal autonomy. If workers were to exercise a variety of abilities, they needed some degree of independence from others for the sense that there has been an accomplishment of results. This necessitated discretion over many facets of the work from its inception to its final completion (Breaugh, 1985).

In order to facilitate learning and improvement, jobs should also possess ample feedback potential. Observing results and making appropriate refinements to actions should be possible from the information gleamed both from things and other people (Hackman & Oldham, 1975, 1976; Hackman et al., 1975). Jobs should, in other words, not be done in a vacuum that denies a performer knowledge of its critical outcomes.

Perhaps the most ambitious element of this theory is the wish for work of significance.

People prefer work that makes a contribution to society and to objectives that are valued by others. This characteristic tends to counter the idea that jobs are only valued for those tangible benefits for which their pursuit can be exchanged. Instead, jobs are a repository of meaning from which those who perform them can take pride.

The last characteristic is task identity. If we are to believe that a sense of accomplishment is important, people would prefer jobs that allow them to take credit for a task that is complete and is identifiable as a unique outcome (Hackman & Oldham, 1975). This notion contradicts efforts to decompose work into small units that only meaningfully aggregate when combined with the efforts of many others.

Taken together, the five characteristics of this theory assert the critical importance of subjective attributes. Task perceptions are socially constructed realities of the workplace that can have objective consequence (Cummings, 1982; Griffin, 1982). When measured with scales using survey data, they have been found sufficiently stable and consistent (Evans et al., 1979).

In that higher levels of performance have been statistically associated with several of the job characteristics, the theory gained momentum. Evans et al. (1979) report strong performance consequences for autonomy, feedback, and task significance. In a meta-analysis of 79 studies, Fried (1991) reports the strongest performance effects concentrated in those three attributes (see also Fried & Ferris, 1987). However, other studies have not found such effects (Griffin, 1980, 1981). Much more uniform is the finding that jobs with the desired characteristics tend to produce higher levels of job satisfaction (e.g., Brass, 1985; Sims & Szilagyi, 1976). This conclusion also holds for different types of satisfaction (Abdel-Halim, 1978) and for different levels of employees (Armstrong, 1971). Although the present research makes no particular claims about these consequences, their possible existence illustrates our proper concern with the configuration of jobs in the tax arena.

METHOD

Interviews were conducted with 28 retired and four currently serving special agents, some of whom had also assumed managerial responsibilities for CI during their careers. The large majority of these people had recently left the organization, ensuring that their working career memories were still fresh. The study design had originally sought active employees, but CI chose not to cooperate to with the study, making such individuals unavailable to the researchers: other than the four active agent who agreed to speak under the specter of losing their jobs is they were identified.

Subjects chosen for interview included people known to one of the authors. These individuals sometimes recommended other retirees who were then interviewed. However, most interviewees were identified through the online membership directory for the Association of Former Special Agents of the IRS (AFSA-IRS) and through an email solicitation sent by the Federal Law Enforcement Officers' Association (FLEOA) on behalf of the authors to its IRS-CI members.

Interviews were conducted either in person or via various communication technologies.

The former involved travel by the interviewer to several different cities. Interviews were conducted between May and August of 2017. Subjects were assured anonymity and were instructed to avoid comments that would specifically identify other people within the organization. Interviews were recorded and subsequently transcribed.

A semistructured approach was taken that allowed subjects ample latitude to reflect upon parts of their now-completed careers. They seemed very willing to share both the high points and low points of their working life. To avoid demand effects, questions did not mention any specific way of looking at these experiences, nor did it offer that any specific values be attached. A protocol of interview questions has been reproduced in the Appendix.

The use of interviews reflects the author's subscription to the value and appropriateness of grounded theory (Glaser & Strauss, 1967a, 1967b). At the time the interviews were conducted, no theoretical template for the analysis of the material provided by CI special agents. The interviews merely provided respondents with sufficient space to describe what they thought about their work. To subsequently define theoretical attributes, we merely translated what the subjects said to amplify and reflected upon its meaning. This approach prioritizes the pursuit of qualitative richness over analytical precision (Strauss & Corbin, 1998).

RESULTS

Skill Variety

Widespread agreement exists among the interviewees that the job of special agents involves the use of a vast number of skills. As summed up by one person, "you can make this job pretty much anything you want (Interview 8, 181)."[1] Several reasons exist for the wide skills inventory. In the vernacular, the job done correctly requires "a lot of digging." Whereas an IRS agent working in the civil divisions needs to know the tax law, that is only the beginning of the skills needed for special agents who also need to "have the skills to do the police part of it (Interview 8, 191)." These skills are often developed on the job apart from formal training; in other words: "you learn a lot in the field (Interview 29, 647)." Agents are encouraged to do whatever it takes: "All of the various techniques available to us. Don't be afraid to do them. Mail covers... trash runs, surveillance, everything that's at our disposal, ... and don't be afraid because that's what you're being paid for (Interview 27, 609)."

Despite this panoply of engagement, special agents also recognize that they possess unique skills within the broader network of law enforcement. "We're the go-to people... to track the money (Interview 27, 604)." As the law enforcement financial experts, special agents are valued because "our eyes don't get blurry when we see a box of financial documents (Interview 22, 487)."

Within the general idea of financial skills, highly specialized abilities exist that are not possessed by your typical special agent. For example, some become information technology experts who are regularly called to assist other agents. Such deep specialties, however, are surprisingly accidental in origin. Several interviewees report becoming instructors of skills to others despite lacking any formal training by merely demonstrating aptitude and interest. This creates some deal of tension as agents still want to function as agents with their own case load and using a more diverse set of skills. As one remembered thinking at this precipice "Let me continue to do what I do (Interview 1, 19)." Even those without such highly demanded special abilities are whipsawed by being unable to delegate the more mundane parts of their work, lacking an abundance of support personnel. Since the flow of work cannot always be controlled: "When you work in cases that have a short cycle time and then all of a sudden, you're working at... putting back work in a case that's going to take a couple of years to complete. It's a different level of agent that you have to have (Interview 11, 254)."

The diversity of skills needed by the special agent would seem to require careful management to develop. Managers are aware of the value of having a "balanced inventory" of agent skills to address the crimes that needed to be investigated. The vagaries of budgets and on-the-job training mean that skills had to be both recruited in and based on prior work experiences. The difficulty of accomplishing this means that new agents often felt overwhelmed at their career's beginning. The acquisition of easier-to-acquire skills does not necessarily build toward mastery of complex ones. One person lamented: "we have very smart young people who have absolutely no exposure to and probably no interest in pursuing complex tax cases (Interview 17, 391)."

The skills needed by special agents change with the crimes that are pursued. The recognition that "everything's electronic now" means that the office has become dependent upon new hires who are more internet savvy. However, some feel that newly hired agents have gone too far in this direction. "I find the newer agents; they want to do a case behind their computer. Whether they then get out and interviewing... I think that, that's a generational thing. Where, they think they can do everything behind the computer (Interview 15, 342)."

The new capabilities are a double-edged sword, sometimes making work more efficient if it relies on the acquisition of public information, but also coming at the cost of other capabilities. One critiqued new recruits as follows: "They weren't successful in their first few years because they had some glaring deficiencies that agents should have in order to be able to put a case together. The critical thinking, the understanding of how does this information relate, and what is my ultimate goal, what am I trying to prove and how am I going to do it, ultimately. (Interview 17, 388)" were often the skills not sufficiently present.

Ironically, the most mentioned change in skills for special agents is the diminishment of ability to deal with complex tax cases: "We had a hard time finding agent[s] that could really handle the sophisticated hedge fund stuff, the tax side of the hedge fund cases, the tax side of the investment cases. It's the big tax schemes really (Interview 2, 44)." While some cast this as the lead item in a process of "losing overall expertise" or a symptom of not appreciating the importance of detail or evidence depth, specific commentary focused on net worth cases. There is an "Indirect Method" of estimating a taxpayer's income by calculating the taxpayer's annual income for the years under investigation by calculating his net worth on the last day of each year under investigation. The difference in the taxpayer's net worth from 1 year to the next is a proxy for the income which should have been reported. Having done even one such case is a badge of honor that most special agents cannot claim. "I was looking to do a net worth case, I wanted to do one. And it took a long time, once I got it, to get it done. And when I got it done, I was very proud of it. That's, I don't think, is the case anymore. I think that there's simpler, lower level cases (Interview 8; 117)."

Those that offered a rationale for a decline of what used to be a central skill for special agents tended to point to the reorientation of agency attention and manpower to identity theft cases, whose pursuit tended to be the antithesis of net worth. Again speaking of colleagues, one person said: "All they knew how to do was ID Theft and I found that we were just getting away from some really good complex cases and the case work kinda became boring to be honest with you (Interview 8, 168)." This might have also been compromised by the adrenaline rush in what could be called the "let's roll up on these bad guys" mentality. Nonetheless, it was acknowledged that "when financial intelligence goes away, it is very hard to recapture it (Interview 17, 391)."

One person asserted that the loss of the ability to do the big complex tax cases would hurt the reputation of CI in the law enforcement community. Those that served as special agents took a great deal of pride in what they were able to do. Reflecting on a long career at CI, one said: "Most of the agents appreciated what I brought to the table as far as my expertise (Interview 7, 126)." Another mentioned how a general orientation to CI work has been leveraged into a post-retirement consulting career: "I get complimented by law firms that I work for because they say to me, 'We can't believe the detail you have in here'. It's like it's second nature to me, it's like I take it for granted now but that just goes to show you how we were trained properly in doing it (Interview 7, 139)." The proper management of agents was believed to begin with a recognition of agent strengths and weaknesses. One interviewee ranked the various jobs he held in terms of the knowledge gains that he realized while in these capacities.

That the special agent job involves a wide variety of skills, some of which are not officially endorsed by the organization, does not mean that all agents possess what most would take to be core skills. Managers appreciate more narrow ranges and must concoct work divisions in accordance with what can be anticipated about different types of cases. As put by one manager in discussing the employee agents that he had to assign: "Identity theft could be the extent of their skill set. So let them have it! (Interview 13, 299)."

In sum, the job of special agent necessitates the possession and regular use of a broad number of skills. Almost all of these are developed on the job and many need to be deployed on a just in time basis. It is the antitheses of the narrow and boring elements of the accountant stereotype (see Bougen, 1994).

Autonomy

The job characteristics model suggests that the most engaging jobs are those that provide a person sufficient freedom of activity. People are deemed to crave a degree of independence in their work, and that facilitating such a space allows good results to emerge.

The activities of special agents could only be described as the existence of radical autonomy. As succinctly put by one, "The policy in our field office is: one agent, one case, one investigation (Interview 32, 689)." This motto (repeated by others) means that special agents are essentially independent contractors, in that they work their own caseloads with minimal involvement of other agents or supervisors.

Agents are expected to develop their own investigations beginning with their inception. In doing so, agents are trusted to know how successful an investigation will likely be, and how much impact it will have in the fight against crime and the underpayment of the federal income tax. Very few employees in business entities or government can have the unilateral opportunity to select their work, and effectively self-determine the interactions that they will have in its pursuit. Agents also possess the ability to close cases, effectively terminating the likelihood that the government will sanction a particular act of deviance.

Granting agents such broad degrees of self-determination has both positive and negative consequences. In that agents effectively own their cases, they became highly engaged: "...any special agent that's really doing what they're supposed to be doing, it's all-encompassing, it's not a job - it's a career, it's a lifestyle. I worked a lot of hours, so there's a lot of things that I've put off, things I told my wife we would always do (Interview 2, 48)." Then again, this autonomy expectation also bred a more than healthy contempt for management. Agents, other than rookies, took umbrage to any attempts to assign them cases. "The last thing you wanted was your supervisor giving you something (Interview 12, 270)." Management quickly learned to leave productive agents alone. That which most employees would not even notice would be characterized by agents as harmful micro-management. The ethos of the office was that no agent could be truly successful when under the wing of another person, even their supervisor.

A certain fit between extreme autonomy and the specific nature of the work existed.

Agents believed that they had the "decisions right in front of you" and that all that was necessary was to do "the next right thing." Agents implicitly believed in their bag of tricks. Special agents working their cases alone brought "new ideas, new ways of doing things, better ways" to the accomplishment of their work.

External motivation was superfluous: "I didn't need motivation to work (Interview 4, 94)." Good independent work also generated prized collateral work for others and "good exposure" for the individual that did it.

The autonomy afforded to agents presents its share of difficulties to the CI. If managers have specific enforcement priorities, autonomy demands make it more difficult to move the office in a particular enforcement direction. Speaking about management, one special agent asserted: "I'm going to finish what I'm doing and then, like I said, I've usually got three things on the back burner that I want to open, once this case is concluded. So whatever their priorities are here, that doesn't affect the things I have in my drawer that I want to open. No, I don't really care at all what their priorities are (Interview 21, 468)."

Very little exceeded the ire of disagreements with management over the termination of cases. When an agent puts considerable effort into a case and continues to believe in its prospects, forced closure of it by management left the agent very bitter. One agent described what happened when the special-agent-in-charge (SAC) refused to meet with him/her after the SAC told the agent through subordinates to close a politically charged case, "The SAC won't meet with me. Can you believe that? Won't meet with me to discuss the case...I'm gonna sit in the garage and wait for him to come to his car. At some point, he's gonna come to his car and he's going to talk" I said, "You let him know that (Interview 23, 526)." Even cases that get reassigned and ultimately not pursued, create skepticism. Some agents go as far as to question the need for as much management as they currently have.

A sensible case for more control over agents could be made. Without a strong central voice, agents do not agree about the primary goal of CI but instead enact their personal balance between pure tax collection and pure law enforcement. To counter this tremendous autonomy, CI management approval is required to open and close cases, conduct enforcement actions, take leave, and procure equipment. Management (at various levels) also conducts quarterly, semiannual, and biannual inventory reviews. Finally, the criminal justice system creates natural limits on the highly autonomous special agents. Indictments and plea agreements can be pursued only by US Attorneys. When those individuals failed or refused to act, the case development work of the special agent goes for naught, producing great frustration. Knowing what the US Attorney's office would and would not do limited the freedom of agents in their case selection and its framing. "...and so you have to be picky on what they look like and what impact they're gonna have and what industry they're in and what part of your jurisdiction that they're in (Interview 17, 363)." Agents learned that this was a highly nuanced process that involved their reputational capital. "It was like, if I do something for them they'll do something for me. That was really the only way we got some of the cases prosecuted that we did (Interview 19, 428)."

While very little teamwork occurred in the autonomous world of the special agent, collaborative effort was occasionally made necessary by departmental policy that necessitated multiple actors. Dangerous work and work that needed to be witnessed required that agents help fellow agents. While many interviewees expressed a general willingness to help on this basis, one reported the gradual decline in the *esprit de corps* that made this involvement truly rewarding. Another pointed to the opportunity cost of helping others: "You're running around all over the place, bad neighborhoods, all hours of the day, time intensive. And it takes you away from your other cases. So that stretched me very thin (Interview 24, 541)." Whenever possible, agents blamed their supervisors for the work obligations that took them from their own cases.

In sum, special agents demand and receive unusually high degrees of autonomy. This seems to fit the particular demands of the work, even as it makes management of the collective effort problematic. Although autonomy is not well recognized in an era that stresses the value of collaboration, it has been viewed as an antecedent to audit effectiveness (Bamber & Iyer, 2009) and aligns well with classic models of professionalism (Greenwood, 1957).

Feedback

Jobs that demand the use of a wide variety of skills and provide people with high degrees of autonomy would almost necessarily involve large amounts of learning. Only with efficient on-the-job and perhaps just-in-time learning would the needed skills develop so that an organization could tolerate the autonomy that has been afforded to key actors. For the most part, the special agents interviewed were not explicit about how and what they learned in the course of their work. If feedback is the subset of all learning limited to situations where the source of the learning is infused in the work results obtained, one would have to characterize the special agent job as not very rich in this job attribute.

One could assert that since the work of special agents is an investigation that a crime has been committed and that a certain individual was its perpetrator, any success is an instance of feedback sought and received. However, no one offered a systematic explanation of information gathering and its relative productivity. If anything, the investigative process appears as an informed trial-and-error one that ranges across a variety of approaches and wraps itself around the general contours of the case: "We had to go on the tools that were available (Interview 27, 610)." The puzzle for the agent takes on a broader tableau in international cases, where agents also have to confront different legal systems.

The best and purest feedback that agents received came from the US Attorney's Office.

There is no advantage in working cases that are not prosecutable, usually rendered so by the assessment that they will not result in a conviction. "We have to go that way" is a recognition that agents must always present a high-quality case. Agents have to learn, sometimes the hard way, that those cases likely to be dismissed at any point along the way, are ones not to be even selected by agents as a good use of their time. Prosecutability also drove how much work on a case a special agent needed to put in before it could be presented to the prosecutor.

People were more ready to discuss what feedback their organization provided to them about moving their work forward. This centered around defensive tactics for avoiding long time delays and procedural rules that might frustrate ultimate success. This informal know-how often pertained to how a case was classified and how the specific charges included were ordered, but sometimes revealed what the interviewed agents characterized as the hidden agendas of others. Agents apparently learned that not all interests that swirled around CI were perfectly aligned. One indignant agent said: "They set out the procedures but then they didn't follow up (Interview 11, 251)."

What constitutes normal progress is itself a social construct that can only be learned through iterative feedback cycles. Other people are a usual source of feedback, but this simple idea receives only mixed support from the interviewees. Some credited a manager or two with well-timed pats on the back that specifically acknowledged their productivity. One hailed a supervisor for "knowing the job" inhabited by the agent, and for always being available for contributory work "including nights and weekends." But others had a different experience to report, telling stories of managers who provided no help or who had no ideas for how to get an agent help from others. Managers were even accused of giving bad advice that worked to the detriment of cases, primarily because they had not bothered to read agent reports.

Managers also gave formal feedback in the form of evaluations. For the large part, agents resented the process and did not find its information to be instructive: "I've written evaluations for people and poured my heart into writing an evaluation and the employee not even read the damn thing. You have agents that really want the feedback, but really they don't need the feedback because they're doing an excellent job (Interview 11, 257)."

The collected interview data also included some ideas about how the feedback environment could be improved. One manager was willing to erode the autonomy of agents by teaming young ones with older ones in an effort to blend new computer skills with "old school" ones. Formalized sources of feedback such as CPE could also be made more available and timely, according to several. Training was often sacrificed when budgets were tightened, despite its implicit team building function, as noted by one of the interviewees here: "It's always very important to bring people together that you work with. Have meetings. To have educational times. I can't remember the last time we had a CPE. That hurt us a lot. Not being able to do that (Interview 12, 267)."

As agents became the managers of other agents, their feedback needs changed. Managers were directed by CI headquarters to ensure that all agents were fully engaged, and therefore tended to fixate on the number of cases that each agent had. This meant that managers were quite reluctant to interfere with agents that appeared to be fully engaged, as determined by these quantitative measures. Interventions with those not fully engaged were not often helpful. Here, managers were not assisted by their management system because it was not sufficiently nuanced to provide managers with the measures necessary to capture what action was needed. Managers were expected to convey enforcement priorities to the agent workforce. This objective was widely resisted by agents, and therefore was poorly and unevenly implemented. Agents preferred cases that yielded asset forfeitures, since this was seen as an alternative source of funding for the agent work that followed its own sense of relative importance. All cases and investigative actions are summarized by the Criminal Investigation Management

Information System (CIMIS), a massive database that tracks a case from opening to closing. "Management by CIMIS" was a complaint often heard by the interviewees. "Management by CIMIS" indicates that the supervisor is managing the case load based on statistical measures, and not by the nature of the case. As one special agent described it, "Management by CIMIS! You can say you're altering reality to make the CIMIS tables look good. We had a manager that he would number cases a certain way to fit the business model... He would say, 'Just number one', and then right before you're ready to write up your report, number up the others (Interview 9, 204)."

Supervisors reported that they felt they were being scapegoated for that which was beyond their control: "Hard work would get a lot of criticism, especially when you worked a big case and something went wrong (Interview 6, 114)." In one case, a SAC took the blame for a spate of bad publicity regarding an explosion of identity theft cases, "...I really feel bad for former Tampa SAC (name redacted). She really became the scapegoat...Until it blew up, nobody in the IRS was willing to do what they did later. So actually, in a way Tampa blowing up like it did, finally got IRS serious about it (identity theft) (Interview 2, 39)."

In sum, feedback has a very specialized meaning for special agents. It tends to come from the work itself and from the larger process of criminal prosecution. However slightly interviewees acknowledged the sources of their learning, it would be difficult to conclude that they did not exist in a feedback rich milieu.

Task Significance

Special agents with CI expressed a strong and persistent belief that their work had great importance. This opinion, which was elevated beyond dispute, held considerable salience for agents. Exactly how significance was defined possessed consequential variation.

In the most general sense, significance was a subjective state that began with the passion that a person brought to the work. Agents talked of the importance of protecting the integrity of the tax collection in terms of righting a personal offense, and of the "fun" involved in stopping abusive behavior. One person reported being humbled to be part of a large group of talented people who felt the same passion. Another said: "I can right wrongs, and I think there's no greater contribution you can make, at least for somebody like me (Interview 21, 462)."

For several individuals, the social significance of their work was co-equal to the furtherance of CI's mission. These people took it as self-evident that what CI was established to do was a good and noble pursuit, and their small contribution to it would be colored the same way. "I've always really strongly supported the mission of CI. I think it's a critically important mission and whatever I could do to help get that mission done, was part of it (Interview 2, 36)." In the private sector, it would be unusual to hear people say that good work was whatever "benefited the team and the mission (Interview 14, 314)," especially when there was no personal gain. Another subscribed to this goal despite the recognition that the specific mission changes over time. However, another person warned against how this might change at the upper organizational echelons with "you probably can't accomplish as much at headquarters (Interview 3, 55)." Others proved to be mission-supportive in that they wanted to ensure that their successes in the field were credited to CI rather than to another involved agency.

A rather basic, but quite persuasive approach to task significance invoked its moral components. Agents tended to see the world in black and white terms in that their work resulted in "taking bad people off the street," an outcome always looked at as a major accomplishment. If the perpetrator was notorious, such as a major drug dealer, a terrorist, or an upper-level member of a criminal syndicate, the good that was perceived to have been done was even greater. Often CI's role was critical, as put by one agent: "Because it was somebody who was doing something wrong that wouldn't have been caught without the financial aspect of the investigation (Interview 22, 487)." In the vernacular, another said "Being a CI employee, I always got to wear the white hat (Interview 3, 50)."

Since CI agents usually were formally trained in school at business and accounting, they tended to see the importance of their work in financial terms. Several denominated the importance of their efforts in terms of its impact on the American taxpayer. In addition to reducing the burden on the honest by making sure that the dishonest also paid their share, agents tried to conduct themselves in a way that was cognizant that their expenses and wages were paid from public money. As one put it "I'm not the one cutting the check, but it was the American taxpayer (Interview 7, 158)," illustrating mindfulness about waste and sloth and feelings of entitlement.

Significance was not an accidental result of agent work, primarily because agents were usually able to select the cases that they worked upon and pursued to completion. Sometimes significance could be denominated in terms of the money involved, where it was not uncommon to be exceptionally proud of multi-million-dollar cases and to eschew "dinky mom-and-pop ones." Agents sought cases that were legally solid and ones for which their managers would fight, if that proved necessary. Beyond that, the best cases were those that were judged to have high impact. Impact was usually understood in terms of the deterrence effect that the case might create. The future behavior of others had to be changed as a result of an enforcement "because there's people cheating on their taxes everywhere (Interview 3, 67)." Specifically, agents sought "to show people that there's a cost to this kind of crime (Interview 6,119)." Convictions are the gold standard of impact, but in their absence, agent work that leads to changes in the tax law (i.e., the tightening of loopholes) is also evidence of worthwhile case time.

Impact often required positive publicity, an attribute that agents deemed important because it demonstrated the importance of CI's work to the public. While explaining a multi-year money laundering investigation, a special agent commented "There were magazine articles, front page, newspapers every week, a book, and he (the subject) was on American Greed (a television show) (Interview 4, 87)." The outcome produced was a very important element of the cases that succeeded in taking down the high and mighty. "We didn't convict but we indicted the governor at one time and that was a huge deal (Interview 18, 402)." Special agents paid more attention to high-level targets who were well-educated and did not have an economic need to cheat on their taxes. As one agent stated, "One was a real estate attorney who should have known better. Another was a very prominent CPA in the county (Interview 9, 198)." On the other side of the equation, fraud victims who were poor, helpless or elderly helped make cases against their exploiters more viable. One interviewee explained why she pursued a misdemeanor failure to file a tax return case on a handyman preying on the elderly, "...he was a scum... and he would just scam them (aged homeowners)... One of them he drove to the bank so she could make a withdrawal...She (the victim) said (to the investigating agent), 'Well I don't want to tell my family because they'll put me in a home'. They think I can't take care of myself (Interview 3, 56)."

Ironically, pure tax cases rarely possessed the significance attributes craved by agents. Quotes on this point ranged from the categorical: "nobody cares about tax (Interview 2, 43)," to the blame worthy: "it (a tax case) will sit over there (the US Attorney's Office) forever, and then it may or may not get look at before its time to kill it... (Interview 20, 444)."

In sum, special agents seem to thrive on the societal importance of their work. They seem to be willing to sacrifice much for the sense that they are making a valuable contribution to their country. This attribute would seem to compare very favorably to accountants that work in the private sector and are themselves not participants in favorable results. This version of significant contrition may respond to an occupational deficiency (see Hopwood, 1994).

Task Identity

The norm established by the oft-heard maxim "one CI special agent, one case, one investigation" suggests that CI special agents will have a high degree of task identity in their routine work. While this result is not unprecedented in the professionalized world, it exists in great counter-distinction to most work in the governmental realm. This imperative also is opposite to the tendency for white collar work to be performed by teams. In any event, the clear outcomes produced by their individualized work might explain the high degree of pride of accomplishment expressed by agents when reflecting upon their CI careers.

Stories told by agents about their favorite cases lean heavily toward a "cradle to grave" range of personal involvement. This entails case development efforts at its inception, protecting it as it matures, and offering testimony at trial as the case is brought to a successful conviction. "So, I pushed extra hard to get that case opened and I felt really good about working it, progressing through it, and ultimately prevailing (Interview 21, 462)."

Knowing that their personal stamp will be clearly imprinted upon the accomplishment, agents are unabashed about their will to be excellent in their case pursuit. However, the justice system also leads to disengagement if such projects are quashed by others. Agents that are redirected to work not of their choosing are forcibly disengaged from completion. Nonetheless, the spirit of all or nothing preference is captured by this quote, which also illustrates how atypical it is in law enforcement: "that's why the US attorney's office really like to get CI agents on the case, because they knew we dig in, we would get a hold, we would work it diligently, we would work it thoroughly, we would stay with the case all the way through trial. Bureau [FBI] doesn't do that (Interview 2, 46)."

Managerial oversight of agents adjusted to this need to work a case's entirety.

Developing cases on this self-directed basis posed some degree of risk for the agent. A very undiversified portfolio of work resulted since some cases took years to reach fruition. Most agents did not mind such lengthy cycle times, but only if they believed in an ultimate payoff. Nonetheless, such cases did require agent defense against implicit assertions that they were slacking. Many reported the pleasure they found in "putting it all together" often by actions such as "pulling out all the pieces and finding the true crime" or "digging through all the records (Interview 1, 5)." Agents enjoyed their self-determining power, despite the omnipresent realization that success was never guaranteed. One manager reported his strenuous efforts to redefine success after agents had spent "three or four years of their lives on this (case) only to lose at trial (Interview 16, 353)."

Agents resented what they saw as unnecessary impediments on their way to closure. They tended to blame management for inadequate support to help move what anyone would call a very inefficient process along. Agents bristled when they saw their work evaporate at the US Attorney's Office for political reasons. Agents bluntly called such events "a kick in the gut" and "something I ain't forgot about (Interview 23, 527)." For some this was akin to a morality play that ended badly: "So that was the most troubling case I ever had. They were guilty. It was difficult to make. It was difficult to document. And they got away with it (Interview 24, 549)."

Perhaps more threatening to the ability of special agents to enjoy the wholeness of their work are changes seen to be afoot at the CI organization. Budgetary pressure has an effect of "streamlining the types of cases that they would prosecute (Interview 27, 606)." CI is seen as developing a strong preference for fast cases with a more certain outcome. The investigation of complex and more esoteric situations is harder to justify relative to the "lower hanging fruit" (Interview 11, 249). The agency looks good when more convictions occur despite a dwindling number of agents (Interview 2, 43). However, such an objective comes at the cost of task identity, as nicely put by this person: "The last two people I worked for there decided that we needed to do more with less. That was really starting to be a big strain. They were even starting to make what I would say were some asinine decisions on, 'Well, why don't you do 10% of this and 10% of this and 5% of that? At least you're doing something toward it'. It's like, 'So if I'm doing pieces of all this stuff all I'm going to do is end up failing at everything'. It makes no sense to try to do bits and pieces. You either have to support an area or not support an area. I wasn't getting the support that I really expected (Interview 19, 421)."

In sum, the quest for doing the entity of a job sets special agents apart from other accountants. Norms of their organization facilitate task identity as a default condition. As such, special agents have considerable ownership over their work.

DISCUSSION

This study was motivated by the need to introduce the working lives of a very special group of accountants. It has contributed a demonstration of how the five attributes from job characteristics theory could organize an inquiry into the nature of criminal investigations work conducted by the IRS. Thus, this paper can be considered a field experiment that validates the importance and salience of the job characteristics for other research into accountants. This might help us understand turnover and job satisfaction as people strive for good work. On a practical level, the paper's application makes visible a rather under-recognized part of the accounting community. This can help students find careers that match their interests and enable faculty to assist them with a fuller range of options.

By interviewing people who have personally conducted criminal investigations for the IRS, this paper has prioritized the individual level of analysis. This approach adds to a topic that is normally addressed at the organizational level. The implicit suggestion here is that the enforcement of the tax laws cannot be properly understood with assessments of what should happen under conditions of normative institutional functioning but must examine the details of what actually does happen under existing imperfect operations and constraints. The latter requires an exploration of the lived experiences of practitioners.

This study has shown that most of the job characteristics specified in theory as the elements of a good job are profoundly perceived by IRS criminal investigators. They tend to figure prominently in the reflections of recently retired agents about their jobs and their careers. Since these people are forced to retire at age 57, and can retire after only 20 years of service, their memories are not the wistful nostalgia of days long gone, but instead constitute the active thoughts of people very much still in their prime. The interviews bear out the value of bringing a large number of skills to the task at hand, and being given the space to deploy them in a self-directed manner. The people interviewed also crave the opportunity to change things for the better and to be able to take near complete credit for steps in that direction.

The full theory of job characteristics requires the comparison of people with and without such elements for the prediction of better job outcomes. Although no systematic effort was made to link evidence of the presence of the characteristics to outcomes, anecdotal information consistent with this linkage is abundant. Special agents are accustomed to ample degrees of all five elements and are certainly willing to complain when any one of them is compromised or eroded. However, a rigorous empirical demonstration would not be possible within the worldview of grounded theory and the interviewing format of data collection. Strong selection bias is also likely with people more receptive to the value of the job characteristics being those more likely to stay with the organization sufficiently long to retire.

Although approaching the job characteristics as a group seems to be a better strategy for this holistic research project, something can be said about the individual attributes as they are expressed in this occupational group. However, since the number of interviews conducted was modest when judged by the standards set by other forms of quantitative research on related topics, care needs to be taken when offering thoughts about the relative importance of individual characteristics. The literature suggests that contexts will produce varying magnitudes in this regard (Evans et al., 1979), and that some attributes will have negative overtones. Along similar lines, some contexts might produce such a high correspondence among attributes usually found distinct that merging them might be recommended. Preliminary conclusions would elevate autonomy and task significance as the dominant characteristics for special agents. The second of these reflects the pro-social nature of the domain, and the first extends the way organizations have historically addressed deviance. We could also conclude that feedback is relatively muted for special agents. On balance, the work is highly enriched and therefore a classic "good job."

Most cases have foredrawn perpetrators against which evidence beyond a reasonable doubt may or may not be assembled in time to prosecute. With the game being more akin to a jigsaw puzzle, feedback is too deeply embedded to be elevated to that which easily can be articulated. Much more research is necessary before distinct conclusions about the work of criminal investigators can be made. For these purposes, more direct questions would need to complement the purposefully serpentine approach used in this research.

Both the psychological meaningfulness of work and the proper way to organize a consequential social task are still in their exploratory stages. The current research can be thought of as both a revival and a step back. The paper is a revival because it articulates the possible value of a theory whose prime contribution to the management literature occurred long ago. The appearance of the theory in the accounting literature is frightfully thin (see Fogarty & Uliss, 2000; Kim & Cho, 2011). The paper represents a restatement in its advocacy of a qualitative way to explore occupations about which little is known and which do not respond as well to quantitative methods. This approach has to be seen as a step back in time because it has abandoned the more ambitious hopes of producing more efficient job design through the identification of causal relationships. Rather than imposing an a priori structure of effects upon respondents, perhaps we need to discover what the people in the trenches actually believe.

Outside the confines of the five job characteristics examined in the body of this paper, many other things could have been said about the work lives of IRS criminal investigators. Once we get beyond the still surprising fact that their work is not strictly, or even mostly, about the federal tax law, we still have to conclude that it is a highly complex endeavor. Complex job environments have been shown to exceed the capabilities of relatively simple models and theories (Abdel-Halim, 1978). The complexity here involves the juxtaposition of the high church theorizing of legal precedents and evidentiary concepts, with the low church gritty realities of life on the street, both of which combine in an effective investigation. This jumble reiterates the wisdom of conducting a qualitative approach to the area, as well as one not strictly limited by one theory.

No attempt has been made to evaluate the psychological profile of the interviewees. Had a contribution to the improvement of the job characteristics model been intended, such an inquiry would have been essential (e.g., Szilagyi et al., 1976).

In its original formulation, consequences from exposure to jobs rich in the core attributes were expected to be stronger for incumbents exhibiting higher growth need strength (Hackman & Lawler, 1971). Subsequent research showed that this condition may also be exacerbated by the quality of inter-personal relations at work (Abdel-Halim, 1978) and satisfaction with supervision (Griffin, 1981). While the interviews conducted contain much data on these issues, it was not specifically considered in the present project. The special agents were educationally and demographically much more homogeneous at entry level than the workforce in general. They were also made even more similar by virtue of choosing a career in the governmental sector. What seems to be more variable was their interpretations of the trajectory of their organization over the course of their careers.

The use of retired criminal investigators in this research could be seen as the obverse of socialization studies that, for the most part, are built upon data specifically collected from newly recruited members of their organizations. We acknowledge the value of inquiries into the sense making that seeks to discover how people come to believe that which they do. We also see the desirability of talking to those with the proverbial "skin in the game" regarding their current organizations. We counter-offer the value of reflections that take in the perspectives made possible only over the entire arc of a career. We also see value in the clarifying distance that no longer being in an organization can provide. With the vantage of retirement, one can avoid the happenstance of a single moment in time and the bias of group think. The salience of experiences is put to a sterner test over a large number of years.

Respondents to our interview prompts typically worked both as a criminal investigator and as a manager of those doing investigations. In organizing this paper, strict care was not taken to differentiate these capabilities. In many cases, whether a person was responding as a manager or as a worker was not clear. Research has shown that position in a hierarchical structure can change one's desire for, and interpretation of, autonomy, variety, and feedback (Sims & Szilagyi, 1976). Level may be similar or different from personal status, another attribute that may change the way jobs are understood (Armstrong, 1971). As government employees, only one real promotion (from GS13 special agent to GS14 supervisory special agent) was involved and compensation was standardized across individuals at these levels. It also was not uncommon for a manager to drop back to a previously held investigator position. The only real mobility for special agents was geographic. All these reasons pointed toward the diminishment of level are an important issue.

CONCLUSION

Job characteristic theory may never have satisfactorily resolved the discrepancy between that which people perceive and that which actually exists (Aldag, 1978). It may also be the case that people think that there are more or less important dimensions of jobs than there are in fact (Dunham, 1976). This study asserts the unique importance of perceptions, especially in jobs where actors are expected to create a reality. Special agents take what is in-your-face deviance and convert it into a stigmatized life, all offered as an object lesson for the community. In that statistical conclusions based on the level of the job attributes were not attempted, the possible existence of overestimates or underestimates of any characteristic due to objective or subjective differences takes on less consequence. Nonetheless, two special agents could very well see the same thing quite differently. Therefore, this paper may have only been a down payment on the reality it wishes to reveal.

NOTE

1. References were ordered according to their conduct by one of the authors. The second number indicates its location in the 700 plus page transcript.

REFERENCES

Abdel-Halim, A. (1978). Employee affective responses to organizational stress: Moderating effects of job characteristics. *Personnel Psychology, 31*, 561–579.

Aldag, R. (1978). Symposium on task design: Calls for redirection. In *Proceedings of the 10th annual meetings of the American institute of decision sciences* (pp. 168–169).

Armstrong, T. (1971). Job content and context factors related to satisfaction for different occupational levels. *Journal of Applied Psychology, 55*, 57–65.

Austin, J. (2017). *Letter dated November 8, 2017 with CI statistical information, 2010 to 2016.*

Bamber, E. M., & Iyer, V. (2009). The effect of auditing firms' tone at the top on auditors' job autonomy, organizational-professional conflict, and job satisfaction. *International Journal of Accounting and Information Management, 17*, 136–150.

Bougen, P. (1994). Joking apart: The serious side to the accountant stereotype. *Accounting, Organizations and Society, 19*(3), 319–335.

Brass, D. (1985). Technology and the structure of jobs: Employee satisfaction, performance and influence. *Organizational Behavior & Human Performance, 35*, 216–240.

Breaugh, J. (1985). The measurement of work autonomy. *Human Relations, 38*, 551–579.

Cummings, L. (1982). Organizational behavior. *Annual Review of Psychology, 33*, 541–579.

Dunham, R. (1976). The measurability and dimensionality of job characteristics. *Journal of Applied Psychology, 61*, 404–409.

Evans, M. G., Kiggundu, M. N., & House, R. J. (1979). A partial test and extension of the job characteristics model of motivation. *Organizational Behavior & Human Performance, 24*(3), 354–381.

Fogarty, T., & Uliss, B. (2000). Auditor work and its outcomes: An application of the job characteristics model to large public accounting firms. *Advances in Accounting Behavioral Research, 3*, 37–68.

Fried, Y. (1991). Meta-analytic comparison of the job diagnostic survey and job characteristics inventory as correlates of work satisfaction and performance. *Journal of Applied Psychology, 76*(5), 690.

Fried, Y., & Ferris, G. R. (1987). The validity of the job characteristics model: A review and meta-analysis. *Personnel Psychology, 40*(2), 287–322.

Glaser, B., & Strauss, A. (1967a). Grounded theory: The discovery of grounded theory. *Sociology the Journal of the British Sociological Association, 12*, 27–49.

Glaser, B., & Strauss, A. (1967b). *The discovery of grounded theory.* Prentice Hall.

Greenwood, E. (1957). Attributes of a profession. *Social Work*, 45–55.

Griffin, R. (1980). Relationships among individual, task design, and leader behavior variables. *Academy of Management Journal, 23*(4), 665–683.

Griffin, R. (1981). A longitudinal investigation of task characteristic relationships. *Academy of Management Journal, 24*(1), 99–113.

Griffin, R. (1982). *Task design: An integrative approach.* Scott Foresman.

Hackman, J. R., & Lawler, E. E. (1971). Employee reactions to job characteristics. *Journal of Applied Psychology, 55*(3), 259–296.

Hackman, J. R., & Oldham, G. (1975). Development of the job diagnostic survey. *Journal of Applied Psychology, 60*(2), 159.

Hackman, J., & Oldham, G. (1976). Motivation through the design of work: Test of a theory. *Organizational Behavior & Human Performance, 16,* 250–279.

Hackman, J. R., Oldham, G., Janson, R., & Purdy, K. (1975). A new strategy for job enrichment. *California Management Review, 17*(4), 57–71.

Hopwood, A. G. (1994). Accounting and everyday life: An introduction. *Accounting, Organizations and Society, 19*(3), 299–301.

Internal Revenue Service (IRS). (2017a, February 27). *IRS: CI annual report 2016.* https://www.taxcontroversy360.com/wp-content/uploads/2017/02/2016-IRS-CID.pdf

Internal Revenue Service (IRS). (2017b). *IRS: CI annual report 2017.* https://www.irs.gov/pub/foia/ig/ci/2017_criminal_investigation_annual_report.pdf

Internal Revenue Service (IRS). (2021, November 18). *IRS: CI annual report 2021.* https://www.irs.gov/pub/irs-pdf/p3583.pdf

Kim, C. J., & Cho, J. H. (2011). Relationship between core job characteristics and attitude of small business employees. *The Journal of the Korea Contents Association, 11*(5), 28–337.

Marr, C., & Murray, C. (2016). IRS funding cuts compromise taxpayer service and weaken enforcement. *Center on Budget and Policy Priorities.* http://www.cbpp.org/research/federal-tax/irs-funding-cuts-compromise-taxpayer-service-and-weaken-enforcement. Accessed on April 4, 2016.

Nessa, M., Schwab, C., Stomberg, B., & Towery, E. (2016). *How do IRS resources affect the tax enforcement process.* Unpublished working paper, Michigan State University, Indiana University, and University of Georgia.

Nimmo, D. (2021). *Letter dated January 20, 2021 with CI statistical information, 2016 to 2020.*

Organization for Economic Cooperation and Development (OECD). (2010). *Main economic indicators-complete database.* https://fred.stlouisfed.org/series/USAGDPDEFAISMEI. Accessed on November 20, 2017.

Sims, J., & Szilagyi, A. (1976). Job characteristic relationships: Individual and structural moderators. *Organizational Behavior & Human Performance, 17,* 211–230.

Strauss, A., & Corbin, J. (1998). *Basics of qualitative research: Techniques and procedures for developing grounded theory.* Sage Publications, Inc.

Szilagyi, A., Sims, H., & Keller, R. (1976). Role dynamics, locus of control and employee attitudes and behaviors. *Academy of Management Journal, 19,* 259–276.

Treasury Inspector General for Tax Administration (TIGTA). (2011, July 25). Trends in criminal investigation's enforcement activities showed improvements for fiscal year 2010, with gains in most performance indicators. https://www.treasury.gov/tigta/press/press_tigta-2011-51.htm

Treasury Inspector General for Tax Administration (TIGTA). (2017, September 13). Declining resources have contributed to unfavorable trends in several key criminal investigation business results. https://www.treasury.gov/tigta/auditreports/2017reports/201730073fr.pdf

APPENDIX

INTERVIEW PROTOCOL

Interview Process

- Introduction Audiotaping Permission
- Format Introduced Purpose Described
- Confidentiality Promised Questions and Answers

Planned Questions

(1) Tell me about yourself and your career.
(2) Tell me about a case for which you are the proudest starting from the beginning to the conclusion.
(3) Tell me about a case where you were the most frustrated starting from the beginning to the conclusion.
(4) Describe a time, if any, where a lack of resources hindered your ability to select or investigate a case with good criminal potential.
(5) Describe how IRS management directs your case selection and investigative steps. Provide specific examples.

INDEX

Academic performance, 98, 101–102, 107–108
Accounting literature, 5–6, 138
Accounting students, 98–99, 103, 109
  gender on, 101
  grade point average, 99–100
  job attainment, 102
  job outcomes, 99
  native, 101–102
Adams' equity theory, 9–10
Additivity axiom, 6
Affect as information theory, 59
Agency theory, 30–31, 33
ANOVA, 40–42
Association of Former Special Agents of the IRS (AFSA-IRS), 142
Attribution theory, 56
Auditing Standard No. 2110, 34–35
Auditor judgments, 36–37
  control environment risk, 48
  family firm structure, 30, 33, 48
  hypothesis testing, 40
  nonfamily ownership, 48
Autonomy, 145–147
Average variance extracted (AVE), 127

Backfire effect
  corporate social responsibility, 56–58
  hypothesized, 64, 70, 84
  insignificance of, 77
  insurance effect and, 57
  limitation of, 62–64
  testing for, 76–77
Banker's modified Shapley value, 2, 4, 10
Behavioral accounting, 2
Behavioral economics literature, 7–9

Big 4 international public accounting firms, 36
Binomial logistic regression, 104
Bonferroni correction, 104
Budgetary participation, 115–118
  business unit innovation, 120–121
  control variables, 126
  employee organisational commitment and, 119–121
  innovation and competitive advantage, 121–122
  literature review and hypotheses development, 118–122
  mediating effect of, 122
  method, 122–126
  results, 126–129
  sample selection and data collection, 122–123
  variable measurement, 123–126

Cell means
  depiction of, 75
  reputation measures, 78
Chinese Institute of Certified Public Accountants (CICPA), 36
Chinese National Accounting Institute, 36
Chi-Square test of model fit, 107
Clean Diesel, 56–57
Cognitive embeddedness, 49
Community college, 101–102
Comparative Fix Index (CFI), 107
Competitive advantage, 116–118, 125, 128
  budgetary participation and, 116, 122
  control variables, 126
  employee organisational commitment, 117
  innovation and, 121–122

mediating effect of, 122
Composite reliability, 127
Continuing professional education (CPE), 49
Control environment risk, 30, 34–36, 38, 42–43, 47–48
competing effects of, 35
family firm structure and, 37, 42
manipulation of, 39–40
Control variables, 126
size, 126
strategy, 126
tenure, 126
Cooperation, 2–4, 8, 11–12, 14, 20
allocation problems, 20
cost allocations, 3–4
fairness, 3
mutual, 8–9
positive outcomes of, 20–21
Corporate reputation, 70
Corporate social responsibility (CSR), 55–59
backfire effect, 62, 64, 76–77
dependent variable, 69
experimental design, 65–66
independent variables, 68–69
insurance effect, 61–62, 64, 75–76
limitations and future research, 85–86
literature review and hypotheses, 59–65
manipulation checks, 71
mediating effect of reputation, 64–65
mediating variables, 69–70
mediation analyses, 77–81
method, 65–70
participants, 65
predicted results, 66
research instrument, 67–70
supplemental analyses, 81
tests of hypotheses, 71–81
Cost allocations, 2–5, 11–12, 15, 19–21
accounting, 5
behavioral economics literature, 5

equality and proportionality, 9
full cost allocation axiom, 6–7
individual contributions, 3, 5
managerial decisions, 5–6
ultimatum game, 12
Criminal Investigation Management Information System (CIMIS), 148–149
Criminal investigations (CI), 137–139, 148–150, 152–153
managerial responsibilities, 141–142
special agents, 139–140, 142, 149
Cronbach's alpha scores, 124
CSR. *See* Corporate social responsibility (CSR)
Cultural-normative embeddedness, 49
Currency structuring, 138–139
Curriculum vitae (CV), 100

Dependent variables, 38, 69
Descriptive information, 39
Descriptive statistics, 16, 103, 125
Dispositional Positive Emotions Scale (DPES), 15
Dow Jones Sustainability Index, 56–57

Early job attainment, 110. *See also* Job attainment, 107–108
Economic decision-making, 3
Economics literature, 6–7
Efficiency axiom, 6
Employee organisational commitment (EOC), 116, 123, 125, 128
budgetary participation and, 119
business unit innovation and, 120–121
competitive advantage, 127–128
components, 123–125
exploratory innovation, 120–121
mediating effect of, 122
mediating role of, 116–118
sequential mediating effect of, 129

Index

Environmental and social corporate activities, 57–58
EOC. *See* Employee organisational commitment (EOC)
Equality, 2–3, 9–10, 21
  accountability principle, 9–10
  cost allocation problems, 10
  economic decision-making, 10–11
  nulls, 17
  philosophers and sociologists, 9
  proportionality, 11
Equitable factors, 3
Expectancy violations theory (EVT), 56
Exploitative innovation, 117, 120–121, 125, 128–129
Exploratory innovation, 117, 120–121, 128–129
  competitive advantage, 117
  employee organisational commitment, 122

Fairness, 10–11
  accounting literature, 5–6
  behavioral economics literature, 7–9
  cooperation, 2
  cost allocation, 2–3
  economics literature, 6–7
  equality, 2–4, 14
  experimental design and hypotheses, 11, 13–14
  method, 15–16
  philosophy and sociology literature, 9–10
  proportionality, 2–4, 14
  results, 16–19
Family business, 30–32
Family firms, 29–31
  additional analysis, 43–47
  analysis of research question, 40–43
  auditors' judgments and, 32–34
  background and development, 31–35
  control environment, 34–35

dependent variables, 38
descriptive information, 39
design, 35–36
experimental task, 36–37
hypothesis testing, 40–43
independent variables, 37–38
other variables, 38–39
participants, 36
preliminary testing, 39–40
research method, 35–39
Federal Law Enforcement Officers' Association (FLEOA), 142
Feedback, 147–149
Firm type X failure type interaction, 66
Fraud risk, 30, 33–34, 38, 43–44, 47
  client explanations and assessment, 35
  financial, 35–36, 39–40

Game theory, 6–7
Gender, 98, 100–101
  accounting students, 101
  bias, 100–101
  comparability of, 103–104
  discrimination, 109
  grade point average and, 98–99
  internship, 109
  job attainment and, 98–100
  job progression, 98, 101
Grade point average (GPA), 98–100, 104–105, 107–108
  continuous independent variable, 104
  gender and, 98–99, 105
  internships, 99–100
  job attainment, 98–99
  responsibilities and hardships, 107–108

Hopkins vs. Price Waterhouse, 100
Hypothesis testing, 40–43

Independent variables, 37–38, 68–69
Institutional investors, 48
Insurance effect, 56, 61–62, 70

corporate social responsibility, 56–58, 76, 84
documented, 56, 61, 63–64, 84
generalizability of, 58–59
investment judgments, 64
limitation of, 62, 64, 75–76
measures, 81
social resilience, 62
Insurance hypothesis, 56
Internal audit function (IAF), 32–33
Internal Revenue Code (IRC), 138–139
Internal Revenue Service (IRS), 139, 142
criminal investigations, 137–139, 153
job characteristics model, 140–141
Internships, 98, 105, 107
experience, 102, 107
gender-based differences, 109
job attainment, 102
Interpretation check tests, 72–73
Investor judgments, 57, 63–64, 84

Job attainment, 98, 107–109
gender and, 98–100
grade point average and, 98–99, 102
internships, 102, 108
supplemental analysis, 105
Job characteristics model, 138, 140–141, 145, 153
Job offer, 98–99, 103, 105, 107, 109
dependent variable, 104
grade point average, 99–100, 110
logistic regression analysis, 105
mediated regression analysis, 106
supplemental analysis, 105
Job outcomes, 98
Joint cost allocation, 5

Law enforcement, 140, 143
Logistic regression analysis, 104–105

Logit models, 18
Low control environment risk, 46

Managerial capture, 60
Managerial control, 30, 32, 34, 40, 47–48
family ownership and, 33
family firm, 32
independent variables, 37
Mediated regression analysis, 106
Mediating variables, 69–70
Mediation, 106
analyses, 77–81
supplemental analysis, 105
Moderated-mediation model test, 67, 80, 83
Money laundering, 138–139

Nash equilibrium, 6, 10–11
Non-Big 4 public accounting firm, 36
Nonfamily firms, 30
Nonparametric bootstrapping, 45

One-way ANOVA, 39
Organisational empowerment, 119
Organizational legitimacy, 62
Ownership concentration, 31–32, 37–38, 47–49

Partial least square structural equation modeling (PLS-SEM), 46
Path model mediation analysis, 46
PCA. *See* Principal component analysis (PCA)
Perceived firm reputation, 70
Philosophy literature, 9–10
Preliminary testing, 39–40
Principal-agency (PA), 34
Principal component analysis (PCA), 69–70
Principal component factor analyses, 124
Principal-principal (PP), 34
PROCESS, 127–128
Proportional allocation method, 3, 7

Index

Proportionality, 2–4, 16–20
  Adams' equity theory, 9–10
  cost allocation problems, 10
  philosophers and sociologists, 9

RepTrak™ Pulse scale, 70, 96
Reputation, mediating effect of, 64–65
Research instrument, 67–70
Resources-based theory, 121
Root Mean Square Error of Approximation (RMSEA), 107

Self-fulfilling prophecy, 100
Shapley value, 2, 6, 10–12
  axioms, 7, 26–27
  Banker's modified, 4, 10
  Nash equilibrium and, 10–11
Sharing economy, 2
Skill variety, 142–145
Social embeddedness theory, 49
Social resilience, 62
Sociology literature, 9–10
Spearman Rho correlation matrix, 104
Special agents, 143–147, 153, 155–156
  autonomy, 145
  central skill, 144
  criminal investigation, 139–140, 142, 151
  with criminal investigation, 149
  diversity of skills, 143
  feedback, 147, 149
  prosecutability, 147

retired, 141–142
skill variety, 142–143
work of, 139, 146–147
State Contracting & Engineering Corp v. Condotte America, Inc., 3
Stewardship theory, 30–31, 33
Supplemental analyses, 81, 105, 107
Symmetry axiom, 6

Task identity, 141, 151–152
Task perceptions, 141
Task significance, 149–151
Tax instructors, 137–138
Tax law enforcement, 137–138
Tax textbooks, 137–138
Temp-Perfect, 68–69, 94
Transfer students, 98, 108–109
  academic performance, 101–102
  accounting programs, 103–104
  community college, 101–104
  gender breakout and, 103–104

Ultimatum game, 12
Unfairness, 2–3
United States v. Atlas Minerals and Chemicals, Inc., 3

Variable measurement, 123–126
Volkswagen, 56–57

World Trade Organization Riots, Seattle, 61–62

Printed and bound by CPI Group (UK) Ltd, Croydon, CR0 4YY

21/11/2024

14596799-0005